Praise for *The We*

"Briana and Peter are passionate creatives dedicat clarity, productivity, and a life filled with blissful joy. Their work is a gift." —Marie Forleo, Founder of B-School and MarieTV

"Health is wealth and if you're ready to start living your most prosperous life, Briana and Peter are the leaders you want to learn from. This book is packed with lessons, stories, and tips that will change the way you live your life. Dive in and join the well life revolution." —Natalie MacNeil, Emmy Award–Winning Producer and Founder of SheTakesOnTheWorld.com

"*The Well Life* is a beautiful guide to living the good life, mind, body, and soul from two people who walk the walk. . . . This book is a healing journey." —Kate Northrup, Bestselling Author of *Money: A Love Story*

"*The Well Life* is a powerful primer on living as we were intended to live— under grace, all systems go, and in love. A great platform for living deliberately and creating consciously." —Mike Dooley, *New York Times* Bestselling Author of *Infinite Possibilities*

"Many of us find that we have come to a place in our lives where we have 'checked all the boxes'—career, home, family—and yet we feel sad, unfulfilled, anxious, or depressed. Good news: *The Well Life* is your medicine. *The Well Life* is not just a book, it is a roadmap—a poignant interweaving of personal stories, professional anecdotes, and crystal clear and implantable tools to help you live a life of abundance, balance, and happiness." —David Howitt, CEO of The Meriwether Group and Author of *Heed Your Call*

"Exceptional! Don't waste one more minute reading the testimonials. Read the book. Briana and Dr. Peter Borten are experts at creating a Well Life. This book covers everything you need to know and do to become the best you and live a happy, fulfilling life!" —Andy Dooley, Creator of Vibration Activation™

"*The Well Life* is a balanced approach that will lead you to find a happy, satisfying life without feeling like you are making sacrifices. Briana and Dr. Peter Borten lay a foundation that will keep you well no matter what is happening in the world around you." —Linden Schaffer, Founder of Pravassa and Author of *Living Well on the Road*

Praise for *The Well Life*

"If you're looking to break out of the excuses and experience more vitality than ever before, *read this book*! Briana and Peter lay out a beautiful prescription for more ease, joy, balance, and fulfillment in *The Well Life*. Quite frankly, if you put even just 5 percent of this book into practice, you'll create incredible results!" —Alexi Panos, Leader in the Emergent Wisdom Movement and Author of *50 Ways to Yay!* and *Now or Never*

"This is such an important book, and a must-read for anyone who feels like the sweetness of living has been replaced by struggle, exhaustion, or endless busyness. It will help you lay the foundation for a balanced life that allows you to truly thrive—body, heart, and soul." —Emily Joy Rosen, CEO of the Institute for the Psychology of Eating

"Captivating and detailed, *The Well Life* offers a straightforward and vivid guide by providing a system that will bring individuals to their destination in life. *The Well Life* is an essential book for anyone who not only wishes to attain balance and happiness but to achieve the life of their dreams." —Izabella Wentz, *New York Times* Bestselling Author of *Hashimoto's Thyroiditis*

"*The Well Life* is a beautifully written book. Briana and Dr. Peter Borten have taken the best wisdom and insights around health, lifestyle, and personal development and created an engaging and easy-to-follow path for a life that's truly well lived. This book is great food for both body and soul." —Marc David, Bestselling Author and Founder of the Institute for the Psychology of Eating

"*The Well Life* is an exceptional guide to architecting a happy life. With humility, integrity, and a wonderful sense of play, Briana and Peter share the system they've created for living a life full of balance, love, and peace." —Elena Brower, Coauthor of *Art of Attention*

"This book is terrific. It gives us a very wholistic approach that makes a lot of sense. Wellness has far more to it than just what we eat and the Bortens really delve into the juicy stuff that betters us and makes life beautiful. I highly recommend it." —Dr. Pedram Shojai, Founder of Well.Org and *New York Times* Bestselling Author of *The Urban Monk*

HOW TO USE STRUCTURE, SWEETNESS, AND SPACE
TO CREATE BALANCE, HAPPINESS, AND PEACE

THE WELL LIFE

BRIANA AND DR. PETER BORTEN
FOUNDERS OF THE DRAGONTREE

Aadamsmedia
AVON, MASSACHUSETTS

For Sabina and Sailor, the main source of *sweetness* in our lives.
We love you.

Published by
Adams Media, a division of F+W Media, Inc.
57 Littlefield Street, Avon, MA 02322. U.S.A.
www.adamsmedia.com

ISBN 10: 1-4405-9624-7
ISBN 13: 978-1-4405-9624-7
eISBN 10: 1-4405-9625-5
eISBN 13: 978-1-4405-9625-4

Printed in the United States of America.

10 9 8 7 6 5 4 3 2 1

This book is intended as general information only, and should not be used to diagnose or treat any health condition. In light of the complex, individual, and specific nature of health problems, this book is not intended to replace professional medical advice. The ideas, procedures, and suggestions in this book are intended to supplement, not replace, the advice of a trained medical professional. Consult your physician before adopting any of the suggestions in this book, as well as about any condition that may require diagnosis or medical attention. The author and publisher disclaim any liability arising directly or indirectly from the use of this book.

The information in this book should not be used for diagnosing or treating any health problem. Not all diet and exercise plans suit everyone. You should always consult a trained medical professional before starting a diet, taking any form of medication, or embarking on any fitness or weight-training program. The author and publisher disclaim any liability arising directly or indirectly from the use of this book.

Cover design by Colleen Cunningham.
Cover images © Getty Images/punphoto; Marina Demidova/123RF; Shutterstock/Snezh.
Interior images by Briana and Dr. Peter Borten.

*This book is available at quantity discounts for bulk purchases.
For information, please call 1-800-289-0963.*

CONTENTS

Introduction to Your Well Life. 7

Part 1.
Foundation ❖ 11

Chapter 1. Three Elements for a Well Life 13
UNDERSTANDING STRUCTURE, SWEETNESS, AND SPACE

Chapter 2. Eight Practices for Mind-Body Health 23
OPTIMIZE YOUR WELLNESS

Chapter 3. Free Yourself 45
RELEASING EMOTIONAL BAGGAGE

Chapter 4. Your Rise to Power 58
CREATING YOUR WORLD THROUGH YOUR WORD

Part 2.
Resources for Thriving ❖ 67

Chapter 5. Energy 69
THE FUEL TO LIVE

Chapter 6. Confidence 89
BELIEVE IN YOURSELF

Chapter 7. Community 116
CURATING SUPPORTIVE CONNECTIONS

Part 3.
Who Are You and What Do You Want? ❖ 123

Chapter 8. Define Your Superpowers 125
DISCOVER WHAT LIGHTS YOU UP

Chapter 9. Choose Your Prizes. 151
DEFINING YOUR WELL LIFE

Chapter 10. Open Up Your Life. 174
REALIZING YOUR INFLUENCE ON YOURSELF AND THE WORLD

Chapter 11. Connect to Spirit 191
ALIGNING YOURSELF WITH THE UNIVERSE'S GUIDANCE

Chapter 12. Intelligent Life Architecture. 220
PLANNING FOR SUCCESS

Chapter 13. Expand. 250
INTEGRATING YOUR WELL LIFE

Acknowledgments 270

Source Materials 273

Index 280

About the Authors 287

INTRODUCTION TO YOUR WELL LIFE

Do you struggle with an ongoing quest to "have it all"—fulfilling work and leisure experiences, meaningful relationships, and quality personal time? Do you sometimes feel like your life is leading you, not the other way around? Are you bogged down with responsibilities that you dread, relationships that leave you drained, and career milestones you haven't achieved? Do you wonder how some people can accomplish so much, yet stay happy and positive?

These goals aren't out of reach for anyone. You can achieve a full, happy, balanced, gratifying life. We're here to show you how.

Our Well Life has been a full one thus far. A couple of years into Peter's acupuncture career and Briana's massage career, we met and fell in love. Peter had returned to school to learn a different style of acupuncture and was flying back and forth between Portland and San Francisco. Briana was flying back and forth between Portland and Los Angeles to attend college in Ayurvedic medicine (the traditional medical system of India). It felt like we both had pretty full plates, between our practices, our relationship, and our studies, but then Briana decided she wanted to create a spa, and she invited Peter to be a part of it.

Over the next two years, while building the business, we got married and bought our first house. Peter went back to school again to earn his doctorate. We had a baby. We had a crazy idea to open an organic café. Healthy, nourishing food seemed like a great comple-ment to the spa. But, *how on earth*, we wondered, *are we going to manage our spa, our medical practices, Peter's doctoral studies, having a new baby, and starting a café?* But we did it.

When Peter was done with his doctorate and Sabina was two, the Portland airport contacted us to ask if we'd be interested in build-ing a spa there. Airports were never our favorite place, but we took it as a challenge to create a space that would feel the exact opposite of the TSA announcements warning you that "Unattended bags will be confiscated and destroyed!" (Drop by if you're passing through!)

Peter has always been something of a mad scientist, and after we opened the airport spa, he began crafting and testing herbal tinc-tures for specific health conditions. We knew these products would expand our ability to help people achieve relaxation and balance. So, we founded The Dragontree Apothecary.

The next several years brought teaching positions for Peter at three colleges in Portland, a move to Boulder, the opening of a third spa, the launch of a magazine, the publication of *The Dreambook*, several online courses, and the best part of all: baby number two!

Through all of this, we always prioritized our marriage and fam-ily, self-care, music and art, play and dance, spiritual connection, and plenty of good friends and food. As the years went by, we became increasingly aware that we seemed to be *doing life* a little differently than most people. Barely a day would go by without some client, friend, or employee asking us *how* we do it.

Honestly, spelling out our accomplishments feels a bit like writing a resume. We don't do this stuff because we think it will look impres-sive to others; we do it because it's gratifying, and we feel extremely blessed for what we have. We're not better or smarter or prettier than our clients, and it's not always easy. We're just a couple of hardwork-ing people who have learned some things worth sharing. But hav-ing been on the consumer's side of many books and trainings, we recognize the importance of knowing that your teacher has actually attained what they're teaching. So, that's what *our* Well Life looks like.

We want to help you achieve *your* Well Life—however you envision it. It could be simple or extravagant. It could be full of activities or have lots of free time. Whatever your goals, we'll show you how to achieve them while feeling balanced and light. We'll do that through our three fundamental principles of an exceptional life:

1. **Sweetness:** Prioritizing the "sweet stuff" in life will bring you many steps closer to the life of your dreams.
2. **Structure:** Learning the art of life architecture will help you achieve tangible goals and give you more spontaneity and freedom.
3. **Space:** Creating openness will give you the capacity to connect to Spirit, to receive and grow, and to access creativity and insight.

We'll get into more detail on these principles in the coming chapters. For now, know that adding and maintaining *sweetness*, *structure*, and *space* to your life will bring alignment, healing, balance, and fulfillment.

Get ready to create a life that's more expansive, rewarding, and enjoyable than you could imagine—your Well Life.

PART 1.
FOUNDATION

There's a part of you that knows that life can be absolutely magical, rather than a perpetual struggle or a series of compromises. You've seen people embody this magic and, chances are, they left an unforgettable impression on you. Although it's far more common to succumb to the doubt, disappointment, and drama that surround us, we're here to remind you that another option is available to you: a life of balance and accomplishment, an experience of trust and ease, a feeling of being aligned with your purpose, and an ongoing awareness of the tremendous gift that is your life.

We'll share some hard science and many pragmatic tools for managing your life, but the drive to write this book had nothing to do with the academic stuff. It came from our having this inner knowing—it came from the awakening part of us wanting to support the awakening part of you. The big question is, when will you be ready to give yourself over to this awareness and allow your life to blossom?

CHAPTER 1.
THREE ELEMENTS FOR A WELL LIFE

UNDERSTANDING STRUCTURE, SWEETNESS, AND SPACE

Look at the Big Picture to Find Your Well Life

Our ability to remain focused, balanced, and healthy in the midst of our busy lives can be partly credited to our background as practitioners of Eastern medicine. Traditional Chinese Medicine (TCM) and Ayurveda emphasize that it's better to recognize and correct imbalances early than it is to mistreat oneself and attempt to make large repairs long after problems arise. The early detection of imbalance stems from the origins of Eastern medicine, more than 2,000 years ago, in the keen observation of nature. These systems teach that the dynamics of the natural world have parallels in all domains of human life—that is, we're not as different or separate from our environment as we may act and think.

From this perspective, human health is seen as an expression of countless factors—from our thoughts, emotions, and bodily functions, to the many ways we relate to our environment, such as through diet, behavior, community, climate, and more. These ancient arts look at the biggest possible picture, and within the vast tapestry of interacting substances and forces, they discover multidimensional patterns of imbalance. The ability to see the connection between imbalances in many different areas of life allows for more complete and effective solutions.

In our medical practices, while we addressed many of the usual things people go to a doctor for, we repeatedly saw the need to help our patients expand their ideas of what good health means. As we were asked with increasing frequency about issues relating to life structure and balance, we grew to understand that the kinds of *full spectrum* skills our clients seemed to see in us—such as earning a living by doing work that's aligned with your values; setting and achieving goals; maintaining sanity and balance in the midst of many projects; and protecting space and time for creativity, family, and community— represent important and neglected elements of whole health. We recognized that our training made us uniquely qualified to identify and understand the bigger patterns that made so many people say things like, "I could never do what you guys do."

> The ability to see the connection between imbalances in many different areas of life allows for more complete and effective solutions.

Whenever someone says something like this, we explain that everyone has different capacities and strengths. The particulars of our lives might not be appropriate or available to them, but the *qualities* that define them absolutely are. Here are some of the qualities that define a Well Life for the purposes of this book:

- An experience of ease—a state of mental and physical relaxation that is with us even when we're working hard
- A sense of openness—a tendency to accept, rather than resist, what life brings us
- An experience of integrity—a quality of physical, emotional, and mental stability that cannot be easily disturbed by internal or external forces
- A periodic experience of challenge (intellectual, physical, creative, or otherwise)

- An inclination to expand—to be inspired, to create, to share, and to grow
- Healthy and fulfilling relationships
- An experience of spiritual connection, or of belonging to something bigger than oneself
- An income that provides for living expenses, savings, and leisure
- An experience of knowing and being guided by our life purpose
- Frequent experiences of play and enjoyment
- The ability to set goals, create plans, and achieve them
- An experience of opportunity—to help, to enhance, to bring peace and love into our surroundings, etc.

You can refine this list of qualities to fit your own lifestyle, but they represent the impressive scope of a Well Life.

True Balance Isn't Static

Fundamental to the medical systems we were trained in is the importance of *dynamic balance*—a range of relative equilibrium that shifts and changes throughout life. In TCM, this balance is usually expressed as the two-part harmony of *yin* and *yang*. And in Ayurveda, it's often expressed as the harmony of three qualities known as *sattva, rajas,* and *tamas.* Both systems also utilize five-element theories of balance. These multipart concepts of balance reflect the interconnectedness of nature—a shift in one component causes a shift in the other components.

Because of the constant push and pull among the elements of an organic system, it's unrealistic to expect yourself to maintain a state of constant, perfect balance. However, the more conscious you become of how you're affected by diverse variables such as your thinking, your eating, and your climate, the more readily you can make adjustments in order to bring yourself back toward center. In this way, you can achieve a dynamic balance that works for you.

In the diagram that follows, the "B" range indicates someone living within about 75 percent of their optimal balance. The "A" range indicates someone living within about 90 percent of their optimal balance. A very healthy and resilient individual might feel okay with a range like "B" or perhaps even wider, but most of us would much prefer a range of dynamic balance closer to "A." Your target dynamic balance should be the range within which you can readily self-correct for any deviation without degrading your function or experience.

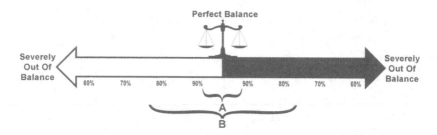

Your dynamic balance range is an expression of all the things you do that compromise your balance, combined with everything you do to bring yourself back. Forty hours of sitting at a desk every week might push you toward a slow metabolism and sluggish circulation, but if this is offset with frequent exercise, the net experience may be close to optimal balance. Of course, mobility is just one of many metrics, and it's not always easy to discern what you need more or less of in order to live closer to center—but that's what you'll learn in this book.

It's important to note that the difference between living in the A range versus the B range has nothing to do with the amount of excitement in your life or the emotional range you're capable of experiencing. You could have an end-of-life skydiving-karaoke celebration with a dear friend who's dying—an experience that includes adventure, elation, and sadness—and stay within the *A range* the whole time. Balanced doesn't mean boring or flat.

Balanced doesn't mean boring or flat.

The further you stray from your optimum (like the *B range*, or wider) the less comfortable you'll feel, the greater your risk of experiencing crisis, and the harder it becomes to correct yourself. One reason it's difficult to correct is that the more severely the scale tips, the more dramatic your efforts to restore balance will tend to be, which may throw you out of balance in new ways. It's a lot like driving a car. If you fall asleep for a split second and notice that you've veered a few inches out of your lane, you can give the steering wheel a little tug and quickly get yourself back on track. But if you fall asleep a little longer and open your eyes to discover that you've drifted to the wrong side of the road and are speeding toward oncoming traffic, you're more likely to swing the wheel far in the opposite direction and risk careening off the shoulder. For this reason, it's best to catch yourself early. Though, even if it's too late for that, you should always begin with moderate, consistent corrections. It's never too late to begin.

Structure, Sweetness, and Space

We've drawn on the dynamic balance of the natural world to create the conceptual foundation we use in this book to guide you toward the attainment of your Well Life. Our system for a life of balance, peace, happiness and meaningful achievement is composed of three elements: *Structure, Sweetness,* and *Space.*

If you're committed to the Well Life, then the good-feeling, soul-nourishing, body-fortifying activities *can't wait* while you juggle your obligations and pursue your dreams. We developed this system so you can incorporate the tenets of a Well Life while still fulfilling your responsibilities. Here's what each of the three components entails.

Sweetness

Playing, being in nature, singing, stretching, exploring, cooking, eating, loving, connecting, creating, and enjoying all come under the general heading of *sweetness. Sweetness* not only makes life more satisfying, it also makes you stronger and better—more authentically *you.*

When we tell people, "Don't postpone the *sweetness,*" it's not because we think you shouldn't have to wait until retirement to enjoy

life (though you should also enjoy it then, too, of course). Don't
postpone the *sweetness*, because when you *feed* your life and soul
with it, you become more effective at bringing your potential into the
world and shaping this life however you choose.

Furthermore, if you fill your life with *sweetness*, you move many
steps closer to the life of your dreams, regardless of the outcome of
any particular goal. If your goals don't materialize when you think
they will (or at all), at least you won't
Sweetness not only makes
life more satisfying, it
also makes you stronger
and better—more
authentically *you.*
have spent years neglecting the sweet
stuff. Just the opposite: you will have
spent the time doing work that feels significant, treating yourself well, enjoying
the world, and living the full spectrum
of this human experience. It doesn't get much better than that! And
then, when you *do* achieve your dreams, if you've been feeding your
soul and growing all the while, you'll be better able to assimilate the
new changes in a healthy way.

Structure

As we've expanded our understanding of health to include the
ability to successfully shape one's circumstances, achieve goals, and
capably manage the responsibilities of a fully engaged human, we've
noticed that *structure* is a challenge for most people. Every goal, from
the smallest to the grandest, requires some form of *structure* to get
from point A to point B. The same is true for the balanced operation
of a life with many moving parts. Yet we've encountered many people who try to avoid *structure* altogether because they simply don't
know how to incorporate it, and/or they believe it will restrict their
freedom and creativity. Or they interpret the Law of Attraction to
mean that everything is accomplished through thought, and therefore
structure and work are needless or misguided.

Other clients willingly utilize *structure*, but not always in a way
that would be most efficient or fulfilling. Perhaps the *structures* they
have in place haven't been consciously updated since childhood.

They're doing things in the circuitous or cumbersome way they came up with decades ago. There may be mechanisms in place that serve agendas that haven't been applicable for years. They may have adopted elements of *structure* by imitating others, but without personalizing them.

When we've examined the *structures* people are using to try to create successful, happy, and meaningful lives, we've found that most folks lack a good education in life architecture. We've seen *structures* like a bridge made of clothesline suspended over a canyon—it seems to go from A to B, but lacks support. Making it across would depend on a massive amount of personal effort, focus, and luck. Other *structures* were more like a concrete pipe—sturdier to walk through, but at the expense of any enjoyment along the way. Still other *structures* were like complicated tangles of trusses, cables, and beams—more likely to get the traveler lost and confused than to their destination.

Structuring your life in a conscious way inevitably means recognizing and abandoning structural elements that are "not to code"—extraneous, unsound, impinging on other needs, or otherwise dysfunctional. A full life and a complicated life are very different things. Complicated structural habits can make a person feel overwhelmed when they only have two things to get done in a day. Likewise, operating from *structures* that secretly serve hidden desires or unhealthy beliefs can be like using an outdated navigation system. You may end up at a used tire stand on a dusty road, trading in one of your less-important organs for a soup can full of gasoline. We really don't want to see that happen. Everyone knows the shortest distance between two points is a straight line, but we're not suggesting that the only good *structure* is one that never meanders. There are rarely any straight lines in life, because there's lots to learn and experience along the way. A good *structure* is one that's forged consciously, incorporates *sweetness* and *space,* and steers you in the direction of your dreams.

You've heard many times that happiness is a journey, not a destination. The same is true for life architecture. Sure, we want you to get to point B. But why take the boring sidewalk there when you could dance across lily pads or ride in a hot air balloon with a pink unicorn on it?

Why not find a way to get there that involves doing something *beautiful* with the resources you're given? Why not take a path that enables you to *use your gifts*? Why not choose a vehicle that's *aligned with your life purpose*? Why not find a way to get there that helps and inspires others along the way? That's what healthy *structure* will do for you.

Space

The key to creating healthy and functional *structure* is to integrate it with *sweetness* and *space*. *Space* is where we connect to Spirit. *Space* is where we really see ourselves. In *space* we can come to understand our darkness and our light, and we can learn the depths of our potential. *Space* gives us the capacity to receive and expand. We need *space* to reflect, adjust, and grow. Alignment and healing can't occur without it. *Space* is where we listen—not to our thoughts or our media, but to the stillness within us where truth lives. Insight and creativity only enter our consciousness through the opening that *space* provides. *Space* is the crucible in which *sweetness* and *structure* interact to yield a life that feels inspired, meaningful, and fun.

Sweetness needs *space* in order to be rooted in authenticity and to penetrate, engage, and feed the deepest parts of you. *Structure* needs *space* for perspective; it doesn't breathe without *space*. Moreover, you need *space* to really understand where you want your *structures* to take you. In turn, within the earthly realm, *sweetness* gives *space* a language, and *structure* provides vessels for *space* to enter the everyday world.

Many traditions have a term like *space* to describe the "emptiness" from which everything is born:

- In Daoism, it's called *Wuji*, the limitless, boundless, or, most literally, the nonpolar. In this sense, it's where our expanded consciousness resides, which isn't polarized, doesn't need to take positions, and is simply open.

- In Buddhism, it's *Sunyata*—emptiness, openness, or spaciousness—the *space* in which the soul is unconfined by the mind.
- In Ayurveda, it's *Akasha*—*space* or ether—the origin and essence of the entire material world.
- In the elemental system of ancient Japan, it's called *Ku*—void, sky, or heaven—representing creative energy, power, and spontaneity.

Besides the expansion and clarity that *space* facilitates in us, there's another great reason to make it a priority: it's the antithesis of the perpetual mental engagement that dominates our lives more than ever. All the time we spend plugged into the massive flow of media, data, and communications, we're disconnected from the magic of the moment and the natural world around us. Inviting *space* into our lives reminds us who we are.

A Few Words on Digesting These Concepts

Certain in-vogue concepts can sometimes make our "bullshit meter" go off, and this makes us hesitant to share them. They may be perfectly valid ideas, but their popularity seems to dilute their value. As a principle becomes widely recognizable, it's common for people to believe that their *intellectual* understanding of it is the same as an *experiential* understanding. "Oh yeah," we think dismissively, "I know about that."

In an age when profound spiritual truths from traditions around the world are easy to come by on Facebook, this shallowness is an insidious trend. Besides the missed opportunities caused by our believing we understand the impact that embodying a concept would have on us simply because we know what the words mean, there's a related belief that contributes to stunted personal growth: that valuable concepts should *produce* change in us, or that, in order for a teaching to be valid, it should be *revelatory*. This rarely happens, of course. Occasionally, a person who is completely ripe for an idea and totally open to it will happen upon the idea and it goes deep. Just through the encounter, they have a life-changing "aha!" moment.

Don't wait for *aha! moments*. It's best to treat them as a fantasy. The information in this—and any—book is highly unlikely to *cause* the change you desire. We often secretly hope this is how it works, and when it doesn't we discredit the information and/or its bearer. Usually, the bearer should be let off the hook, because any smart teacher knows that this isn't usually how learning occurs. Making new information work for you is a process of assimilating it, applying it to your own situation, and consistently using it. It's like building any skill. In the same way that reading about pitching a baseball isn't going to cause you to become a great pitcher, reading about psychological health isn't going to automagically produce psychological health.

In applying the concepts we present for promoting change, it's important to remember that you're up against *habits* of behavior and thinking. It's likely that you've thought the same negative thoughts thousands of times. Breaking habits is challenging. Therefore, whatever approach you take to replacing them with new ones, you *must practice consistently*. Practice doesn't happen while you're reading a book. So, if you finish reading a personal-growth book and then go on to your next book without a period of focused practice, you can expect the book to have little positive impact on you. We repeat: Don't expect an encounter with a valuable idea to produce a revelation in you.

If you're like us, you probably don't actually need to find more, new, and better ideas—you just need to practice what you've already learned. You'd be much better off choosing a single book or teacher and spending a year or more working on the teachings they present before moving on to acquire more ideas.

⬦

In the chapters ahead, we'll show you many ways to cultivate *sweetness*, to build intelligent *structure*, and to open your *space*. We'll also point out many opportunities to notice and shape the *structure*, *sweetness*, and *space* already present in your life. By balancing these elements and utilizing the many tools and exercises we'll share, you'll be powerfully equipped to create the Well Life of your dreams.

CHAPTER 2.
EIGHT PRACTICES FOR MIND-BODY HEALTH

OPTIMIZE YOUR WELLNESS

Building a Solid Foundation for Your Well Life

Creating a strong foundation is crucial to forging a Well Life. Without one, you'd probably still have Well *moments*, but when it's in place you'll have an abiding wellness that sustains you through your ups and downs. This chapter is about the basic health maintenance practices that will allow you to *get the most life out of your life*.

As practitioners of healing systems that regard the body and mind as entirely intertwined, we couldn't imagine advising a client to embark on a journey to great achievement and joy without first ensuring that they had basic measures of self-care in order. We've seen too many cases of unhappy, unmotivated, and uninspired people, irritable people, and people with poor concentration, all of whom incorrectly assumed their problem was psychological in origin. They wasted what little energy they had feeling guilty and looking for ways to change their thinking. But when directed to follow the fundamental maintenance routines we discuss in this chapter, not only did their bodies feel healthier, they regained their lightness, motivation, concentration, and inspiration.

We've also seen too many self-help books that suffer from the same simplistic thinking: *If your mind isn't right, the problem must have started in your mind and can only be fixed through your mind.* Nowadays, with the huge popularity of the Law of Attraction, many authors go one step further to say, *If* anything *about your life isn't right, the problem is your mind—in your flawed thinking.*

Your mind is indeed powerful, but it's just one facet of all that you are. Even if the mind is sick, the issue may not *originate* there. We're lucky to live in a time when even the mainstream medical world recognizes the fact that many physical problems may actually be psychological in origin. It's now equally important to recognize that the opposite is true: Many psychological problems are actually physical in origin. For example, insufficient sleep can cause poor mental focus, a short temper, moodiness, and difficulty making good decisions. Sometimes direct work on psychological issues is necessary, but since basic self-care will serve you on multiple levels, why not get this in order *first*? If the true origin is in the body, you'll never achieve lasting success if you only address the mind.

Many psychological problems are actually physical in origin.

We see health maintenance as a vital part of integrating *structure, sweetness,* and *space* into your life. It's the most basic prerequisite for a life that works. It affects not just your physical capabilities, but your mental function and psychological outlook.

The eight practices outlined in this chapter will get you the most bang for your buck in terms of the effort required relative to the outcome in improved energy, focus, sleep, and overall sense of well-being. Your health is imperative for your purpose. Even if you're technically healthy but sleep deprived and caffeinated, as so many people are, your ability to be creative, insightful, and wise will be compromised.

Incorporate Self-Care Mindfully

In a culture that values instant gratification, comfort, and productivity, self-care is often an afterthought, partly because its rewards aren't always immediate. If you're someone who has a hard time with self-care, try adding these routines one at a time. Give each practice a chance for a few weeks. See if you can find a friend to join you so you can motivate and encourage each other. You *will* feel better, even if you don't notice a difference right away.

Try to avoid thinking of self-care like an oil change—that is, as a mere obligation. We usually don't notice any change in a car's performance from getting the oil changed; it's just something we feel guilty about when we *don't* take care of it. Instead, we offer you the challenge of bringing your presence to these routines with an eagerness to see how much satisfaction you can derive from them. Doing good things for yourself has great potential for connection and enjoyment—in the very moment that you're doing them. It's like a more evolved form of instant gratification! And this potential hinges entirely on mindfulness. The more of yourself and your attention you bring to the task, the greater the opportunity there is to experience it in a special way.

Just try it while eating, exercising, or bathing. Meditate on this for a minute:

What would I do if I were intent on getting the most possible enjoyment from this activity?

As we see it, the most significant thing you could do, no matter the activity, would be to simply give it all of your attention. *Devote* yourself to it. Nobody has any trouble keeping their attention on what they're engaged in if it's thoroughly enjoyable. Who has to remind themselves to focus on what's happening when they're in the middle of good sex or an excellent massage? Although using your attention in this way with self-care means working a muscle you probably haven't used much, the good news is that it will immediately increase your satisfaction.

Besides enhancing your self-care experience and beginning the process of making it a ritual, it will give you a break from the tendency to put your attention on your thoughts instead of your actual *now* experience. Making this a habit will help you stay more anchored in the present, which always feels more alive and inspired than your thoughts, and it can also help alleviate feelings of anxiety, grief, and depression.

Now, for your eight fundamental self-care practices: sleep, healthy eating, breathing, movement, being in nature, play and laughter, stillness, and connecting with others. As a whole, these practices can be understood as enhancing *sweetness* since they feed us and they should absolutely feel good, but certain practices offer special support in one or more of the three S's.

1: Sleep

Despite how good it feels to get a refreshing night's sleep, and how off-our-game we can be when we're deprived, sleep is one of the first things we sacrifice when we get busy. Countless times, our clients have told us they get only four to six hours a night—or just enough to function without drooling.

STRUCTURE, SWEETNESS, AND SPACE

Sleep is vital for all three S's. It's an experience of *sweetness*, in that we make ourselves as comfortable as possible and then simply surrender. While asleep, our body undergoes tremendous *structural* healing and renewal, and every day is *structured* around it. And, we access *space* in the act of sleeping, through which ideas and experiences are processed and insights enter our consciousness.

You can't treat sleep as a luxury if you want to thrive. Essential processes occur while we're sleeping, such as cell renewal, repair of damaged tissue, memory consolidation, restoration of the nervous system, and hormone production and regulation. Good sleep is critical for concentration, problem solving, immune function, energy, growth, and learning.

Research clearly indicates that people with insufficient sleep have a greater tendency to gain weight, have accidents, and feel irritable, anxious, and depressed. Sleep deprivation is also associated with diminished sex drive, worsening of pain, and higher risk of illness, including heart disease, infection, obesity, and diabetes.

Virtually all adults do best with seven to nine hours of *quality* sleep a night. The operative word here is "quality." Eight hours of tossing and turning and checking Facebook won't get the job done. For this reason, we recommend giving yourself at least thirty minutes of winding-down time before bed, when you

> You can't treat sleep as a luxury if you want to thrive.

dim the lights, slow your movements, turn off the television, and put away electronic devices. Try taking a bath before bed, or even just a foot bath. To enhance the tranquilizing effect, you can add a few drops of one or more of the following essential oils to the water: lavender, Roman chamomile, valerian, orange, mandarin, cedarwood, ylang ylang, and vetiver. You can also use a diffuser with any of these oils in your bedroom.

TIPS FOR OPTIMIZING SLEEP QUALITY:

- Make your bedroom as dark as possible while sleeping, and if you have to get up to use the bathroom, don't turn the light on (it can stop production of the sleep hormone, melatonin, in the brain).
- Keep your room on the cool side.
- If you get sore in the night (or already are) consider a better mattress and/or pillow.
- If you have cold feet that make it hard to fall asleep, try using a hot water bottle at the foot of your bed.
- Reduce or eliminate caffeine and other stimulants, especially after noon.
- Exercise during the day.
- Try going to bed and waking up at the same time every day.
- Before bed, write in a journal, intend to let go of your day, and mentally set aside your problems.
- Avoid beverages close to bedtime if they make you wake up to pee in the night.
- Consider relaxing sounds, such as a white noise generator.

- If you tend to wake up in the middle of the night, try eating a protein-rich snack before bed, such as an egg or Greek yogurt to keep your blood sugar stable.
- If possible, reduce interference such as noise, pets, and children.
- Try falling asleep to a guided meditation crafted to assist you in dropping into deep sleep. We created one for you that you can download at www.thewelllifebook.com/resources.

Ultimately, there's no substitute for sleep. No amount of vitamins, green drinks, yoga, or kombucha will replenish you in the same way. You know this. We're just reminding you.

2: Nutrition

Nutrition is a hot topic, with so many "experts" arguing about which foods are good and which are bad. Rather than focusing primarily on specific foods you should or shouldn't eat, we prefer to emphasize broad, timeless principles, which will help you make your own wise choices. Because there's so much to say about how we feed ourselves, we've broken this section down into the *structure, sweetness,* and *space* of healthy eating.

Structure

In our Eastern traditions, the body and mind are said to thrive on a consistent routine. This actually pertains to all parts of life, but since we're on the topic of nutrition, this means eating at roughly the same times each day, and roughly the same amount of food each time.

It means not being erratic about mealtimes, not skipping meals, or suddenly gorging yourself at the all-you-can-eat buffet. Don't skip breakfast, don't go more than about four hours between meals, and don't snack between meals. As for the *structure* of the meal itself, we recommend incorporating into each meal:

- Some **good fat**, such as avocado, oily fish, chia, hemp and flax seed, walnuts, almonds, coconut, olives and olive oil, and egg yolk. Good fats are essential for healthy neurological function and they benefit energy, hormone production, skin and joint health, and more.

- Some **high-quality protein**, such as egg white; beans; fish; lean, clean, antibiotic- and hormone-free meat; and Greek yogurt or cottage cheese if you tolerate dairy well. Protein helps us build and repair tissues, including muscle, skin, nails, hair, cartilage, and bone. It provides sustained energy and lasting blood sugar stability.

- **Green vegetables.** The chlorophyll we see in green vegetables is evidence of plants' almost magical ability to turn solar energy into biological energy. It's an essential step in the nutrition of virtually all inhabitants of our planet, and a part of every food chain. Green vegetables are nutritional powerhouses, and their abundant fiber content helps clean us out.

- **Foods with vitality.** The more fresh and alive your food feels, the better. Go check out the farmers' market. Meanwhile, reduce your consumption of processed foods. The more steps of processing the food went through and the less it resembles a living thing, the less healthy it is.

Space

When we speak of *space* in nutrition, we mean it both literally and figuratively. First, the figurative. Make *space* in your life for the act of nourishing yourself. You are worth it. When you eat at your desk or while driving, or you gobble up your meal because you only have five minutes, you're telling yourself that your own nourishment isn't that important.

Likewise, when you eat while watching television, or while having a heated conversation, or while doing anything else that takes your attention away from the act of eating, you're degrading the nourishment process. If you're stressed while eating, your biological stress responses literally divert resources away from the digestive organs and impair digestive effectiveness. Instead, set aside time for a nice meal. Slow down. Put your stresses aside.

Second, the literal. Leave *space* in your stomach. Don't let *fullness* be your indication to stop eating. Most people eat until the stomach is packed to capacity, or even to overcapacity. Overeating is taxing to the body. It stretches the stomach and damages the lower esophageal sphincter that closes the top of the stomach. If you rely on the feeling of fullness to know when to stop eating and you routinely stretch out the stomach, you'll need to keep eating more and more food to feel satisfied. It's a clear sign that you're in some way "disconnected" in the act of eating.

Think of your stomach like a clothes dryer. If you overstuff it, the clothes won't have *space* to move, the air won't circulate, and your laundry will take hours to dry. In a similar way, if you pack your stomach, chances are you won't digest and absorb your food optimally, and you'll undoubtedly exceed your caloric needs. Instead, stop eating as soon as you're satisfied and no longer have a feeling of true hunger. Usually this will feel like about 80 percent or less of your stomach's capacity—or a volume of food about 1½ times the size of your closed fist.

Sweetness

If you let the most thorough enjoyment of food be your guide, you'll be steered in the right direction. When you feed yourself, think what a marvelous thing this is, that you get to savor this delicious fare and your body will get the fuel it needs from it. Imagine the food is entering your cells and rejuvenating you. How delightful can you make this process?

By the same token, you may notice that certain habitual behaviors don't really work if you're prioritizing total enjoyment. For instance:

- Eating when you're not hungry (if you wait until you have an appetite, you'll enjoy it more)
- Putting food in your mouth when there's already food in your mouth (how could you be savoring what you're chewing on if you're thinking about the next bite?)

- Eating while doing other things (you can only fully give your attention to one thing at a time)
- Eating in the midst of intense stimuli (loud music, upset people, etc.)
- Eating with a feeling of guilt or shame about it
- Overeating (as soon as you exceed your need, your body starts giving you unpleasant signals that it's had enough—even if you've learned to tune them out—and this degrades the enjoyment of any additional food)

Now for the literal side of *sweetness*. In the traditions we practice, foods such as whole grains, sweet potatoes, fruit, and poultry are considered natural sources of mild *sweetness*, and they're a healthy part of a balanced diet. But modern diets are full of super-*sweetness*—excessive amounts of grains, fruit juice that represents much more sugar than the whole pieces of fruit it came from, and many kinds of concentrated sweeteners. In comparison, these are overwhelming and destabilizing to the body. In medical terms, they contribute to inflammation, obesity, diabetes, and other health problems, so make them a very small part of your diet.

3: Breathing

Since breathing happens automatically it's easy to not think about it. But there's a big difference between the shallow rapid kind and the slow deep kind. Deepening your breathing opens your body, alleviates pain, relaxes you, promotes circulation, and slows down a stressed mind. Shallow breathing does the opposite.

There are a few reasons people get in the habit of shallow breathing. Let's take a look at the most common:

1. **Poor posture** is probably the worst culprit. When you sit hunched over a desk, computer, or phone, your abdomen gets compressed, your shoulders round, your chest caves in, and your neck cranes forward. (Check out your posture right now

as you're reading this. How, in this moment, can you improve it?) Besides hindering the breath, poor posture is a major cause of muscle strain, and it probably impairs digestion and other organ functions as well. Good posture is essential to healthy physical *structure;* as we allow *space* in the cavities of the body, the breath naturally deepens. So, lift yourself up—your mood will improve, you'll look more attractive, and your body will feel better.

2. Another source of restricted breathing is **modern humans' tendency to suck in our bellies.** We think a flat abdomen is attractive, so if we've got some extra insulation here, we may try to hide it by habitually contracting our abs. It's impossible to breathe deeply while doing this.

3. The third common reason for shallow breathing is as **an unconscious response to stress.** When we resist unpleasant thoughts and circumstances, there's often a physical expression of this resistance, which occurs as some form of clenching or tightening of the body. The diaphragm doesn't rise and fall freely, perhaps our chest or abdomen becomes constricted, and the breath is confined to just the very top of the lungs. It's as if, in an effort to avoid experiencing the unpleasantness, we're unconsciously keeping it compartmentalized in a small area. Of course, this doesn't actually improve either our circumstances or the way we're feeling. If anything, by restricting our breathing as a response to unpleasant thoughts or circumstances, we compound and prolong the unpleasantness.

There is a principle in Eastern medicine that could help so many people: "The mind follows the breath." What this means is that when your breathing is shallow and rapid, your mind tends to race and constantly chew on the same thoughts. When your breath is slow and deep, you access *space* more easily, the mind becomes tranquil, and your thoughts slow down. You'll also notice that this phenomenon works in the opposite direction. When your mind is agitated or processing a lot of data, your breath will get fast and shallow, and when you're peaceful, you're naturally breathing more deeply. So, if you notice that you're anxious, slowing and deepening your breath will help. For this purpose, we find that lengthening the exhale (making it longer than the inhale) usually works even better.

As a general practice, we encourage you to focus more on the *depth* than the length of breath. That is, try to bring the breath *deeply* into your body. Imagine the pelvis as a bowl that you're filling with the breath. Feel your hips open from the inside as your lower abdomen expands. The rate should be slow, but if you focus too much on making your breath very long, it can easily become forced. Keep it natural. We have a deep-breathing meditation available for you at www.thewelllifebook.com/resources if you would like a guide.

STRUCTURE, SWEETNESS, AND SPACE

A single deep breath, given the total focus of your attention, can dramatically change how you feel. It creates mental *space* and opens the physical *space* within the body. The constant rhythm of the breath can be understood as a form of *structure* that's with you throughout your entire life. And when you become a connoisseur of the breath, it's a free, inexhaustible form of *sweetness*.

To mindfully incorporate proper breathing into your day, start with a few minutes of deep breathing each morning and night, plus a few moments of tuning in to your breath throughout the day. If this isn't possible at first, try just ten deep breaths once a day. Or even better, make yourself a reminder, such as an alarm on your phone or computer, or place stickers in your home, car, and office, and each time the alarm goes off or you see one of these stickers, take a moment for a deep breath.

4: Movement

If you look in a textbook of Traditional Chinese Medicine, the potential causes of each disease are listed, and in a great many cases one of

these causes is "imbalance between movement and stillness." Historically, the imbalance was usually one of too much movement and not
enough stillness, such as a life of hard manual labor with insufficient
rest, but in the urban centers of the modern world, we almost always
see the reverse. Huge portions of our lives are spent sitting. Sitting
on chairs to eat and work, sitting in cars and buses to commute, and
sitting on couches to relax. Exercise has become optional for many
people. But it's best if we don't think of it that way.

Movement is essential for healthy *structure*. The benefits of exercise are so tremendous and diverse that nearly any health issue will
benefit from it, and nearly any life will be enriched and prolonged
by it. The body needs to be moved, stretched, and worked in order
for both it and the mind to stay healthy. We used to accomplish this
naturally by fetching water, chopping wood, digging, walking, climb-
ing, carrying, squatting, scrubbing, and playing. Now that we have
the questionable "luxury" of sitting all day, exercise is something of
an artificial construct that must be deliberately scheduled into our
lives. Be that as it may, you might as well embrace it and find forms
of exercise that you enjoy.

TWENTY REASONS TO MAKE EXERCISE A NON-
NEGOTIABLE PART OF YOUR ROUTINE:

- It improves our quality of sleep.
- It reduces our risk of certain cancers (breast, colon, perhaps
  lung and uterine, and probably others).
- It helps prevent development of type 2 diabetes.
- It makes us look better. Beyond weight loss, we simply look
  more vibrant with exercise.
- It lowers our blood pressure and improves our cholesterol
  profile.
- It reduces our risk of cardiovascular disease and stroke.
- It improves self-esteem.
- It reduces anxiety.
- It improves erections in men.
- It alleviates depression.

- It may reduce hair loss.
- It improves our ability to deal with stress.
- It increases libido.
- It helps prevent cognitive decline in old age.
- It improves brain development in children.
- It makes us more creative.
- It reduces cigarette cravings in smokers.
- It reduces alcohol cravings in drinkers.
- It makes us more energetic.
- It lengthens our lives.

STRUCTURE, SWEETNESS, AND SPACE

As you can see, exercise has benefits in all three realms—*structure, sweetness,* and *space.* In terms of *structure,* exercise supports the physical *structure* of your body and promotes a clear mind that is better able to track your daily *structure.* It supports mental calm and alleviates anxiety and depression, enabling you to more readily access an experience of *space.* And it encourages you to fully enliven this body, your vehicle, to revel in the *sweetness* of movement and sport.

If you want to thrive, aim to engage in some form of movement every day. This doesn't need to be a two-hour, herculean workout— that would verge on imbalance in the opposite direction. Just get moving. We recognize that making exercise a consistent habit can be an ongoing struggle for many people, so utilize the mindfulness approach discussed at the beginning of the chapter.

5: Stillness

In the previous section, we explained that humans have shifted from too much movement and not enough stillness to too much stillness and not enough movement. However, that's not really the whole story. While this happened on the physical level, the opposite trend occurred on the mental level. In the past, most people engaged in much less mental activity (movement) and had much more opportunity for mental stillness than we do today. Nowadays, the balance is dramatically skewed toward excessive mental activity, and the more full our minds are, the more difficult it is for us to access *space.*

People who work with their bodies, as more of us did in the past, tend to have calmer minds. Today, we have more mind-based jobs than ever before. And during our leisure time, most of us engage in more mental diversion, such as social media, e-mail and text, television, and reading.

We have seen an alarming increase in the percentage of our clients who complain of anxiety, of feeling overwhelmed, of depression, and we believe that a major contributor is mental overload. This trend has directly paralleled the explosion in the use of mobile phones, tablets, and laptops. Computers and televisions used to be bulky and resided in one spot in our home or office. When we left the room, office, or house, we had to disconnect. But now we can stay engaged with a device with a screen almost perpetually. It has severely encroached on our *space.*

In order to be balanced and healthy, we need mental stillness, and the most basic solution is to be less immersed in what we call the Human Data Stream—the collective multimedia flow of all shared information. Not only does constant immersion make us unbalanced, it promotes disengagement from the real world around us—from our immediate experience.

Instead of being fully immersed in what's happening around us, we've become concerned with recording it, editing it, and sharing it. Further, due to the sheer volume of material we have to process in the form of e-mails, texts, status updates, photos, and other media, we have learned to browse through life—to stay shallow—which makes it harder for us to go *deep* and hold our focus for an extended period.

Besides reducing your screen time, we recommend two things.

1. First, practice deliberate patience and depth. Engage more deeply with the real world on a regular basis. Whatever you happen to be doing, give it your full awareness. Let yourself be fascinated in simple, everyday things. You'll have an experience not just of *space* opening up, but of a quiet *sweetness* within.

2. Second, have a practice of pure mental stillness. There's really nothing that recharges us in the same way as intentionally not using the mind. Creating *space* for the sake of *space*. Not trying to manipulate our thoughts or consciousness. Not trying to produce a particular state or result. Just sit, close your eyes, and let go of everything.

If you need to watch something, watch your breath (that's all the *structure* you need). Even just a single minute of this each day can be rejuvenating. If you absolutely must have more *structure,* you can try following a guided meditation, such as the ones on our website, www .thewelllifebook.com/resources. Ultimately, we hope that you'll use at least a portion of your stillness time free from any sound or talking.

6: Being in Nature

Once upon a time, nature wasn't *outside* and it wasn't *scenery.* It was just *home.* And our lives were inseparable from it. It profoundly shaped our existence, and we were perennially conscious of the fact that it provided everything that sustained us.

But all that has changed. In the past few centuries, we have built lives that increasingly isolate us from our origins. We can live entirely in climate-controlled buildings and cars. We can eat foods that come in cans and boxes and bear no resemblance to plants or animals. We can ignore the limitations of our natural resources and the environmental consequences of our lifestyles.

This trend may seem benign, but we believe it has serious negative consequences. Without our connection to nature, we miss out on something essential. We lose our sense of *space*. We forget what we are. We miss out on nature's example of harmonious *structure* and the recognition of our place in it. We feel isolated. We deprive ourselves of the most awe-inspiring *sweetness* and a great repository of wisdom. Writer Richard Louv coined a term for this new problem: Nature-Deficit Disorder.

The wisdom traditions all began with observation of nature. They studied the subtle and majestic dynamics of the natural world and used them to illustrate how these dynamics exist in human psychology, physiology, politics, business, and relationships. If you spend enough time in nature, you get a sense of how things move and change, the rhythm and balance of it all.

You'll feel at peace, at home. Breathing clean air, getting our feet on the ground, and being surrounded by life, grounds, aligns, and recharges us. It also provides a break from the usual bombardment of countless forms of pollution—from artificial light, to noise, to electromagnetic radiation, to household and industrial chemicals, to the Human Data Stream—so it's an excellent place for stillness. New research from Gaétan Chevalier, PhD, and others even shows that being in contact with the earth improves mood, reduces the viscosity of our blood (diminishing a risk factor for cardiovascular disease), decreases inflammation, improves circulation, lowers stress, benefits our sleep, and regulates the immune system.

STRUCTURE, SWEETNESS, AND SPACE

Nature is a free source of *space* and *sweetness,* and it displays majestically the *structure* of seasons, change, and interdependence. Go outside. Find ways to incorporate more of the natural world into your everyday life. Walk to work or the store. Take a detour through the grass. Eat outdoors. Make plants, rocks, wood, shells, flowing water, and other natural objects part of your home decor. Grow a garden.

Have you ever been in the woods, and all the stimuli that usually seem random and disunited—the songs of the birds, the movement of the wind, the swaying of the trees, the croaking of the frogs, and the ebb and flow of your own breath—suddenly feel connected and synchronized? It's a magical thing, and we believe that spending time in this space integrates and tunes us. The more we practice falling into this groove ("practice" is kind of an unfortunate word to use in this situation, but probably necessary for modern humans), the more we naturally stay there, and soon, without even thinking about it, we begin to perceive the groove in our home, on the highway, and in the office. We slip into it, we do our thing, and before we know it, we have a magical life.

7: Play and Laughter

George Bernard Shaw said, "We don't stop playing because we grow old; we grow old because we stop playing." We know it's hard to schedule time just for enjoyment, but play is important stuff. It's pure *sweetness*. Playing and laughing are good for our cardiovascular health. They foster bonding with our family and friends. They're relaxing. They promote development of social skills. They're uplifting. They teach us cooperation. They help us learn to manage our emotions. They improve brain function, learning, and cognition. They relieve stress. They enhance healing. They stimulate creativity and problem solving. They keep us feeling youthful.

Build at least a few minutes of play time and laughter into every day. Tell jokes, tickle, play games, make funny faces, watch funny movies, listen to comedy on your way to and from work, or join a laughing group (people who get together to induce themselves and each other to laugh—yes, that's a real thing). Full belly laughs are best—they get the whole body involved. Meanwhile, reduce the degree to which you expose yourself to "feel bad" media, such as violent and tragic films and news stories. Beyond dedicated playtime, we encourage you to infuse play into your life. Become a *playful* person. Don't be so serious. Cultivate *lightness*—it's always available. We've played games to become healthier, games to support more income, and games to make mundane or unpleasant chores more enjoyable. You can do this, too! Try asking yourself, "How much fun could I have with this?" whenever you're faced with something that doesn't seem inherently fun.

If you get motivated by incentives and disincentives, keep this in mind: if you're going to build in a disincentive to losing (or, rather than losing, let's say, *winning the least*), consider choosing something that you'd feel good about doing anyway, like a community service, a donation to a charity, a way to help a friend, or a task you've been procrastinating. And if you're the one who has to "pay up," make that a game, too! Competition can be healthy.

STRUCTURE, SWEETNESS, AND SPACE

Play is *sweetness* because its main purpose is enjoyment. In the act of play, much of what we've been mentally chewing on falls away, naturally opening *space* for us to connect, receive, and grow. Finally, the spirit of play is one of the most precious ingredients you could add to your *structure*. It can make an otherwise boring, difficult, or painful process more bearable. One of our favorite dramatizations of this idea is Roberto Benigni's film, *Life Is Beautiful*, in which he plays a father who is imprisoned in a concentration camp with his young son during the Holocaust. By convincing his son the whole thing is actually a game, he is able to shield the boy from the horrors of the experience.

Reflect back on the fun and motivating competitive experiences you've had in your life, and remember times when you worked harder than usual because of a competitive element. As a child you had less control over the atmosphere of competitive events—and some of the little shits you were playing against—but now that you're an adult, you get to choose the conditions of your competitive endeavors. You can keep them healthy and playful, and choose goals of enjoyment and achievement. You may occasionally find yourself in competitive scenarios with others who are decidedly *un*-playful, but this doesn't mean you can't keep it light and fun on your end.

Remember, play isn't just the specific fun activities you engage in, it's an attitude. When you have the perception that the world is your playground, with endless opportunities for exploration, and that your challenges are games, well, that's pretty much the definition of a good life.

8: Connecting with Others

Besides enabling our disconnection from nature, modern life has allowed us to be increasingly disconnected from other humans. We're busier and more independent. There's less intergenerational contact than ever. Online communities have allowed us to abandon our local communities. And high-profile cases of sexual abuse and harassment have made us paranoid about affection. It's a major loss of primary sources of social *structure* and *sweetness*.

STRUCTURE, SWEETNESS, AND SPACE

Connecting with others is like gathering around a fire on a chilly night. We smile more in the *sweet* warmth that's kindled through our interaction. Our life *structure* is bolstered by the support of others—both material support and the internal strength that develops through the exchange of ideas. And when we get out of our heads and really feel what's happening in community, we perceive the *space* between and around us that we're cocreating, where the magic of our synergy arises.

University of Chicago psychologist John Cacioppo has written that our need for social connection is tied to our most primal urge to survive; our brains even feature neurological circuitry specifically for processing social cues. We are pack animals. Yet, research shows that over the past few decades Americans have reported having fewer intimate friends, fewer people with whom they can discuss important matters, and a greater sense of isolation and loneliness. Many people are embarrassed about admitting their loneliness—which Cacioppo says is a feeling more similar to hunger, thirst, or pain than to mental illness. Lack of community also makes us more prone to form addictions and more susceptible to disease.

The solution is to let people into your life. Look for opportunities to meet like-minded folks. Although the Internet has in many ways made us more isolated, it has also spawned some great real-life get-together tools, like Meetup. Find ways to serve your community, to help someone, and to build friendships. We'll explain more about community building later in this book.

Let people into your life. Look for opportunities to meet like-minded folks.

Beyond casual social contact, there is a special therapeutic value to giving and receiving touch. This includes both platonic forms, such as massage and partner dancing, and intimate forms, including sex. Safe touch is good for the soul.

How Touch Impacts Us at Various Ages

Sadly, many people are not altogether at ease with touch. Nearly everyone goes through three difficult transitions that involve a withdrawal of loving touch. Within the womb, we are perpetually embraced by our mother's body. We're always held and never alone. All our needs are met; it's a state of perfection. The birth process is the first withdrawal of touch, and though we don't consciously remember it, it's the initial trauma of our lives.

Luckily, most of us continue to receive lots of physical affection after birth. We're kept close against our parents' bodies, we nurse from our mother, and family members and friends want to pick us up and touch our soft skin. We are properly adored. But within a year or two, the second process of withdrawal begins. Our parents need to get better sleep and have work to do; this requires putting us down more and moving us into our own bed. We're left alone for increasingly longer periods, but we don't have the language or competence to understand why contact is decreasing.

Around the time we enter school, our parents are likely to start warning us of inappropriate touch and "bad people" who may act friendly but actually wish to harm us. We learn that humans can be predatory and touch can be invasive. We're also increasingly in the company of other children who are as new to this as we are. There's a push-pull dynamic, whereby we're encouraged to join and submit to the will of the tribe while simultaneously experiencing hostility from other tribe members.

In our teenage years, the third degradation of innocent affection occurs as touch takes on new meaning. More than ever, it's premeditated and it's a communication. As we learn about sex, nearly every touch initiates a question in our mind: *What does this mean?* This coincides with a growing peer pressure to always know what *everything* means (teenhood is, after all, the *I know everything* time of life). We're reluctant to ask and scared to misinterpret, so we may endure or inflict unpleasant or unwanted touch.

Meanwhile, we're bombarded with a tremendous array of mixed signals, from the constraint imposed by religious groups, to the abusive touch perpetrated by their own representatives; from the hypersexualization of our media, to the media's own hypervigilance for sexual behavior it can condemn as scandalous. If you had excellent guidance through your developmental years, you may have made it to adulthood completely unrestrained about giving and receiving platonic physical affection; with very clear boundaries between platonic and sexual touch; and with the confidence to communicate whenever necessary to ensure that both parties are happy with the exchange. But, if you're like the 99 percent of the world that turned out somewhat less healthy and clear about touch, it's time to let yourself off the hook. Recognize that you've been through the unfortunate process just described and give yourself credit for being even remotely functional in this arena.

Inviting Healthy Touch Into Your Life

If you have had difficulty with giving and receiving healthy touch, we encourage you to begin the process of healing from the past. We tend to think of women as being most in need of this work, due to their higher likelihood of having been on the receiving end of bumbling and possibly abusive sexual contact, but men have a greater tendency to become emotionally shut down, so this work is also for any guy who can't share a hug with another man without inserting a handshake between your two bodies.

Obviously, if you've experienced severe physical or sexual abuse, this is a process worth navigating with a professional. But for all those with the garden variety of weird touch experiences, remember, there is abundant opportunity for safe touch. Though your mind may be scathed by your programming and experiences, your soul yearns for it. It may feel contrived and somewhat uncomfortable at first, but over time, you will relax into it. You'll be less conscious of every touch as it becomes more natural. And you'll return to your native state of comfort and enjoyment with touch.

The next time you're speaking with a friend, put a hand on their shoulder. Take a breath. And release. Whew.

⚜

These eight health maintenance practices aren't all-encompassing, but if you take care of yourself in these ways, you'll find it easier to navigate whatever challenges come along. Plus, you will feel vibrant and relaxed in your body and mind, which will spill over into all parts of your life.

CHAPTER 3.
FREE YOURSELF

RELEASING EMOTIONAL BAGGAGE

It's Time to Release the Past

In order to maintain a strong foundation that supports your progress toward a Well Life, there are all sorts of things you can do to fortify yourself, including the practices we covered in the previous chapter. But all the fortification in the world can be thwarted by the ways in which you simultaneously undermine that foundation. You can only get so far before unresolved conflicts, withheld forgiveness, and limiting beliefs from your past impede your progress. Therefore, you've got to get really *real* about your baggage in order to achieve the Well Life.

Are you carrying around nagging broken agreements, dysfunctional relationships, grudges, or limiting stories? It can be an uncomfortable process to clean this clutter up, but chances are, you're already living with a certain burden of discomfort because of not having dealt with or released these issues.

Sadly, our magic wands aren't powerful enough to turn your childhood into one long, happy visit to Disneyland, and we don't want to lead you to believe that you're going to fix your relationship with your past by the time you're done reading this section. What we aim to do is to make you aware of how you may be limited, and to teach you how to start the process of freeing yourself.

STRUCTURE, SWEETNESS, AND SPACE

We'll guide you through exercises to help uncover, clean up, and release thoughts and experiences that are sabotaging you from below the radar. Happily, this is work that yields immediate relief and greater access to *space* and *sweetness*. If that's not incentive enough, consider this: you simply *can't* move forward cleanly and lightly, or fully express your gifts, or experience life in an entirely unfettered way, if you aren't willing to release the hooks that are keeping you bound to the past. The rest of this chapter will show you the *structure* to help you do just that.

What's Wrong with Keeping the Past in the Past?

Now, before you think, "Oh boy, this is going to be heavy," we want to tell you that *this doesn't have to be a heavy experience*. In fact, it's an opportunity to feel lighter. It's just that, between the heaviness and the lightness, there's often something that one of our former teachers calls a "veil of discomfort." The discomfort is only a veil because it's really quite insubstantial. As soon as we become willing to experience it, we readily pass through it. And on the other side is lightness and opportunity!

Let's talk about how these loose ends from your past can undermine you. One thing that may happen when you prepare to go for something big (whether it be a new relationship, a career change, or a cross-country move) is that your mind quickly runs through all your baggage—unresolved issues, past traumas, mistakes, losses—and tells you this is a bad idea. Rather than hating your mind for this, it's important to remember that you programmed this mind. You started out as a baby with a clean mental slate, and little by little you trained your mind to look out for things that might threaten your survival or happiness. That's how your mind is built to work. It just happens that most minds are overly eager to do this job (especially if it means that your mind gets to monopolize your attention). The more intense the bad experiences of your past, the deeper the groove they cut in your mental record. The mind looks for anything in your present that even remotely resembles these past experiences so that it can steer you clear from repeating them. It produces warning thoughts and initiates intense emotions to grab your attention.

So what can you do? Thank your mind for its efforts to protect you, but inform it that it's working from outdated beliefs and overly generalized data. There's no purpose in blaming yourself for how your mind functions. You've done your best with the resources that were available to you in each moment. But if you want the freedom to show up to each moment without being restrained by your past, it's imperative to recognize that your baggage impedes this. Limiting beliefs and the echoes of past emotions are an intrusion on your *space* and the peace that lies within.

> If you want the freedom to show up to each moment without being restrained by your past, it's imperative to recognize that your baggage impedes this.

Figure Out What's Holding You Back

The key to identifying past incidents that get priority cleanup status is that when you bring them to mind and then check in with your body, you don't feel altogether light and clean. Instead, you might feel heavy, tight, agitated, or constricted. Or a negative emotion might come up, such as guilt, fear, shame, anger, regret, sadness, or grief.

It's possible that something you did that was objectively bad, like stealing the Statue of Liberty and burying it in your backyard, doesn't actually provoke an especially strong physical or emotional response when you focus on it. In such cases, it's important to remember that the objective "sin rating" of an event is less significant than how much of a hook it has in you. On the other hand, you might have accidentally thrown away your child's first finger-painting and experience a tremendous feeling of guilt when you think about it—this would be something worth addressing.

Think of this process like cleaning your living space. When your house is filthy, there are piles of documents, dishes, laundry, and areas needing repair. It can feel so daunting you don't know where to begin. You don't even *want* to begin. But once you start, and then you have one room that's clutter-free, it feels more manageable. Eventually, the whole house is pretty well in order, and then it's fairly easy to stay on top of it. In the same way, as you clean up your life, you'll find it both easier and more appealing to continue to clean, and to nip any new messes in the bud so they don't impede your future.

Use the following table as a way to release the baggage that is holding you back. You can replicate this on a separate piece of paper, or download this worksheet as a PDF from our website, www.thewell lifebook.com/resources.

MY BAGGAGE LIST				
ISSUE	BLAME	CONSEQUENCE	OPPORTUNITY	FIX

Let's look at how to fill in each column.

Column 1: What Are Your Issues?

In this column, write three unresolved situations. These could be:

- Things that happened in the past that you haven't let go of and still affect you (Perhaps you got your period while giving a speech to your school in white pants)
- Problems that are occurring right now (Maybe you're overweight and you hate it, or you're in the middle of an ongoing argument with your boss)

- Issues that involve other people (You ran over Mrs. McGil-licuddy's hairless cat)
- Situations that live entirely in your own experience (You stole a candy bar from the grocery store)

If you're having trouble thinking of issues, try asking yourself: What do I dislike or regret about myself, my life, other people, or the world? Or, who (from my own life) would I least want to be stuck with in an elevator? Then search through your answers for unresolved conflicts. Most people have enough issues worth clearing that it's a good idea to get some recycled paper in order to reduce the environmental impact of all the pages you could fill. Don't try to go through your entire life at this point, though. Just start with the first few things that come to mind.

When you choose the issues you want to work on, you don't need to explain the whole situation in the Issue column; just use a few key words ("candy bar") that will help your mind connect to it. Leave a bit of vertical space between each issue so that you're using the whole column for just three or four issues.

Column 2: Who Are You Blaming?

For each of your issues, it's now time to determine whom you are blaming for their existence. Whom are you holding hostage in your mind? From whom are you withholding forgiveness? Write their name or names in this column. It's quite possible (and common) for your response here to be *myself*.

The Power of Forgiveness

Think of letting your hostages go as a mental cleanse before you start building your new life. There's so much talk in the natural-health world about ways to cleanse our bodies, but so little about how to cleanse our minds. The most powerful mechanism for mental cleansing is *forgiveness*. Here's how to do it.

Recognize that most people are just confused children (or at least we can be when we're emotional).

Our bodies have gotten bigger and older looking, but our minds have no such built-in maturity program. In all likelihood, we never got the expert training we all could have used in conflict resolution, nonviolent communication, navigating the socialization process, and developing our emotional intelligence.

We're still looking to get our needs met, still wanting everyone's approval, still perhaps wanting to cause hurt when we get hurt. So when we're upset, we are often operating from a perspective that's not much different than it was when we were six years old.

In the process of stumbling through life, we often cause pain for others. If you've been on the receiving end, it may be worth considering that the perpetrators of the hurt were acting out of confusion: not really understanding that they could get their needs met without hurting someone else, not really understanding the impact of their actions, not really conscious of the love that's always available to them, and not really understanding the nature of their connectedness to you. This may not make their actions *okay* for you, but hopefully it makes forgiveness an option.

Consider the possibility that lifelong punishment may be unreasonable.

If it's your intention to withhold forgiveness of someone (possibly yourself) for the rest of your life, maybe this qualifies as "cruel and unusual." It's a uniquely human thing to hold a grudge and never let it go. Ask yourself: *How long will I hold on to this before it will be enough?* Or, *how much longer am I going to pollute myself with this?* Then experience your reaction to this question—feel it, accept it, let it move through you, and be done with it.

View forgiveness as something we do for ourselves as much as for the other person.

When you withhold forgiveness of others, you basically take on the job of administering an ongoing punishment. So, you're playing warden in the mental prison you're keeping them in, and it demands energy and mental "bandwidth." Do you really want to *give* your energy and peace of mind away to the very person you believe wronged you? Does corrupting your peace and restricting your inner freedom make the situation better in any way?

Resentment is an emotional poison in your system. Even if you don't want to do anything nice for the person you've been resenting, for your *own* sake you need to get that poison out. The nice part is that it will bring you immediate relief. You get to quit that warden job and detox from the poison in the same act.

See forgiveness not as a single act, but as an ongoing commitment.

Often it may not be possible for you to just pronounce someone forgiven and have that be the end of it. As we said, strong feelings cut deep grooves; it's easy to fall back into them. Instead, you might need to make a commitment with yourself that from now on you're going to recognize any time you've begun harboring resentment toward them again. And every time you notice that you've picked it back up, you're going to let it go again. You're not going to analyze why you picked it up again, you're not going to scold yourself for having picked it up again, and you're not going to indulge in the resentment again. You're just going to drop it (forgive them again) as efficiently as possible. And you'll immediately feel lighter. Soon, the habit of dropping it will begin to replace the habit of holding onto it.

If you feel so emotional that forgiveness seems impossible, choose anger over despair.

As soon as you have enough distance from the situation to wonder, "What do I do with this intense emotion I'm carrying around?" remember that anger can be more easily transformed into action and determination than hurt and sadness can. So, if you're stuck, find the part of you that is angry about whatever happened.

This adversarial part of you insists to yourself (and probably others) that someone did something *wrong*. That something *shouldn't* have happened that did happen. And simultaneously that you and your current perspective on the matter are *right* about this. Perhaps you build your case in the shower and while driving.

The thing is, when you're stuck in needing to be right, you block your progress in life. You diminish your *perspective* by hanging onto this. You keep yourself from seeing the big picture of what will most efficiently get you to a life of happiness and fulfillment.

When you're harboring a grievance against someone or something, you can hang out in the mental place of "he/she/this was wrong" forever, but if this is your way of pushing back against something that someone did to you, in a way they're *still* sticking it to you as long as you live in this mindset. As long as you continue to cripple your own life and happiness for this mental argument, they're *still* hurting you. As long as you replay these conversations and events, you reopen your own wound.

The river of life continues to flow, but you're clinging to a rock called "This Wasn't Supposed to Happen." The silly part is that you're probably not *really* stuck in a fight. Chances are, this is a one-sided war that's happening in your mind, where it's only you who continues to get punished. You who pretends that there's value in carrying on with it, sorting it out, perpetuating a fight that the other party isn't present for. You who's corrupting your own happiness and potential, corrupting the quality of presence you have with others, and investing energy into something that will never give you back anything.

If the best you can muster is anger and the desire to cause hurt, then the ideal way to stick it to the other person would be to not let them have any more of your soul than you've already given. Instead, pull back *all* the energy you're spilling on them. If you can't manage to shake the anger, if you find yourself wanting to cause hurt, try to approach it from the angle of self-preservation—forgive them so they no longer have their hooks in you. Divest completely. Forgive completely so that they don't get the tiniest bit of your consciousness anymore. Eventually the need to withdraw your energy will be replaced with a feeling of neutrality.

Remember: the person who needs the most forgiveness is you.
If you're like nearly all other humans, to some degree you blame yourself for everything about your life that isn't the way you think it should be. You may not be aware of it, and you may also be blaming someone else, but chances are when things aren't perfect, your mind has an explanation that amounts to: *there's something wrong with me,* or, perhaps more specifically, *my body is wrong, my mind is wrong, I'm making the wrong choices, I messed up my life,* etc.

The focus of this self-blame is so broad that we believe it's simply an inevitable product of the way children are raised. The emphasis during our early years is to learn, and the goal of every lesson is to be *right.* You got approval when you ate all your food or named the correct color (you did it right) and disapproval when you drew on the wall (you did it wrong). And since most of this positive and negative feedback came from your caregivers—the people responsible for your very survival—you made being right one of your highest priorities.

You became an expert at being—or, at least, appearing—right. Two important secondary behaviors developed from this training:

1. First, you taught your subconscious to habitually identify *wrong* things—because it's at least as important to know and avoid being wrong as it is to be right.
2. Second, you learned to internally preside over the judgment of your own behavior. By policing yourself, scolding yourself, and withholding approval from yourself, you could get better at presenting only rightness to the world.

Our self-criticism is such a constant thing that many of us barely even notice it. Even in psychologically healthy folks, it's likely that there are dozens of thoughts each day that go something like: "I'm not working fast enough," "I should be thinner," "I shouldn't have said that," "I should have done that differently," "I should be better at . . . ," "I'm so bad at making money," "I haven't done anything impressive compared to other people," and more. Self-blame thoughts like these make us less happy, and they cause us to withhold self-approval, even if the thoughts aren't actually that bad. Even if we think, "But it's *true.*"

Self-limiting beliefs are like sandbags weighing down your hot air balloon. And when you forgive, it's like cutting the strings. When you start forgiving habitually, not only do you begin to experience a lightness and freedom that for many of us has been absent for decades, but you also begin to recognize just how powerful you are.

Column 3: Consequence

It's time to return to your Baggage List. In the third column, given the grievance you listed in the first column, the person or people you're blaming and withholding forgiveness from in the second column, and the discussion earlier, what is the consequence of allowing this to remain unresolved? Even if you can't think of an objective consequence, there's always the toll it takes on your peace of mind and *space.* For example, if you're in an unresolved argument with your boss, maybe this is causing you to dread work, which you normally enjoy. If you ran over a cat, perhaps the consequence is the foul smell in your apartment from having adopted dozens of strays out of guilt.

Column 4: Opportunity

What if you could just stop struggling with it and be at peace about this? What would be possible if you let the issue go? Greater happiness? More energy? Freedom? The ability to move on with your life? Write your answer here.

Column 5: Fix

This column is where you look ahead to how you can work to resolve this issue to free yourself to build your Well Life. What action will you take to fix this issue? A commitment to let it go every time it arises? A communication to achieve resolution? A demonstration of your trustworthiness? A ritual to release yourself or someone else from your prison?

Here are a few more ideas:

- If you broke an agreement, betrayed someone's trust, acted without integrity, or in some other way caused harm (and the recipient of this harm could have been you), acknowledge what you did, don't make excuses, and *clean it up*. Do something that displays the sincerity of your apology. Go above and beyond—especially if your aim is to regain someone's trust (or your own). Show up for them (or yourself) 110 percent. Replace or repair what was broken, or repay what was stolen. (We'll get into fixing broken agreements in greater detail in the next chapter.)

- There are times when admitting a past wrongdoing or openly fixing an old trauma in order to clear your side of things would do more harm than good. If the other party has moved on, or it wouldn't be safe or productive to involve them in your resolution, *don't*. Although we want you to repair the wounds you have caused, this isn't always possible. In such cases, our concern is *your* healing, forgiving *yourself*, re-establishing trust in *yourself*, and your putting this behind *you*. In order to accomplish this, besides a commitment to forgiveness, you may consider an anonymous act of kindness toward them, a donation to a charity, or a ceremony by yourself, such as planting a tree to symbolize new hope and healthy growth.

- Most of the past transgressions that weigh on us involved ways in which we didn't honor ourselves or actually did ourselves harm. Besides forgiveness—fierce forgiveness—we encourage you to actively demonstrate love for yourself. How can you show yourself how much you love *you* today? What nice things could you do for yourself? How could you *listen* to yourself even better? How could you honor yourself more completely?

- Consider trying a forgiveness practice used by Dr. Ihaleakala Hew Len based on the ancient Hawaiian art of reconciliation known as *ho'oponopono*. See yourself in your mind and repeat these four statements, as if speaking from your soul to yourself: "I love you. I'm sorry. Please forgive me. Thank you." Using these words like a mantra can help release you from your own bondage and return you to health. It can also be applied to others.

- As rituals go, we like the use of fire when the intention is closure. For example, you could write a letter to someone who is no longer alive or available, explaining your actions and asking forgiveness. Or you could write out the whole story of a traumatic event, imagining as you write that all of your emotion around the subject is entering your words and being put onto the paper. The story you tell yourself about this issue lives in your mind, and your mind thinks in words. As you bring up all of the most charged feelings that are within you, choose the charged words that most accurately reflect the words you use in your mental story. When you're done with your story or letter, feed it to the fire, declare your intention to let this issue go, and leave it up to the universe to take care of it from here.

No matter what fix you choose, make sure you *do* these fixes, and as you do them, fully expect that the opportunities you listed in the fourth column will come to be. Moving forward, return to this five-column format whenever you're stuck. All you need is a scrap of paper and a pen.

Reducing Baggage on a Daily Basis

Healing your past takes effort and a willingness to be uncomfortable, but it's absolutely worth it. Every time you resolve one of these issues, it's like letting go of a suitcase full of rocks. As you experience increased freedom and lightness, you'll start *wanting* to identify and clean up conflicts and grievances because you'll perceive their weight on your spirit.

As a smaller scale daily practice, it's a great habit to let all the "snags" go at the end of each day—or, better yet, as soon as they happen. Anytime something occurs that you have resistance to (dirty dishes left out, someone using a condescending tone of voice, a piece of bad news, a stiff back), it encroaches on your *space*. The encroachment is more a function of your reaction to the incident than the incident itself. Forgive your body, forgive your mind, forgive the world, forgive everyone for everything you think they're doing wrong. Dissolving these conflicts as they form will help minimize the accumulation of new stuff to clean up. If there's a conflict you can't let go of, communicate immediately to restore clarity and authenticity with the other person—or yourself, as the case may be.

⟡

The cleanup process entails getting a little dirty. If you aimed to scrub down a stable without getting a smudge on your pristine clothes, it would be a very uptight, arm's-length experience. But if you were to accept the dirt, tie back your hair, and jump in, it would go faster, easier, and you'd do a better job. We urge you to take the latter approach. Your future plans are more likely to succeed with a clean start.

CHAPTER 4.
YOUR RISE TO POWER

CREATING YOUR WORLD THROUGH YOUR WORD

Formulating Honest Agreements

If you're committed to not creating new baggage, it's essential that you bring your full consciousness to your agreements. As you embark on integrating intelligent *structure* into your life, this *structure* will hold up only if you have integrity and self-trust. This means only entering into agreements with yourself and others that you fully intend to keep, and following through on your agreements with a spirit of enthusiastic participation. The cleanness and self-reliance this fosters in you will feel refreshing and energizing.

This is one of our favorite subjects to discuss, because we've both had experiences of profound clarity around the significance of our agreements and what happens when we keep or break them. We feel that this one idea—*do what you say you're going to do*—could be the most life-changing habit a person could adopt.

When you make an agreement, it's like planting a seed. You have a desired outcome in mind, and the agreement is a declaration of the intention to achieve this outcome. A union is established between you and another person (if someone else is involved), between you and the universe (including all the surrounding variables you intend to have align in your favor), and between you and your highest self.

Any time you say you're going to do something, you're making an agreement. Following through on an agreement to its completion is a matter of integrity. When you honor this process, it supports the power of your word as an expression of truth and a tool of creation. However, when you break an agreement, your sweet little creation is aborted and it weakens the strength of your word. The late Sikh leader Yogi Bhajan is quoted in *Energy Maps* saying:

> Only enter into agreements with yourself and others that you fully intend to keep, and follow through on your agreements with a spirit of enthusiastic participation.

The highest, most effective energy on this planet is the word. When we understand the power of the word and we apply the whole mind behind the word, then we create the word, which can create the whole world for us. One who does not know how to live to his word does not know how to live. But if you will honor the word, you will be honored in this world.

Beyond honoring our agreements, we bolster the power of our word by speaking the truth, speaking with kindness, never polluting our environment with our words, and following our words with actions that support them (i.e., "walking our talk").

When we have honed our words to be precision tools of creation, they are indeed magic. But if we have undermined their value by repeatedly breaking our agreements, they cease to be a tool we can depend on. As the contractor of your own magnificent life, would you want a faulty, unpredictable, or even potentially harmful tool on your job site?

Early in our spa business, we hired a massage therapist who was amazing in her interview. She was professional and talented. She trained for a week, and we were eager for her to start work the following Tuesday. When Tuesday came and it was time for her shift, she was not at the spa. We called her repeatedly and she didn't answer. Like any good spiritual folks who endeavor to control their emotions, we were pissed off.

That evening she called, completely panicked. She had made a mistake in her schedule and left town to go skiing, thinking that she didn't start work until the next day. Rather than firing her on the spot, we decided to give it some thought and told her we'd call her back in the morning. If this was just a one-time honest mistake, it would be a shame to lose someone so talented, but flaking out on five clients on her very first day? It didn't bode well.

An hour later, she showed up at the spa with a little gift for us and chocolates for the rest of the staff, plus a note saying she was very sorry and that she understood how this must have affected both the staff and our clients. She offered to call the clients to apologize personally and to give each of them a free session with her. She also let us know that she would always double-check her schedule from then on and make sure it was in her calendar correctly.

We were impressed. She took complete responsibility for her actions, didn't give us any excuses, and made significant gestures to show her commitment to gaining our trust. We gave her another chance, and over time we came to consider her one of our most trustworthy team members. She was always on time, very reliable, and never missed a shift again. Because of her willingness to clean up her mistake rather than run away or deflect responsibility, we got a great employee for nine years, and hundreds of clients benefited from her healing work at our spa.

The Importance of Agreements with Yourself

If your plans don't often work out, it will be valuable to look at their underlying *structure*—your agreements. When we make agreements with others, most of us understand the consequences of breaking those agreements. If you break agreements with your boss, you might lose your job. If you break agreements with your friends, you might lose your friends. If you break agreements with family, you might hurt their feelings and lose their trust. In all cases, a relationship will be damaged.

So, what happens when you don't keep an agreement with yourself? It's not so different, really. A relationship is damaged; it's just harder to see. Let's say you decide to work out every day for a month but you quit after five days. There doesn't seem to be anyone getting screwed by breaking this agreement. Nobody is mad at you. Of course you'll let yourself off the hook. But your self-trust is eroded.

If you forgot to pick up your children from school, you'd probably make it a priority to regain their trust because you care so much about the relationship. But, chances are, you don't do that when you break an agreement with yourself. You may be barely aware that an agreement was broken. This matters in many ways, big and small.

If you serially break agreements with yourself—you don't get things done when you say you'll get them done, you don't wake up when you say you'll wake up, you don't treat your body as healthily as you tell yourself you will—the material consequences are unfortunate, but usually small. The bigger consequences are things like not being able to count on yourself, or giving up your big dreams for ones that are more realistic, given your history. If you have a habit of breaking agreements and now you want to do something big and important, your mind will have a lot of evidence to undermine you. Why should this time be any different than the past?

Four Steps for Re-Establishing Trust

If your trust with yourself or others has been eroded in the past, rebuilding it is key if you plan to make new agreements that everyone can rely on. Here are four ways to approach that process:

Be Clear When Defining an Agreement

Become clear about what constitutes an agreement and be conscious of the agreements you make. Generally, whenever you tell another person you will do something, this is an agreement. If it's left in a nebulous way, this may indicate that one or both parties are ambivalent about making the agreement, or that one or both parties has a track record of breaking agreements and is deliberately avoiding getting specific because they want to give themselves some leeway. For the sake of your *own* integrity, get specific. What *exactly* are you agreeing to?

If you had a passing thought about washing the car and then it didn't get done, is this a broken agreement? Well, you need to decide (before it's too late to get it done). Choose a format for making official agreements with yourself and stick to it. If you want to make an agreement with yourself to wash the car, you might think to yourself, "I agree to wash the car today," or you might say it out loud, or you might write it down. Just decide what constitutes an actual agreement.

Be forthright and *clean* with yourself and others. You know whether you meant something to be an agreement or not, and you can't really hide from yourself. The more nebulous you are, the more you allow yourself and others off the hook, the cloudier your mental *space* will become.

Look out for thoughts such as: *Did I say* one *more game of Candy Crush, and then I'd walk the dog? I think I meant to say* sixty *games. . . .* Or, *I know I planned to work out today, but what I meant was that I would work out unless something more important came up.* Be honest. As you distractedly lift your two-pound dumbbells while watching *The Late Show*, ask yourself: *Is* this *what I intended when I agreed to work out every morning?* Think about the quality of participation a boss or client would expect of you, and deliver at that level, whether it's for a friend, your spouse, or yourself.

Communicate Any Changes in the Agreement

If you anticipate that you won't be able to keep an agreement, communicate ahead of time and look for ways to make it work and avoid a loss of trust. This means, if you're running late to meet a friend at 3:00, you don't text them at 3:05 to say "on my way" if you genuinely care about the relationship, your integrity, and the power of your word. A more noble option would be to let them know well in advance so that they can go later or bring a book, or, if they wish, to change the agreement altogether. Even if you haven't yet broken the agreement, if you're calling to change the agreement, the responsibility is yours to make sure the other person understands that they matter to you and that they are satisfied with the arrangement.

If you're changing an agreement with yourself, again, do it well in advance, apologize to yourself, tell yourself that you matter, and find a way to stay in harmony. If you find yourself repeatedly changing agreements with yourself or someone else, you're likely to begin losing trust, even if you're *technically* not breaking these agreements. In this case, it's worth asking yourself if you're really backing up your agreements with an attitude of enthusiastic participation.

Even if the other party doesn't mind letting you off the hook over and over again, remember that this is about building up your own sense of self-trust. It's *your* integrity that's at stake, and even if *they* don't care, almost everyone will appreciate that *you do*.

STRUCTURE, SWEETNESS, AND SPACE

The biggest motivator for most people to stay clean around agreements is that broken agreements significantly degrade your ability to enjoy sweetness, they shrink your sense of space, and they undermine the stability of your structure. But we prefer to lead you through positive reinforcement. Agreements are structures, and healthy agreements make for a healthy life. When you get clean with your agreements, you'll discover a unique quality of sweetness there— like living in a clean house. This cleanness also brings an opening of space. When your mind isn't cluttered with feelings of obligation and guilt (because you've cleaned up broken agreements and you trust yourself to keep your current and future agreements) your "bandwidth" increases and you pick up on subtle gifts, such as beauty, intuition, and grace.

Clean Up Broken Agreements

Unfortunately, despite everyone's best efforts, sometimes agreements get broken. Whether the broken agreement is with yourself or another person, the steps to repair it are the same:

- **Express that you broke an agreement and take responsibility for it.** No excuses. Making excuses—*even if they're true*—is a deflection of responsibility and indicates a disregard for the health of the relationship, whether with yourself or someone else, and whether or not you feel it was actually your fault. Blame only degrades the communication.
- **Be sincerely apologetic.** Remember, you value this relationship. Try to understand the other party's experience. If you broke an agreement with yourself, understand that this divides you—you're frustrated with your own unreliability in this situation—and apologize to yourself for this.
- **Making a gesture that is meaningful to the other person shows them that you care,** and demonstrates that you're working on re-establishing trust. Simply letting someone know the steps you've taken in your own life to make sure that you don't make that same mistake again can go a long way.
- **Remind yourself that you matter.** Your showing up with integrity matters to you, to others, to the world. You add your own specialness and value to every circumstance.

If you broke an agreement with a friend, you'd acknowledge the damage that was done: "I feel terrible about missing your show. I'm really sorry. I cherish you as a friend and I want to be there for you." You would do something special the next time you saw them (like bringing them flowers or helping them with a project) to demonstrate your commitment to fixing the relationship. And you'd remind yourself that your presence matters. Even if your friend is willing to let it slide, your own consciousness is watching, too. Are you making a statement of self-worth or the opposite?

When cleaning up a broken agreement with yourself, treat yourself like a friend. Rather than beating yourself up, acknowledge and repair the damage. Believe it or not, there really is a hurt part of yourself— a part of you that takes these broken agreements to mean, *I don't need to keep my agreements with you, because you don't matter.* Affirm to yourself that you *do* matter and that you *can* be trusted. Then make a new agreement that goes beyond the one you broke, and be sure to keep it. Or, if you broke the agreement because it wasn't a realistic agreement (which means you had no business making it in the first place), make a new agreement about something that supports you in another way (some act of self-care, for instance), and keep it.

Having a bunch of broken agreements equates to a lot of loose ends in your life. It's sloppy and it pollutes your *space.* You're in charge of your life. With a spirit of kindness and virtue, clean it up.

Don't Make Too Many Agreements

Not taking on too much is especially important as you begin this process. If you wanted to get an estranged friend to trust you again after you missed five lunch dates, you wouldn't start out by offering to edit their thesis, refinish their floors, and meet them to watch the sunrise every day for a year. You'd just be setting yourself up for more damaged trust. Instead, you might ask them earnestly to give you one more chance at lunch, and you'd make sure to get there early.

Your Word Has Value

The process of re-establishing self-trust starts with baby steps. For the first few days, you might want your only official agreements to be things you'd probably do anyway, like, *Wake up no later than seven o'clock*, and, *Have dinner ready by six thirty.* Do this so you can become more conscious of your agreements with yourself and then be sure to keep them. Over time, you can add a bit more to your list. But never make an agreement you think you're likely to break. Eventually, you'll have an impressive dossier on your trustworthiness.

You will have demonstrated to yourself and others hundreds of times that w*hat you say is going to happen . . . happens.* Your word will be as good as law. When you say to yourself, *I'm going to change the world,* there will be a mountain of evidence to indicate that big things are coming. And because the words of a person of integrity initiate a series of predictable behaviors, the world *understands how to support you.*

One of our mentors said, "When you keep your agreements, your life works." Over the years, we have noticed that when we're managing our agreements well, life feels easier, cleaner, and more magical. In contrast, when we have a broken agreement, something feels *off.* In fact, whenever something feels off, we check to see if there's an unnoticed broken agreement that needs our attention. If anything is out of whack in your life, turn back to your agreements, start keeping them, and watch how things fall into place.

❖

There's more potential for your buttons to get pushed while holding yourself to agreements, but this foundation work is vital. If you were to commit to only the work of this one chapter, your life would be forever changed in a positive way. You will feel healthier in body and mind, you'll feel lighter with regard to your relationships, and everything you set out to do will be more likely to succeed with the power of your word behind it.

Regarding the pushing of your buttons, if the buttons are there, they're going to get pushed (because it's tempting to push buttons— just ask any kid). We're reminded of one of Peter's earliest spiritual mentors, SiriNam Singh, who, upon getting any of his buttons pushed—especially ones he had been unaware of—would jubilantly exclaim, "Thank you for showing me my buttons!" He said this with real gratitude, because he understood that when you don't know your buttons, you get pushed around by life. When you know your buttons, you can begin to deactivate them, take away their power, and experience more and more freedom. With that, we encourage you to join our lifelong button-finding quest, and we applaud you for taking these first steps toward a deeply rooted Well Life.

PART 2.
RESOURCES FOR THRIVING

We want to help you bring your potential into the world—to innovate, to connect, to heal, to create, to make it a better place for everyone—and doing work of this magnitude requires having good resources. Your internal and external sources of support give you a sense of solidity and promote the courage to take risks. It's important to get your resources in order before you take on big goals, and this part will explain how to do that.

Just remember that you don't need to be prepared for every possible obstacle before you can start. At some point, you'll look at your resources and say, "This is pretty good, and I'll keep cultivating these resources even as I move forward with my plans."

Resources can be understood in a number of ways. They primarily serve as structure, *though they also provide opportunities for* sweetness *and hold us as we access* space. *While different people have different needs when it comes to resources, we're going to cover three of the most valuable: energy, confidence, and community.*

CHAPTER 5.
ENERGY

The Constant Quest for More Energy

Energy is big business. Our demand for more of it has produced a market for 20,000+ Starbucks stores. Then there's Rockstar and Red Bull and Coke and all the other caffeinated beverages. Sure, people could be drinking this stuff for the flavor. Or they could be going to Starbucks for the pastries. But we all know the main driving force behind the industry is our desire for *more energy.*

To a mind that thinks it needs to get more done, more energy appears to be the solution. The difference between you and the savant entrepreneur who writes a book every year and sold her first company at age twenty-five? Perhaps you've told yourself, "I just don't have that kind of energy," and such a life therefore seems unattainable.

The more important discussion may be whether your underlying beliefs about productivity are valid and useful, but we'll get to that later. For now, we're willing to agree that energy is important. With good energy, your gifts are more likely to be shared with the world. With fatigue, you're more likely to tell yourself it's not important that you do anything, or you just beat yourself up for not being more productive. So, let's talk about energy.

Understanding Your *Jing*

One of the most valuable lessons we've garnered from the study of Eastern systems of medicine is the concept of *essence*—known as *jing* in Traditional Chinese Medicine and as *ojas* in Ayurveda. It's an idea worth sharing with the West. Our *jing* can be roughly understood as our life potential, stored deep inside us. It's a combination of genetic inheritance, Divine and parental contributions, and innate gifts. When allowed to emerge into the world at our own pace, we tend to live long and productive lives. But if we stress out, burn the candle at both ends, and try to rush life along, we can habitually exceed our resources, and we may exhaust our *jing* prematurely. When our *jing* begins to decline, our body shows signs of aging.

> Jing can be roughly understood as our life potential, stored deep inside us. It's a combination of genetic inheritance, Divine and parental contributions, and innate gifts.

Inherited *Jing* vs. Acquired *Jing*

There are actually two kinds of *jing*—prenatal or inherited *jing*, and postnatal or acquired *jing*:

1. As you can probably guess, **inherited** *jing* is what we're born with. It's essentially unreplenishable. You get what you get, and if you burn it up too fast you can't have it back.
2. **Acquired** *jing* is what we accumulate every day through eating good food and extracting the life in it; through getting deep, restful sleep; through having loving interactions with the world and its inhabitants; through recognizing the gifts in our lives and letting that recognition really soak in. In essence, acquired *jing* is replenished through everything that really nourishes us.

Your inherited *jing* is best left alone. As life proceeds, this potential is manifest in physical growth and development, the unfolding of your life, and the expression of your gifts and purpose. This facet of your essence is often described as being like a well—a well with enough water for one lifetime. Every time you pull an all-nighter, you tap into this well. Every time you ignore your fatigue and use caffeine to keep going, you tap into this well. Every time your fight-or-flight system gets triggered, you tap into this well.

Aside from the rare emergency, there should be no need to draw your inherited *jing* into the world before its time. If your inherited *jing* is represented by a well that gets its water from a subterranean reservoir, then your acquired *jing* is more like a rain barrel, which catches the rain that falls each day as an expression of the nourishing things you do. Why tap into the well when you can drink right from the rain barrel?

How Do You Handle Energy Crises?

Using your two kinds of *jing* the way they were intended is mostly a matter of expanding your consciousness (i.e., paying closer attention to your relationship with your resources) and exercising discipline. Think of your acquired *jing* as your daily allotment of energy. It's energy that feels good—grounded and solid. When it runs out and you tap into your inherited *jing*, it feels like "emergency energy." If you really pay attention to it, you'll notice a qualitative difference. It's like the difference between the energy you have after a great night's sleep and a healthy breakfast (plenty of acquired *jing*) and that of a strong cup of coffee after a terrible night's sleep (the raw feeling of inherited *jing* released too early). The energy of burning inherited *jing* may have a deep fatigue beneath it. It may feel edgy, jittery, and rushing. In biomedical terms, it often corresponds to activating the sympathetic nervous system (the fight-or-flight mechanism) and getting hormonal energy by tapping your adrenal glands.

If you pay attention, you may notice at some point in your day that your energy is waning, and you can choose to respect this or ignore it.

If you ignore it and push through, you may well shift from consuming acquired *jing* to consuming inherited *jing*. Sometimes we call this "pushing through the wall." If you do this frequently, it becomes taxing.

When you crash into bed having exhausted all your acquired *jing* and also having tapped into some of your inherited *jing*, you're at an energy deficit. You've used more resources than you had available. A better option would be to go to bed as soon as you get to the natural end of your daily allotment of energy. But the best option, especially if you have a past of not respecting your limits and you're exhausted as a result, would be to go to bed with some of your acquired *jing* still left. It's a rare thing to encounter someone who's committed enough to their future health to practice this. In this way you'd actually be *investing* some of your acquired *jing*, and over time, you're likely to build up richer reserves.

Certain diseases—and the signs of aging in general—are attributed to depletion of *jing*, such as graying and thinning of hair, loose and devitalized teeth, osteoporosis, hearing and vision loss, incontinence, poor memory, and muscle wasting. The concept is simple, really—*don't use more energy than you have*—but we often have a hard time convincing patients to take this seriously. Heck, plenty of practitioners, ourselves included, have a hard time abiding by this rule. Modern life makes us feel we always need to do more and to do it faster, and harder, and that it's noble to *push* every step of the way to achievement. However, you simply can't exceed your available resources without paying a price, and with recurrent violation of this law, the price becomes increasingly steep.

Early in Peter's medical practice he met an older professor of Chinese pulse diagnosis, and they started talking about this concept of not using more energy than you have—and how nobody takes it seriously. He himself had spent years breaking this rule as he strove to make a living as an acupuncturist in San Francisco. One day he asked his own mentor, a true elder in our field, to treat him. But his mentor felt his pulses and refused. "I won't treat you," he said. "You need to work less. I can feel it in your pulses. There's no reason to try to build you up until you get this under control."

The professor started making arrangements to cut back on work. Ultimately, he was able to stop working for a year and a half, and during that time he looked at all of the ways in which he was unintentionally expending energy. Things he did that got him upset, he realized, consumed energy. That meant not reading the newspaper and watching the news so much. Things that made him afraid or on edge, like scary movies, got his adrenaline flowing—needlessly. *Little by little, he became tuned in to everything that took an energetic toll without yielding something of value in return, and he cut these things out of his life.*

When he began this hiatus, his health was declining, he felt old, and he believed things could only go downhill. Afterward, he saw this time off as the single most life-changing act he had ever taken. He had his health back and his life back. It forever altered the way he related to his resources. He became conscious of the energy cost of all his choices and the potential return—or lack thereof—he stood to gain. That didn't mean he never stayed up late dancing—that might be an energy expenditure he could recover from quickly and which would yield a huge return in the form of fun, connection, and a feeling of vitality.

Sure, there might be some merit to burning through life fast. If that's your choice, please make sure you're doing it consciously. You might as well burn through it loud and bright too, with no holding back and no regrets. What good is a life consumed prematurely due to fear or an obsession with work? Hopefully, you're at a place in life where there's ample opportunity to heal your relationship to your resources, to bring greater awareness to how you expend energy, and to evaluate whether the resource-demanding habits you engage in are actually worthwhile.

The Impact of an Energy Deficit on Your Body

In case that *jing* discussion was too out-there for you, let's look at what's happening biologically when you push yourself beyond your means. The adrenal glands are probably the closest anatomical analog to the well of inherited *jing*. We demand more from them when we're stressed, and they oblige by giving us some extra energy and suppressing our pain.

Historically, depleted adrenals weren't recognized as a medical condition by doctors unless they were essentially nonfunctional—a condition known as Addison's disease. But progressive healthcare practitioners have been diagnosing and treating the milder condition of "adrenal fatigue" for a few decades. Now we see it so much that it's kind of absurd that most mainstream doctors still don't know how to test for it or treat it.

If you have really low energy, feel exhausted after exerting yourself, feel lightheaded when you stand up, and you have a history of stress—either psychological stress or the physical stress of not getting enough sleep, not eating well, working long hours, being chronically ill, or managing chronic pain—there's a good chance your adrenals aren't performing as they should, and it's worth seeing a naturally oriented healthcare provider. They can do a saliva test for adrenal hormones known as cortisol and DHEA to confirm this and then help you through the rehabilitation process.

The recommendations that follow in the rest of this chapter are for anyone who doesn't have an abundance of energy. For those with true adrenal insufficiency, additional help may be needed, but these lifestyle changes are still an important part of the recovery process. Whether you're just a bit less energetic than what seems normal or you're deeply fatigued, chances are you got there, at least in part, by pushing through life and ignoring your limitations. (And if your energy is great, congratulations! This stuff is still worth reading so that you *stay* energetic.)

Our intention is not to scold you but to educate you. You get to a state of energetic depletion by:

- Pushing rather than trusting
- Paddling against the current of life rather than going with the flow
- Demanding that your desired future be here *now* instead of fully accepting and relishing the present

* Allowing yourself to go unconscious around the impact of your lifestyle, your stress, and the habitual arousal of your nervous system

Before we get into the specifics of energy awareness and enhancement, rate your energy on a scale of zero to ten, where zero represents total exhaustion, and ten represents a state of being fully charged (not manic, just the maximum of positive energy you could see yourself having). Overall, how has it been for the past two weeks? Stop reading for a moment, check in, actually choose a number, and write it down somewhere like so: "Self-evaluation of my energy on [date]: seven out of ten."

Factoring in Stimulants

Now, were you rating yourself with stimulants in your system? If so, you didn't evaluate your *actual, unmedicated* level of energy. Therefore, reconsider what your energy would be in the absence of caffeine, sugar, chocolate, or other stimulants, and record this value instead. Modest amounts of these substances aren't a problem for most people, but this varies based on each individual and how much is consumed. While a single cup of coffee could have no negative impact on one person, it could give another intense agitation and insomnia. Wherever you fall on the spectrum, if you consume stimulants, it's worth asking yourself why you use them and what's wrong with being unstimulated. If your energy is low, figure out and address what's *actually* causing it. You know that the energy you get from caffeine is artificial and involves a tradeoff.

We see caffeine as having something of a mixed effect. In modest doses, it activates our metabolism, mobilizes sluggish energy and fluids, and gives us a mild energy boost. In larger doses, it revs up the nervous system and consumes resources. The line between modest dose and large dose varies from person to person, and only you can know if you're on the healthy side of that line. If you feel edgy, anxious, fatigued, or have sleep problems, it will take smaller doses to cross into the unhealthy range. Coffee, black and green tea, and choc-olate all have certain well-documented health benefits, but it's impor-tant to consider what else you're consuming when you have them. For instance, the sugar in your chocolate or coffee makes them less healthy.

Other Stimulants

Beyond consumable stimulants, you may find that you stimu-late yourself to stay energetic—or even hyperaroused—through things like social media, exercise, video games, endless task lists, or simply pushing through when you hit your wall. This isn't necessar-ily unhealthy, but it's important to pay attention to these behaviors because of their potential to deceive you as to your true energy. What would happen if, in the middle of the day, you were asked to sit alone in a dark room? Would you fall asleep in a matter of seconds? If so, you're probably fatigued.

Structure for Optimal Energy

The *structure* that will allow you to have great energy builds on some of the basic concepts we've discussed so far. There are four funda-mental aspects to this practice:

1. Understand how energy comes to you and how it leaves
2. Learn to feel yourself expending energy and reduce your expenditure
3. Learn to feel how you build energy and enhance this process
4. Respect the limits of your daily allotment of energy and strictly reduce demands on your reserves

Abiding by these principles isn't all that different from earning money and balancing your bank account. Tapping into your inherited *jing*, on the other hand, is like drawing on credit and going into debt. We already discussed numerous factors that contribute to excessive expenditure of energy. Following are some more to consider.

ENERGY DRAINERS

- "Feel bad" movies, horror movies, thrillers—any media that makes us tense
- Being especially empathetic (feeling bad on behalf of someone who is experiencing a challenge)
- Getting outraged about politics, upset about tragedies, sad about other people's problems, etc.
- Being deeply invested and stressed about work projects
- Addictions
- Illness, injury, pain, and disability
- Food sensitivities
- Poor diet or unhealthy eating habits
- Being involved in unresolved conflicts; these could be current or from your past, but in any case, they demand mental energy
- Harboring negative thoughts and emotions—anxiety, depression, fear, anger, pessimism, outrage, grief, sadness, judgment, or any other state that feels unresolved
- All other stressors, good and bad—moving, change of job or school, change of relationship status, death of a loved one or other loss, pregnancy, financial strain, health problems, travel, new responsibilities, etc.

To restore your energy (and nourish acquired *jing*), you can start by embracing the eight health maintenance practices we covered in Chapter 2. In particular, the following items are worth integrating into the *structure* of your energy optimization plan:

- **Good nutrition and hydration.** Besides the nutrition concepts we already discussed, when it comes to the *structure* of nutrition for optimal energy, it's worth considering whether you're eating foods that are appropriate to your metabolism and constitution. Some of our patients have felt considerably more energy with a high-protein diet, a high-fat diet, or a high–complex carbohydrate diet. Others have found that a certain ratio of carbs to fat to protein works best. Figuring out the ideal foods for optimal energy for *you* will require some experimentation and perhaps the help of a naturally oriented healthcare provider. Furthermore, if you get tired after eating, this could result from overeating, eating too fast, eating a food you have a sensitivity to, or possibly a deficiency of stomach acid or pancreatic enzymes (these break down food and prepare the nutrients for absorption).

- **Restful sleep.** The word "restful" is key here, since the number of hours you spend in bed isn't all that meaningful unless it's spent in deep, restorative sleep. Along with nutrition, sleep is the main way we replenish energy. There is simply no substitute for good sleep. Look back at Chapter 2 for tips on improving sleep.

- **Weight optimization.** A bigger body requires more energy to maintain it, heat it, move it around, circulate blood through it, etc. Moreover, the factors that led to weight gain in the first place (such as unhealthy eating habits) may have contributed to compromised digestive function, and this may continue to impede energy production from food. Losing weight and repairing compromised digestion can yield huge improvements in energy.

- **Exercise.** If you want more energy, it's vital to *structure* exercise into your routine. Exercise—especially the aerobic kind—is effective at liberating pent-up thoughts and emotions that can bind up a significant portion of your energy. Muscle-building is also important. We believe it increases a person's *energy-carrying capacity* by creating more *structure* to hold blood and energy.

- **Breathing.** You'll keep living even if you never think about it, but correcting a habit of shallow breathing and learning to breathe fully and deeply can help you feel more alive and energetic.

When we perceive fatigue as a feeling of *not enough* energy, it's natural to conclude that it must signal a need for *more* of something.

But we can also be tired because of something the body or mind has *accumulated*. This can cause a demand on our energy and may produce stagnation or blockage, which interferes with proper replenishment, distribution, and availability of energy. Some examples of accumulations that drain energy are infections, excess body weight, mold, toxins, and negative thoughts and feelings — any of which could produce fatigue that's likely to disappear in its absence. Therefore, if your energy doesn't respond positively to the recommendations in this chapter, consider seeing a skilled healthcare practitioner who can do a more thorough investigation into such possible causes.

Sweetness for Optimal Energy

The *sweetness* of energy optimization lives primarily in recognizing and cultivating the things that nourish you, and in appreciating them as *sweetness* rather than perfunctory routines. Consider how much more you could enjoy these practices, and, because they're such an ongoing and prevalent element in your life, how much your life would thus be enhanced, if you chose to really savor them.

Communal Energy

Another type of energy to consider is *communal energy*. By communal energy, we're referring to the ambient energy around us, which is always available for our use. Some people tap into communal energy quite well without ever thinking about it. For others, it might take a greater focus of consciousness to draw from it. You can tune in to communal energy through acts of *sweetness* — by engaging with community; by getting inspired; through spiritual connection; by singing, dancing, or laughing; and through *direct* practices, such as *Qi Gong*, which entails deliberately focusing our consciousness on this reservoir and drawing energy into the body.

Elements of *Qi Gong* theory and practice (pronounced "chee gong," roughly meaning "energy skill") are present in Traditional Chinese Medicine, calligraphy, and martial arts. In *Qi Gong* terms, communal energy is one of many expressions of *qi*—the broader term for the energy matter that makes up everything. Mostly, *qi* is used to refer specifically to *life energy*—the stuff that animates us, gives us awareness, vitality, and power. *Qi Gong* practices are meditative, and may include slow, graceful movements, rapid forceful ones, or no outward movement at all. One's attention is nearly always on some facet of the energetic anatomy of the body. In our opinion, the greatest gift of *Qi Gong* is a concept called the "lower *dan tian*"; whether or not you have any interest in pursuing a *Qi Gong* practice, this element of *Qi Gong* is worth knowing about.

Getting in Touch with Your *Dan Tians*

In *Qi Gong* theory, our energetic makeup consists of a "central channel," like a vertical axis that runs from the very top of the head to the very base of the torso at the perineum. When our energy is relatively focused and consolidated in this central channel, we feel strong and centered. Along the central channel are three highly significant energetic centers, called *dan tians* ("dahn tee-en"). Often translated as "elixir field," a *dan tian* is a place where energy is stored and transformed. Here are your three centers:

1. The **lower** *dan tian* is located a few inches below the navel and a few inches deep (about halfway between the front and back of the body).
2. The **middle** *dan tian* is located at the level of the heart.
3. The **upper** *dan tian* is located between the eyebrows, all centered on the midline of the body.

The lower *dan tian* is considered to be the foundation of our energy. It's our center of gravity, and it's the place from which movement and power are initiated. When someone without training throws a punch, the movement usually starts at the shoulder or elbow. By comparison, a kung fu fighter activates the movement in the lower *dan tian*, and like a spark of electricity, it ripples through the pelvis, then rushes up the torso and out through the arm to the fist. The arm needs barely to move. Using this form of "inner training," Bruce Lee was famous for what was called the "one-inch punch." Starting with his fist just one inch away from an opponent's body, he could deliver a blow that would knock the other man over. Lee explained that it wasn't the thrust of a single inch of arm movement, but the power of his *qi.*

When you're under stress, it's easy for you to lose energy because your survival mechanisms are engaged. Your energy goes to the surface of the body to make you more alert for danger. You breathe more shallowly and become unanchored from your core. According to *Qi Gong* theory, your energy is more prone to be scattered or drained when it's poorly consolidated in your core. In order to better contain your energy, you need to bring your energetic focal point back down to your energetic center. Learning to focus on and strengthen your lower *dan tian* will counteract stress, make you more resilient, and build energy.

Try getting in touch with your lower *dan tian* now:

1. Let your abdomen relax completely, and allow each breath to descend the whole way down to your pelvis. For a minute or so, imagine that you're opening this bowl, including your hips, with every breath.
2. Next, focus on a point about two inches below your navel and deep at the center of your body. By scanning around in this area, you can find a point that feels most powerful and solid.
3. As you breathe in, imagine that you're drawing in pure light from every direction, funneling it into the lower belly.
4. With each exhale, imagine that you're condensing the light into the center of the lower *dan tian* to a ball of light the size of a pearl. The idea is that the more dense and solid you make this storehouse of energy, the more powerfully anchored your mind and energy will be, and the harder it will be for your energy to unconsciously "leak out."

We've created a guided meditation to walk you through this process. You can find it at www.thewelllifebook.com/resources.

If you make this a daily practice—breathing into your belly and focusing on your lower *dan tian*—you'll begin to notice that stressful events don't throw you off the way they used to. You'll bounce back quicker, too. Practice shifting the center of your consciousness (which usually resides in your head, since that's where most of your sense organs are) down to your lower *dan tian* as often as you think of it. See if you can tune in to the uniquely *sweet* experience of feeling solid in this region. How does it feel to stir a pot of soup or beat eggs with the movement coming from the lower *dan tian*? How does it feel to initiate the movement of walking from the lower *dan tian*? How about painting, or writing, or dancing, or speaking, all from the lower *dan tian*? We strongly encourage you to give it a try.

Savor It

When building energy through *Qi Gong*, sleep, nutrition, or any other nourishing practice, you can *sweeten* the practice by asking yourself:

> *What could I do to enhance the enjoyment or fulfillment of this act? Or, how would I relate to this act if my goal was to get as much enjoyment or fulfillment as possible out of it?*

For example, if you were to ask yourself what you could do to maximize the enjoyment and fulfillment of sleep, the answers might be things like making your bedroom the perfect sleeping space, getting a better mattress and bedding, letting go of stressful thoughts, and avoiding anything that might compromise your sleep, such as caffeine, electronics, or going to bed with a full stomach.

If you were to approach eating from the perspective of maximizing enjoyment and fulfillment, you might find yourself eating more slowly, you might savor the flavors and textures more, or you might visualize the energy from the food being absorbed by your body and distributed to all your cells.

If you were to focus on heightening the *sweetness* factor in your approach to exercise, water consumption, spiritual practice, and community, at the very least you'd enjoy these activities more. But in addition, you'd likely find yourself feeling more "charged" by them than ever before

KEY WAYS TO BUILD ENERGY THROUGH *SWEETNESS*

- Look great, even if you don't have to.
- Let yourself be fascinated by everything around you. If you look closely, you'll find amazing things everywhere.
- Practice gratitude. Be alert for gifts! Think about how your anticipation of gifts filled you with a bubbly eagerness on Christmas, Hanukkah, your birthday, or other gift-giving occasions. What if you knew each day would be full of gifts? They may be slightly hidden, but you can find them if you're alert.
- Serve others. There's nothing like witnessing the value you can add to others' lives.
- Do something lovely for yourself.
- Appreciate beauty. It's everywhere.
- Accept with delight whatever comes to you.
- Share love. Whether you're expressing love or receiving it, spending time in the conscious experience of love connects you to communal energy and gets you in a mindset conducive to healthy energy.
- Visualize that you're absorbing energy from the natural things you interact with—trees, clean water, air, the ocean, food, etc.

Once you tap into the reservoir of energy that issues from the experience of *sweetness,* stoke it. Bounce from one sweet experience to the next—not by stimulating yourself through force of will, but by keeping yourself sweetly engaged with the world in a way that uplifts and nourishes you. When you feel you're steeped in this energy, try sending some down to your lower *dan tian* and hitting the "save" button.

Space for Optimal Energy

Abundant energy requires *space*. *Space* is essential to be able to listen to and to feel the influx and outflow of energy. Only by making *space* within ourselves, to shift a portion of our consciousness to what's happening on an energetic level, are we able to feel if we're needlessly pouring our own vital energy into a project, or giving it away to a troubled friend.

Your Energy Is *Yours*

Learning to perceive the distinction between your personal energy, others' personal energy, and communal (or ambient) energy is a valuable skill. Specifically, knowing how not to give your personal energy away will preserve your energy and promote cleaner relationships with others. Except for perhaps deliberately giving some of your own energy to a mortally wounded loved one, your energy is *yours* and nobody else needs your personal *qi*. Giving a good massage doesn't require pouring your own *energy* into your client. Cheering up a sad friend doesn't require it. Loving someone deeply has nothing to do with giving them your energy. Even making a big difference in the world doesn't demand *your personal energy*.

Get It Done with Less

While you may be habituated to using effort to accomplish everything, there is nearly always a path of least resistance (or *less* resistance) available—a way to get the same task done with less of an investment of your own energy. You've seen it before. There are people who find drama in everything, conflict around each corner, and several emergencies a day. People who are drained by anything unexpected. At the other end of the spectrum are folks who are easygoing about everything. Nothing is worth getting their feathers ruffled about.

If a person of each type were given the same day's work, the first would likely be worn out by the afternoon, while the second would be wondering what kinds of fun activities were planned for the evening. People tend to think this variability comes down to how we're "wired"—a matter of personality that rarely changes—and while that can certainly be a factor, it's also something that can be learned.

FOUR WAYS TO CREATE SPACE FOR ENERGY

1. **Cultivate** *spaciousness.* Accumulating and storing energy requires *space.* If you don't have *space* in your days, in your mind, and in your heart, the flow of energy through your life is constricted. *Qi Gong* and meditation are especially valuable in this capacity. If everything is made of energy, having more of it shouldn't be a difficult task. Imagine that you're a vessel for receiving energy efficiently, and that it flows through you freely.

2. **Routinely let go of anything—physical, mental, or emotional— that isn't serving you.** Clear your mind and release clutter. While people tend to exercise for its physical benefits, it's also quite effective at "cleaning out" negative thoughts and emotions and neutralizing deep neurological ruts that drain us.

3. **Avoid fighting with life.** Stop creating a struggle where there doesn't need to be one, going about things the hard way, and investing more of your own energy than necessary. Be light.

4. **Take advantage of ambient energy and the currents around you.** Harness the prevailing flows of energy in the world in order to accomplish more with less personal cost. In more mundane terms, this means paying attention to how the world works, noticing how change happens, and being clever enough to take advantage of this momentum. In aikido and other "soft" martial arts, this means exerting minimal force to beat one's opponent. Instead, through a graceful combination of timing and biomechanics, you use the opponent's energy and simply redirect them—to the floor. In more everyday terms, don't create something from scratch if someone else has already done some or all of the work; don't work against the system when you can work with it; don't fight with someone when you can

ignore them or get them on your side; and carpool whenever possible—and we don't just mean in the sense of sharing a car. The more you consciously expand your *space* and experience the heightened awareness that it brings, the more you'll notice opportunities to harness the energy around you.

Your Resources Are a Gift

When the excrement hits the rotary cooling device, having good resources is a godsend. One of the most poignant experiences of this truth was in 2012, when we decided to move from Oregon to Colorado. We had spent fifteen wonderful but soggy years in Portland, and leaving was a big deal. We had friends and family there, and we were deeply rooted in the community. We owned two spas and several pieces of real estate in town. And we chose to leave all of it. It felt simultaneously exciting and insane.

We settled in and began learning how to run our Portland operations from Colorado. We hadn't specifically planned to open another spa in Boulder, but then a commercial space opened up in one of our favorite locations. It seemed that it was meant to be. Our bank was supportive, so we decided to go for it. Although we were "pre-approved" for a construction loan, we had some hoops to jump through, like signing a lease on a very pricey building that wasn't generating any income, and hiring a contractor. But we had every reason to believe it would be a smooth process.

Almost immediately, things started to go wrong. The contractor was never on site, and the foreman spent most of his time chewing tobacco and talking on the phone. For weeks, there was no sign of progress. Finally (after numerous angry conversations), the contractor replaced the foreman and the space slowly began to take shape. Meanwhile, there were unforeseen miles of bureaucratic red tape with the city that slowed down construction and required expensive upgrades to the building.

Five months in—well after our loan should have come through—new employees took over at the bank who informed us that if we were "still interested" in a loan we had to meet all sorts of new requirements. This included spending tens of thousands of our own dollars to do extensive environmental testing on the building in Portland that we were using as collateral. We were in so deep at this point that the only thing to do was to throw more money at it. But even when soil tests came back clean, the bank decided, seven months in, that they were no longer interested in giving us a loan. We were on the receiving end of a lot of anger. When the builders found out the bank had dropped us, they walked off the job. When the landlord heard, he was furious. People called daily to yell obscenities at us. And our staff, whom we had hired in anticipation of being open for business at this point, were jobless and in limbo. We had an unfinished spa, a ten-year lease, and a mountain of debt. If we couldn't get another bank to fund it, it threatened to take down our other spas, our credit, and our home.

But we somehow managed to keep putting one foot in front of the other. What allowed us to persevere were our *resources*—resources we had built up before undertaking this move and business venture. These resources acted as a buffer against the stress of this process and a well to tap into for support. We continued to spend time with friends and family, even though it was an effort to act sane. We kept eating good food, even though we had no appetite. We kept dancing and stretching, even though we were physically and emotionally exhausted. We kept spending time in nature, even though we were sometimes too lost in our thoughts to fully enjoy its beauty and serenity.

Through it all, we persisted. We kept our agreements, we bargained with the contractors (they finally came back to the job), we met with more banks, we trained our staff, we negotiated with building inspectors, we assembled furniture, we decorated the space, we networked with other business owners, we began marketing. Our resources helped us maintain perspective: No matter what, we had our family, we had our health, we had food and shelter, we had our spiritual connections, and we had the purposeful, valuable work that we do in the world—all of which would probably be intact regardless of the outcome of this story.

In the end, we did end up borrowing from pretty much everyone who would loan us a dime. And, eventually, we found a local bank that believed in us. They wanted to support our mission.

But, without our deeper resources, it's unlikely that we'd have had the sanity to make it through this ordeal intact, to say nothing of the dedication to see this thing through and turn it into a thriving business. It was undoubtedly the hardest year of our lives. When we look back on it now, we still don't laugh. The whole experience taught us a lot about resources, though. If it had been this difficult to open our first spa a decade earlier, before we had such resources, we never would have made it.

⬧

Take anyone who has accomplished huge things in life, and beyond whatever intelligence, connections, luck, and persistence they had, it's likely they also learned how to channel communal energy really well (probably unconsciously) and/or they had an abundance of energy to begin with.

You may be wondering, *How do I do this?* The answer is to make *space* in yourself. Feel. Feeling the contours and trajectories of life is tricky if you're pushing and spending all of the time, so, at least at the beginning, try to access your *space* during simple, relaxed activities. Perhaps a good *Qi Gong* instructor could give you more detailed instructions, but ultimately, this is something that can only be learned by practicing it. Pay attention to what energizes you in a healthy way, and do more of that. Notice what makes you tired, and either stop doing it or figure out how to do it in a way that doesn't tax your personal reserves. The energy to actualize your Well Life will come.

CHAPTER 6.
CONFIDENCE

BELIEVE IN YOURSELF

Don't Diminish Your Light

We have all known individuals who had great talent or amazing ideas but lacked the confidence to pursue a life that fully utilized these gifts. Maybe we've all worried at some point that our life was such a case. Perhaps you've thought something like, "If I could just be more confident, then everything would be easier. Life would start to go my way." But most people don't know how to change this. Building true confidence is more than just mustering the nerve to do something that scares you. And, unfortunately, you can't get it from your friends, your family, or your partner. You have to build it yourself.

By defining confidence as four separate but related qualities and teaching you how to upgrade yourself in each area, we'll help you attain a measurable improvement in your confidence that will translate into your taking advantage of more opportunities, experiencing more of life, and really getting to step into your gifts. It may not be possible or prudent to postpone your dreams until you feel fully confident in every arena, but you'll start the process, launch your plans, and then continue the confidence-building as you go. The four qualities we'll explore are: Self-Worth, Self-Trust, Competence, and Courage.

Confidence Ingredient #1: Self-Worth

Self-worth is defined as "the sense of one's own value or worth as a person." Some sources consider the terms self-worth and self-esteem to be synonymous, and others make a distinction between the two. We believe a distinction is useful. For our purposes, we'll define self-esteem as "a person's perception of who they are in the world." In other words, it's the impression we have of ourselves in the context of the world we're part of, and it's shaped by how we act, what we accomplish, how others relate to us, and our interpretation of all these things—whether accurate or not. Recognition of your self-worth will make you stronger in yourself; good self-esteem can help you take this value into the world and put it to use.

While we believe that both healthy self-esteem and a clear sense of one's self-worth can be valuable, we're emphasizing self-worth because it's not variable and subjective the way self-esteem is. It's a more objective and durable foundation. Self-esteem can be manufactured, and it can be devastated in an instant, depending on how much stock you put in, say, what a particular person thinks of you, or what your achievement on a particular challenge means about you. But your self-worth just *is*.

Your self-worth is a fact. It's not variable at all. The only variability is in your *awareness* of this fact. The deeper and more constant your recognition, the more your confidence will be bolstered and your life guided by it. What we're really talking about here (and we're hesitant to break out the G word, lest we alienate anyone) is the recognition that you are an expression of God. We're not talking about organized religion, and if you're averse to the word God, you can go with Divine, or Spirit, or Dao, or Highest Self, or Oneness, but to us, it's all the same thing. You are a *vastness* that is being expressed through the life of a human being, and as you connect more with this vastness, you'll come to feel more certain of your worth. This worth is *undiminishable,* and because it's your true identity, it's also the thing of absolute greatest value—a value that we believe transcends even the lifespan of the body you occupy. The awareness of this identity is often shrouded by a veil of mental noise, so the primary means of reconnecting to your inner knowing of this fact is through the deliberate practice of making *space.* (*Sweetness* can also be a means of connection, but *space* is still a requirement.)

Therefore, "working on" self-worth is kind of a funny thing, since it's not your worth that needs to be worked on, but your remembrance of your worth. In any case, we're going to offer some advice for building your connection to this truth, and for simultaneously enhancing self-esteem in a more stable and meaningful way.

Competence Doesn't Define Your Worth

It's common when embarking on a challenging endeavor to question your ability to succeed. As long as this doesn't thwart your progress, that's okay. But when you let this feeling get in the way, it's important to do some investigation and grow through it, rather than letting this be the end of the line. You might notice thoughts like, "Maybe I'm just not good enough at . . . ," but underneath, perhaps, are thoughts like, "Maybe I'm just not good enough. Period." The first could be a case of (real or imagined) lack of competence, while the second could be a case of unhealthy self-worth.

When we interpret our lack of confidence as a lack of competence, we often respond by trying to learn more or improve our skills. There's nothing wrong with this; it's just not likely to improve our self-worth or self-trust.

How Does Self-Esteem Fit In?

Beginning in the 1970s, there was a growing belief that healthy self-esteem was among the most important qualities a human could have, and this greatly affected the way teachers and parents related to children. Wary of damaging kids' self-esteem, they criticized less and praised more. But it turns out these efforts were probably overly simplistic. In recent years, numerous studies have been conducted to gauge the impact of this movement, and most have concluded that the benefits are superficial at best. Some research indicates that this trend has even contributed to a dramatic rise in narcissism. For instance, in 1952, only 12 percent of teens agreed with the statement "I am an important person." By 1989, this number had risen to 80 percent.

They were told, "Good job!" countless times by adults, and, lo and behold, they think they're great—regardless of what they do. We're certainly not opposed to people feeling good about themselves— or believing they're important—however, we can now see that this "artificial" self-esteem, derived more from what others told them rather than from an objective self-assessment of their accomplishments, didn't translate to happier, more productive, or more successful individuals. Instead, as compared to past generations, this population is prone to experience a lack of drive to grow, to achieve, and to develop their abilities. They feel anxiety to achieve at a level that matches their (possibly inflated) self-image. They see dissonance between their perception of themselves and their lack of objective success. And they experience depression from the realization that they may not be as impressive as they thought.

STRUCTURE, SWEETNESS, AND SPACE

The nutshell version is this: Allow *space* to connect to who you truly are, beyond what the world tells you. Experience the *sweetness* of your intrinsic worth. *Structure* a habit of consciously witnessing your mental dialogue, and learn how to keep your self-criticism from undermining your self-esteem and obscuring your sense of self-worth.

Self-worth, as we've said, is a value that doesn't change even if we go bald, or lose all our teeth, and it has nothing to do with worldly accomplishments. Healthy self-esteem urges you to face challenges and triumph over them. Together, they are an exciting and gratifying part of life as a human.

Perhaps more importantly, there are innumerable ways to use self-worth and self-esteem to serve the world, to help others in need, to help the planet itself, and to preserve the beauty that the confusion of human expansion threatens.

The recommendations that follow are for three purposes—first, to help you tune in to your self-worth; second, to help you overcome beliefs that serve to obstruct or deny this truth; third, to help you be more honest in how you construct your self-esteem.

- **Don't define yourself through your looks, your skills, your accomplishments, or your reputation.** Through the vast awareness that is You, you have the capacity to experience the deepest peace, the most complete love, lightness, grace, awe, and unimaginable beauty. This gift yearns to be shared with others, to help, to heal, and to illuminate the world. You deserve it.

- **Make *space*.** Find the *space* between your thoughts and the golden *sweetness* there. The *sweetness* is in the *space*. Ask, "What am I really?" and listen.

- **Love yourself.** To love anyone deeply and completely, not holding back at all, makes most people afraid, at least a little. It makes us feel vulnerable and fearful of losing this love. The same is true of loving ourselves in such an unrestrained way. Plus, we face the added challenge of seeing ourselves so close that there are an infinite number of mistakes and flaws for us to scrutinize and to use as reasons to withhold love. Love yourself anyway.

- **Don't feel selfish.** Loving yourself deeply and completely may strike you as narcissistic. It seems more noble and selfless, perhaps, to focus your love on others, or on God. But, if anything, withholding love from yourself is an insult to the Oneness (the Universe, God, Dao, or whatever your term of choice) that created you and *is* you. Imagine the absurdity of saying to the Universe, "Thanks for everything. I love it. You know, except for the *me* part." Withholding love from yourself also makes

you a less effective conduit of love to others. If you cherish this
life and the greatness that gave it to you and that *is* you, love
the gift that you are.

- **Stop comparing yourself to others.** There's nothing to be
gained from comparing your life to someone else's life, other
than inspiration. If you tend to fall into negative comparison,
reduce your exposure to triggers such as magazines and social
media, and remember that others' lives have nothing to do with
your worth. Let them only serve as an example of what's possible. Cheer them on. Enjoy seeing other people succeed. Do you
scorn a peacock for its fancy plumage? Do you scorn architec-
turally spectacular buildings, or a gorgeous painting? No? Then
neither should you scorn people who create impressive lives.

- **Don't let others' opinions define your value or dictate your
self-esteem.** But do accept the compliments that are offered
by people you trust, and consider even asking a handful of
friends and family to tell you what they see as your three greatest strengths. Write them down and revisit them when you
experience a lack of self-esteem. When someone compliments
you, inhale, see if you can open and let it in without analyzing,
deflecting, or objecting to it—either in your mind or verbally.
Just say, "Thank you."

Disempower Your Inner Critic

Most of the negative stuff we say to ourselves happens below the
radar. These thoughts are usually quiet or familiar enough that we
barely notice them. Yet they sabotage our self-esteem and cause us
to deny our self-worth. Turn up the volume on these thoughts so
you can "hear" them loud and clear. Mostly, this means paying closer
attention so that you're able to discern the specific words that make
up these thoughts and the tone in which you're mentally speaking
them to yourself. Often, they're more than just recurrent ideas but
entire "subpersonalities" that tell you, year after year, that you're
doing something wrong or that there's something wrong with you.

As you tune in, see if you can perceive the voice of this critic (or you may have multiple destructive subpersonalities with different voices). Dramatize the voice as you listen to it. Perhaps the voice is that of a bratty child who wants everything his way. Maybe it's a snooty know-it-all who points out your imperfections. Or a monstrous tyrant who relentlessly berates you. Whatever the personality, make it more tangible, more caricaturized, and give it a name, so that you begin to recognize it every time it shows up.

Instead of letting it attack you, you'll be changing your response. Different ways of responding work more effectively for different people, so if one method doesn't work, try another. And if no methods work, get the help of a skilled counselor. Here are some approaches to consider. We suggest giving each one an earnest go for at least a few days until you find the method that works best.

Thank you, I love you, I'll take it from here.

The first approach is to consider that, in some confused way, your mind is trying to protect you. It's feeding you these negative messages because it believes the issues it's pointing out actually threaten your survival or happiness. Love the inner you that was once hurt, scared, or threatened enough to create a habit of overly cautionary (or downright critical) thoughts. Thank this personality for its help — then tell it firmly that you're going to take it from here.

Arouse Your Fierceness

Numerous spiritual traditions speak of adopting the attitude of a warrior when seeking the truth. Humans are subject to many kinds of internal and external forces, such as social pressure, yearning for acceptance, wanting material goods, family and community drama, etc. These forces have the potential to dominate your attention and monopolize your life, causing you to forget deeper truths — like your gifts and purpose, like the blessing that your life is. Instead of a life filled with awe and gratitude, you might end up in a life dominated by staring at screens, yearning for the past, and worrying about the future. Being a *spiritual* warrior means cutting through whatever stands in the way of your living in accordance with the truths you know in your soul.

With this method, we apply this approach to your inner critic, which means recognizing how the conflict you're engaged in undermines your peace and happiness, *and* you must remember that the restricted life your inner critic perpetuates is not all there is. When it rears its head, don't take its bullshit for a second. Retort inwardly or out loud. For instance, if you catch your critic saying, "You're not getting anything done today," you might retort, "No! You will not dominate my life," or, "I'm exactly where I need to be," or, "I am an expression of love and truth in the world." Remember, you are not your mind. Stand up for yourself!

One caveat: the human psyche is already so full of conflict that we're hesitant to suggest an approach that resembles more conflict. But we're actually promoting that you cut through conflict itself. This method works well for many people, and the key is not the *fight*; it's the fierce assertion of your power and purpose, your light and love, and your commitment to these truths.

Get Silly

We usually get all serious when we're criticized. But humor is one of the most effective ways to take the power out of an assailant's attack. You could imitate your inner critic's statement in an absurd voice, like Bugs Bunny or Bart Simpson. You could say something really goofy in response to the criticism. Like if your inner critic just told you, "You're not as pretty as she is," you could respond with, "Oh yeah, look how pretty I am now!" and make a pig nose, stick out your tongue, and fluff your hair. Go ahead—be childish. You'll be surprised at how well this can defuse the negative message and take the wind out of that bully's sails.

Choose an Empowering Alternative

Let yourself hear the critic's words clearly and then choose a counter statement that draws your consciousness in the opposite direction.

These should be statements that you can *believe*. If your critic has been telling you, "You look ugly today," for twenty years, a response statement such as, "I look beautiful today," probably isn't going to cut it, because it's likely that you don't really believe it.

But if you use a response more like, "I choose to let my inner beauty shine through me today," this has more power, since it's not something your mind can readily argue with. It's a choice you're making, rather than a totally subjective statement about what kind of person you are.

Consider statements that include phrasing such as "I choose," "I trust," and "I allow." You might even use a counter statement that takes the attention off of your qualities and directs it at others. Here are some examples: *I trust that I'm doing the best I can with the resources that are available to me. I choose to shine my light on the world today. I choose to come into my power now. I allow myself to be guided to purposeful action that serves my community. I allow God to use me as an emissary of Love. I choose to trust myself to manage my life.*

So What? Who Cares?

Oldies but goodies, *so what?* and *who cares?* are meant to shake up the tendency to attach importance to the mind's cries for attention and to instead guide us back to the truth.

We once knew a psychotherapist who claimed these were his most used questions in counseling sessions! When the inner critic comes up with some negative thought, however true or desperate it may seem, you can repeat the critic's statement (for instance, "I'm never going to succeed!") and then ask yourself, "So what?" and see what follows. If the intensity lingers, ask yourself, "Who cares?" and see what follows. If the intensity lingers, return to "So what?" and repeat.

Sometimes the issue seems *so* important that this exercise feels worthless. Other times, it has an almost magical way of dismantling the urgency and bringing you back to a state of lightheartedness. It can also force you to push past the surface issue so you can unearth what's really behind your fears and doubts.

Don't Engage

This is different from ignoring your inner critic—which is what most of us have always done, even though we still get damaged by the critic's attack. We're suggesting you consciously witness the critic's statements and consider them *part of the critic's campaign to engage you.* The critic only lives as long as it has a victim or an opponent. Each nasty statement is like a hook that wants to catch you and hold onto your energy and attention. It would prefer that you buy into its garbage and let it run away with your mind, but it would be satisfied to have you engaged with it in an ongoing fight. In either case, you're hooked. But in this approach, you'll instead commit to not giving it any of your energy at all. Imagine that the hook just passes right through you.

Vadim Zeland has a description of this concept in his book, *Reality Transurfing,* in which he refers to all these highly charged ideas as *pendulums.* Like a giant, swinging pendulum, every political movement, every religion, every trend, every common human thought-form is perpetuated and strengthened through the energy of all those who subscribe to it. When you align yourself with a particular pendulum, it carries you along with its momentum. As more people latch onto them, they swing all the more strongly and are increasingly influential.

Pretty much anything your inner critic comes up with is a pendulum. According to Zeland, we can never truly win when we fight with a pendulum. Both subscribing to the pendulum and fighting with it mean engaging with it, and therefore giving it our energy and being taken for a ride. The only real solution is to avoid engaging with it. Become indifferent to it. Let the pendulum swing through you as if you were a ghost. Don't let it stir you, enroll you, or engage you. Don't give it an iota of your energy.

Share Your Worth

Finally, although your worth isn't derived from what you do in the world, it may be easier for you to *recognize* your worth when it's shared. Put it out there. Make art, make music, teach what you know, give a rescued animal a better life, foster a child, speak the truth, listen carefully, inspire, be a healer in every context, enhance what you're presented with, *and the mark of your worth will be made visible.*

If you know your value and you're able to act, then you'll feel a drive to act. Then, pay attention: *Notice* how your value promotes the expression of others' value. There's little that is more gratifying than this. And remember, inherent in recognizing your self-worth is recognizing *everyone else's* self-worth.

The Impostor Phenomenon

Hand in hand with self-worth and self-esteem is your assessment of what you deserve in your life. If you have ever had the feeling that you're not as talented as people think you are, or that you don't deserve the success you've had and that it's only a matter of time before people figure out what a fraud you are, well, you're in good company. So many people feel this way, in fact, that there's a name for it—"The Impostor Phenomenon," a term coined by doctors Pauline Rose Clance and Suzanne Imes, in 1978, after they discovered it was exceedingly prevalent among high-achieving women.

Since then, it has been observed in many successful people. Clance and Imes also described certain behaviors that go along with the belief that one is a phony:

1. Relentless hard work and diligence—in an attempt to become the person one believes other people think they are.
2. Inauthenticity—trying to sound and act as impressive as one believes other people think they are (this, unfortunately, can help "prove" to them that they're a phony).
3. Using charm (friendliness, looks, sexuality, etc.) to win the approval of people that one admires. "The Impostor Phenomenon" is, of course, just an expression of the Inner Critic. Try the preceding strategies on it; they'll make a difference.

Confidence Ingredient #2: Self-Trust

When you begin peeling away layers of negative beliefs about yourself, and you experience an emerging knowing of the preciousness and potential that you really are, this automatically leads to a sense of reverence for this authentic Self. From that reverence comes an urge to be a person of integrity. And there's really no greater fortifier of confidence than to have integrity—to know that you can be trusted.

In order to be confident in yourself, you must be able to trust yourself. The most critical areas of self-trust are the ability to trust yourself to honor your soul, to abide by your core values (which we'll discuss in Chapter 8), to keep your agreements (as we discussed in Chapter 4), and to manage whatever hurdles life throws at you. Having a clear sense of your self-worth can help in the development of self-trust. When you recognize your value, you tend to honor yourself and practice integrity in your relationships with yourself and others.

Self-trust is essential to creating your life the way you want it to be. When you trust yourself, you know that your word is a guarantee, and so does everyone else. What you say will happen happens. When you trust yourself, fear melts away because you know that you'll manage whatever comes up. When you trust yourself, you get to explore the outer limits of your creative potential because you know you have a solid foundation to fall back on.

Assessing Your Self-Trust

Self-trust isn't a static thing and it doesn't apply equally to all areas of life. For instance, you might be able to trust yourself to show up for your kids no matter what, but perhaps you don't trust yourself at all to eat well. It's important to evaluate your self-trust in each of the different arenas of life so you can see clearly where your behavior may be undermining your self-trust. Go through the following list and rank your level of self-trust from one to five. (If you don't want to write in your book, or you're reading this as an e-book, you can download this chart at www.thewelllifebook.com/resources.) It's important to have these values recorded, so please write them down and put today's date on it. Rate yourself as follows:

5: Strong trust of myself in this area.
4: Moderate trust of myself in this area.
3: I could go either way.
2: Moderate lack of trust of myself in this area.
1: Serious lack of trust of myself in this area.

SELF-TRUST PERSONAL ASSESSMENT			
AREA OF LIFE	LEVEL OF TRUST (DISTRUST 1 — 2 — 3 — 4 — 5 TRUST)		
	DATE:	DATE:	DATE:
Communication How much do you trust yourself to tell the truth, to say what needs to be said in order to have healthy relationships, to speak kindly and respectfully, and to express yourself authentically?			
Dependability How much do you trust yourself to show up for friends and family, and support them when they need it?			
Nutrition How much do you trust yourself to choose foods that you know are good for you, to avoid foods that you know are bad for you, to eat in a healthy manner, and to stick with the agreements you make with yourself around eating?			
Punctuality How much do you trust yourself to be on time to work, to social meetings, or to anything else with a specific time?			

SELF-TRUST PERSONAL ASSESSMENT			
AREA OF LIFE	LEVEL OF TRUST (DISTRUST 1 — 2 — 3 — 4 — 5 TRUST)		
	DATE:	DATE:	DATE:
Follow Through How much do you trust yourself to follow through on the projects you start, in the time frame you intended, until they are complete?			
Money How much do you trust yourself to stay conscious of what you have, to maintain a positive attitude around money, and to avoid taking on unnecessary debt?			
Health Maintenance How much do you trust yourself to treat your body and soul well, to get the care you need, and be kind to yourself?			
Focus How much do you trust yourself to stay focused on what you have chosen to work on, and avoid indulging in distraction?			
Work Performance How much do you trust yourself to honor the work you do, to do your best, and to show up enthusiastically to do the work you have agreed to do?			
Values How much do you trust yourself to live by your core values?			
Other			
Other			
Other			

How do your numbers look? Besides becoming more tuned in to your integrity in a general sense, choose one area at a time from this list to work on. You'll feel cleaner and stronger. In the downloadable version of the chart, we have provided several columns for ratings, so that you can track your progress over time.

Build Self-Trust with Intentional Language

In 2012, a fascinating study was published in the *Journal of Consumer Research* called "'I Don't' versus 'I Can't': When Empowered Refusal Motivates Goal-Directed Behavior." We believe it was a landmark paper in the emergence of our understanding of how the language of our thoughts affects us. The researchers specifically investigated whether the phrasing "I don't" was more empowering than "I can't" in terms of helping a person to refuse temptation and stay on track with a goal. The authors stated:

> We theorize that saying "I don't do X" connotes a firmly entrenched attitude . . . it emphasizes the personal will that drives the refusal . . . [and it] serves as a self-affirmation of one's personal willpower and control in the goal pursuit, leading to a favorable influence on feelings of empowerment, as well as on actual behavior. On the other hand, saying "I can't do X" connotes an external focus on impediments. We propose that this . . . results in less feelings of empowerment and thus also hinders the self-regulatory goal pursuit in question.

Researchers conducted multiple experiments to test this theory. In a healthy-eating study, participants in one group were directed to use "I don't" language when faced with the temptation of eating unhealthy food—for example, "I *don't* eat junk food," while those in the second group used "I can't" language—for example, "I *can't* eat junk food." When offered the choice of a chocolate bar or a healthy granola bar, 64 percent of those in the "I don't" group chose the granola bar, compared to 39 percent of those in the "I can't" group. In another study, women were enrolled in a ten-day health program.

Ten women were instructed to use "I don't" self-talk when they were tempted to lapse in their participation, ten were instructed to use "I can't" phrasing, and as a control, ten were told to just say "No" when tempted to quit. Eight out of the ten women in the "I don't" group stuck with the program for the whole ten days. Three of the women in the "Just say no" group stuck it out. And just one woman in the "I can't" group finished the program.

When rebuilding self-trust while simultaneously taking on new goals, there's a risk that failing or aborting the plan could cause greater damage to your self-trust. So, pay attention to your self-talk when considering breaking agreements. "I don't" phrasing, such as, "I *don't* skip my scheduled workouts," "I *don't* put junk food into my body," and, "I *don't* get on Facebook during my workday," may help empower you to stick with the plan. Of course, "I don't" is just one example of empowering self-talk. With experimentation, you may find that other phrases work even better.

Confidence Ingredient #3: Competence

When we feel unconfident in some arena, our most natural tendency is to assume we're not adequately competent. We may assume that if we were good enough at something, we'd feel confident. If you've been teaching Spanish for ten years, chances are you feel confident in a Spanish classroom. If you went to Miss Manners' School of Social Etiquette, you're competent in social decorum, and therefore probably confident about going into a variety of different social settings. But this isn't always the case. There are plenty of people who are highly competent yet not at all confident. There are talented singers and artists who can't muster the confidence to put their art on display. There are scholars who have spent their lives accumulating college degrees, but who still think they're not smart enough.

Therefore, if you feel unconfident, it's important to figure out why. You may be adequately competent but just don't recognize it. Or you may indeed lack competence in your chosen arena, but have some block around taking action to improve:

- You may be failing to improve your competence because you're utilizing poor sources of information or ineffective training methods.
- You may have started out lacking competence and then improved your knowledge and skills, yet haven't revised your self-assessment, and therefore believe you need to continue to get better.

Developing competence and recognizing your competence must often be supported by recognition of your self-worth, building self-esteem, and developing courage.

Commission an Honest Assessment of Your Skills

Try to find objective and accurate assessors of your competence. This is something very few of us do when we endeavor to enter a new work arena or to go further in our current field. Find resources to assess your knowledge and/or skills. There may be written tests available or online exams. There may be people in your life who will tell you objectively what they think of your competence. Ask them to be honest. If an assessment of your competence can only be accurately made by someone in your field, seek out a professional you respect and inquire to see if they would be willing to tell you where you could improve (if anywhere). There may also be job placement experts who can make such an assessment for you. They will probably be able to see things you can't. It's best to get at least a second (if not a third or fourth) opinion.

If your assessors (tests and/or humans) tell you that you don't need to build competence, yet you still aren't sure of yourself, go back to the sections on self-worth and self-trust and follow the forthcoming recommendations in the courage section. If it turns out that you do need to learn more, ask others in the field what the best avenues are for growth. Can you get it from a book? An online course? Is there a hands-on apprenticeship available? Seek out others who have done what you aim to do and get their advice. Would they be willing to mentor you or let you shadow them?

In our own experience, we've found that experiential training is best—both in terms of the value of the education and the impact on your confidence. For instance, we've done consulting for several health coaches who attended schools that lacked any real-life supervised clinical work. When they told us they felt unsure of their skills, we admitted that we felt unsure of their skills, too. Lots of educational programs are available online these days, and while they may be cheaper, easier, and more flexible, they may carry a higher likelihood of leaving you feeling undertrained for the real world. Would *you* choose a professional who had the training you're considering for yourself?

Embrace a Growth Mindset

We already looked at what didn't work in the self-esteem movement. So, what *does?* Some of our best answers to this question come from Carol Dweck, PhD, author of *Mindset: The New Psychology of Success,* and a leading researcher in learning and motivation. Based on her studies of children, she defined two distinct mindsets around intelligence. She saw that kids with a "fixed mindset" felt that their intelligence was an unchanging trait. However smart or dumb they thought they were, they believed that they were stuck with whatever they got. Children with a "growth mindset," on the other hand, believed that regardless of their current ability, they could improve through effort, creative thinking, and getting help.

Which of these two mindsets seems to apply to you? Do you tend to feel that your abilities are relatively fixed? Do you make statements like, "I'm just not good at math," or do you feel that, if you put your mind to it, you could learn pretty much anything? If not, why? Is it because you have a fixed perception of your skill? Well, it's just not true. Our learning styles vary, but we all have the ability to learn—even those with learning disorders. Learning to trust your ability to grow may yield great benefits in terms of your competence, and therefore, your confidence.

If you catch yourself thinking that you could simply never get good at something, challenge these thoughts. A lack of innate talent really only becomes a limitation when we strive to be a champion at something. It may be true that you'll never be a virtuoso on the cello, and if you've never played music before, it may take extra work for you to even become a decent cellist, but you absolutely have the potential to grow.

STRUCTURE, SWEETNESS, AND SPACE

If you decide that you need to build competence and your objective assessors agree, remember that you can further your education even while working in your chosen career. Often, high-level competence isn't even possible without being immersed in the challenges of your field, because until then you may not know what you don't know. Find a learning *structure* that allows you to balance this quest with the rest of your life. You'll need *space* to expand and grow. The entire process is made easier if you incorporate *sweetness*—pursue a skill that aligns with your purpose, and make learning fun by finding a teacher who inspires you and peers who make the process enjoyable. Learn enough to get started, but don't make being an expert a condition for pursuing your dreams.

Questioning your skill level can sometimes be helpful if it drives you to learn and improve, but if your self-evaluation is completely disconnected from your actual skills and achievements, insecurity becomes a relentless taskmaster who never gives you a break from acquiring more knowledge and proving yourself. Chances are, you're the only one who's evaluating you.

Confidence Ingredient #4: Courage

It's a virtue mentioned in nearly every fairy tale, but the need for courage in pursuit of the Well Life is sometimes diluted by an emphasis on things like business skills, education, networking, and hard work. These other qualities are nothing to scoff at, but timidity, risk-aversion, and fear can undermine the best-laid plans and the most impressive skill set.

We understand that not everyone is adventurous, nor extroverted. But even for the introvert who wants a stable and peaceful life, there will come times when courage will allow for a deeper experience of peace and a richer experience of life's wonders. Although not everyone faces overt conflict, physical danger, or great financial risk (where the need for courage is clear), each of us has areas of life and areas of our own mind that we have chosen to avoid. Each of us has "shadow work" to do, to heal the unilluminated parts of ourselves, and it takes courage to willingly face our pain, fear, and darkness. On the other side, a more liberated and joyous existence awaits us.

Some of the most powerful ways to build courage have already been discussed. We'll review these now, and introduce a few more:

1. Building self-trust, which we discussed in this chapter and the previous one, makes us more courageous because we know we can trust ourselves to manage with honesty and integrity whatever comes up.
2. If you've begun the cleanup work in Chapter 3, you probably have a sense of the courage required and the "return" in the form of immediate lightness that results from this work. It's likely you also have an emerging understanding of just what's at stake when you're *not* courageous. The conflicts you didn't resolve, the communications you didn't make, the agreements you didn't keep, these all leave a weighty residue that degrades this precious life. Moreover, while much of what we've repressed (into what Carl Jung called the "shadow aspect") is painful memories and negative parts of our personality that we disapprove of, sometimes we discover virtuous and powerful facets of ourselves hidden there, which, for whatever reason, we were previously unable to accept. It takes courage to fully embody our power, but it awakens us to a new magnitude of possibility.
3. Strengthening your lower *dan tian* gives you power to draw on and anchors you so that you'll be less prone to be overcome

by strong emotion. Besides an ongoing focus on this point and breathing deep into the pelvic bowl, a more regimented practice of *Qi Gong*, tai chi, or traditional martial arts will yield a faster and more significant benefit to your courage.

Following are a couple of new ideas you can use to build your courage:

1. **Rehearse.** Before a performance or a challenging task, visualize or act out the scenario exactly as you want it to go. Start your mental movie a few moments before the task begins, seeing and feeling yourself experiencing peace and confidence as you enter the scene. Guide yourself through the situation with as much detail as possible. Imagine that you're creating a precise script of exactly how the story will go. Run over the script repeatedly, feeling your courage and calm throughout the story, so that you feel it has been memorized by both your mind and body.

2. **Acknowledge your acts of courage.** Get a piece of paper, open your journal, or start a blank document on your computer and write "My Acts of Courage" at the top of the page. (You can also download a PDF version of this worksheet at www .thewelllifebook.com/resources.) Then (after reading the list of examples that follows) make a list of ten examples where you have been courageous in the past or are courageous on a daily basis. Remember that the need for courage is subjective. Based on different backgrounds, what might be natural for one person (say, jumping into the ocean) may require mustering courage for another.

Practice Courage

Just like any other skill, it helps to do something frequently to get more proficient at it. Following is a list of potential ways—both big and small—to boost your courage:

- Striking up a conversation with a stranger
- Standing up for someone
- Stating an unpopular opinion
- Asking for help
- Choosing what's right over what's easy
- Speaking in front of a crowd
- Taking responsibility for your life rather than blaming the world
- Protesting against an injustice
- Expressing your own style
- Persisting when things get hard
- Applying for a job
- Choosing to grow from your mistakes
- Declaring an alternative sexual orientation
- Admitting your weaknesses
- Letting go of someone or something that isn't good for you anymore
- Apologizing
- Quitting a job that isn't right for you
- Being open to ideas and opinions that differ from your own
- Trying something new or unusual
- Pursuing a dream
- Helping someone without regard for what you'll get out of it
- Keeping your commitments
- Requesting a raise or promotion
- Loving and accepting people whom you dislike or disagree with
- Remaining calm even when those around you are freaking out
- Challenging your own deep-seated beliefs or stories
- Being kind to strangers
- Making an important but uncomfortable communication
- Leaving an abusive relationship
- Being grateful and optimistic even when life sucks
- Reconciling with an estranged family member
- Saving a baby from a burning building

We all experience varying degrees of fear and discomfort on a regular basis, and anytime we proceed anyway, our courage is activated to enable us to push through. Unless you feel that nothing in the list above is daunting (except maybe saving the baby), please *do the following exercise!*

Anticipating and Overcoming Discomfort

This exercise will help you plan some ways to practice courage. In so doing, you can identify what feelings you experience as you look ahead to the act, and you can reflect on the event and see what came of it. Look back at the list of examples and think of your current challenges, then choose five courageous acts you'll perform in the coming week. Write these acts in the first column, allowing some space between each act in case you need to write several lines of text in the other columns. Either right now, or before performing each act, write in the second column how you feel in anticipation. It might be as simple as, "Slightly nervous," or as detailed as, "I'm worried that as I'm talking to my boss I'm going to start crying and then I'll run out of the room."

ACTS OF COURAGE			
COURAGEOUS ACT	HOW I FELT BEFORE	HOW I FELT AFTER	WHAT I GAINED

Don't choose acts that are so easy there's really no courage involved. The key to identifying prime opportunities for courage development in your life is that you feel uncomfortable when you think about going there. You have to *use* your courage to build it; if you don't, it starts to shrivel. If you've been avoiding discomfort for a long time, you're probably averse to even minor discomfort. But the uncomfortable situations you avoid act as infringements on your freedom and they squelch your expression.

We're not suggesting that just because you're uncomfortable with the idea of skydiving or singing the national anthem at the Super Bowl that these are things you must do (although doing them may serve to boost your courage in a general sense). We're specifically addressing the discomfort that is part of *your life path*: the discomfort of existing, unresolved conflicts, the discomfort of obstacles to your dreams, the discomfort of whatever blocks the expression of who you truly are, the discomfort that gets in the way of your being in love with yourself and in love with the world. The more you willingly face what makes you uncomfortable, the easier it becomes, and little by little you'll find yourself expanding into a genuinely ecstatic life.

If you feel distinct anxiety coming up as you anticipate facing an area of discomfort, here are a few additional tips to experiment with:

- Don't resist the feeling in your body. Feel it as willingly as possible. Ride the feeling like a wave. Remember: it's just a feeling. It doesn't mean something is actually wrong.
- Keep breathing into your lower belly. Make your exhale as long as possible.
- Put your feet flat on the ground. Imagine you're anchored into the earth.
- Forgive yourself for whatever unpleasantness you're experiencing. Let yourself off the hook for not being more peaceful.
- Stop trying to analyze it. More thinking is unlikely to stop this feeling.
- If you're intensely anxious, in all likelihood it's a garden-variety panic attack—something millions of people experience. *Everyone* thinks they're going to die when they're immersed in it, *everyone* thinks they're going crazy when they're in it, and *everyone* worries that it's going to last forever. None of these things will come true.

- Remember that, biologically speaking, your fear stems from the primitive, animal part of your brain, and it's telling your body to fight for your life, run for your life, or freeze and hope for the best. It's a protective mechanism and, chances are, *it's an error.* Thank your brain for trying to save you, reassure it that your survival isn't at stake, and tell it that it can shut down the alarm system.
- Also remember that you're more likely to fall into reactive, animal-brain thinking when you haven't gotten sufficient sleep, when you haven't been eating well or enough, when you're sick, or when you're stressed in other ways. The smarter, more evolved, reasoning part of the brain—the prefrontal cortex—demands more resources in order to prevail over your thinking, resources that aren't available when you're taxed.
- Do at least twenty minutes of vigorous exercise. For many people, this helps clear the jittery nervous system energy and restores us to a calm state.

After you do each of these five courageous acts, go back to your Acts of Courage page and fill in the column for "How I Felt After." Your response may be as simple as, "Relieved" or as in-depth as, "I felt like I was finally able to have a genuine relationship with my dad." Finally, fill in the "What I Gained" column. Once more, a simple answer might be something like, "Stronger" or "Lighter" or "A promotion!" and a detailed answer could be, "Greater confidence in my ability to get what I want."

Start to Live Courageously

Keep up those acts of courage. Remember, the more consistently you willingly approach uncomfortable situations, the easier it becomes, and the more your courage and self-trust will grow. As soon as you avoid making an important but difficult communication or procrastinate something you're nervous about, it will seem more challenging to gather the courage to proceed. Focus on your lower *dan tian*; relax your belly completely; relax the rest of your body; breathe deeply into your pelvic bowl; if a friend is available, hold their hand; if not, just imagine that you're holding the hand of a loved one, or that a helper has their hand on your back; know that you're moments away from feeling relieved and proud of yourself, and go for it.

Confidence Assessment

Now that we've explored four elements of confidence, fill in a bar graph to measure your assessment of yourself in each of these areas. (If you'd rather not write in your book, or you're working from an e-book, you can reproduce a blank version of this table yourself or you can download a blank one at www.thewelllifebook.com/resources.) These aren't qualities that can be measured precisely, so don't over-think it. Just make four bars to represent your self-ratings and see how it turns out. (The bars shown are just an example of how yours may look. Also, you don't have to use numbers along the left side of the chart.)

This visual representation of these four elements of your confidence will help you see better where it may be most productive to devote your efforts. If you feel a lack of confidence around making a change in your life or pursuing a new goal, see if you can determine if the issue is a disconnection from your self-worth, a lack of self-trust, inadequate competence in this arena, or simply a lack of courage. In a month or two, redo this chart as well as the self-trust assessment and the courage worksheet. See what has changed and shift your focus, if necessary.

⚜

Remember, even if you become highly competent and have great self-esteem, there may come a day when you're out of your element, you have a big zit on your nose, you have uncontrollable gas, someone just pointed out that there's been a fifteen-foot piece of toilet paper trailing behind you for the last three hours, and now it's time to get on stage and give a speech. You're not going to be feeling very good about yourself, but all that is going to matter is whether you do what you said you would do (and hopefully stay light about it).

Confidence feels great, and we want you to have it. But when it's not there, if you're truly committed to getting the life of your dreams, you have to just keep on going. Even Marilyn Monroe, despite being so widely beloved, suffered from lack of confidence. She said, "There was my name up in lights. I said, 'God, somebody's made a mistake.' But there it was, in lights. And I sat there and said, 'Remember, you're not a star.' Yet there it was up in lights." Even through her self-doubt and self-deprecation, she kept moving toward stardom. A teacher of ours used to say, "The starving children in Africa don't care if you feel good enough or confident enough. They only care that they get the food." Don't wait until you feel confident before you'll share your brilliance with the world. We want it now!

CHAPTER 7.
COMMUNITY

CURATING SUPPORTIVE CONNECTIONS
.

You Need Local Community

In a recent conversation about community with an older friend, she told us, "Before everyone had a television, it was different. Someone was always stopping by to say hello in the evening. But once there was a TV in every living room, people became concerned about interrupting a show, so they made fewer unannounced visits. And if they did stop by during a television show, the conversation might be stifled—or nonexistent—because everyone was distracted." Television dealt one of the hardest blows to local community engagement. Community was hit even harder with the later advent of the Internet, cell phones, and then smartphones. As Robert Putnam so thoroughly detailed in the book *Bowling Alone,* our participation in local social, political, and religious groups has withered over the past few decades. Our sense of involvement in a tangible community has declined, and our definition of community has changed.

We now have huge online communities, but they don't provide the same kind of support and closeness that physical communities do.

In fact, they have been instrumental in enabling our withdrawal from local community. Online social forums can certainly have a value in our lives. They may enable us to connect with a group of like-minded folks that doesn't exist in our local community. They allow us to easily stay in touch with a geographically diverse set of people from different times in our life. But, like most of our media engagement, these connections tend to be a bit shallow. Your geographically distant friends are unlikely to know if you've been taking care of yourself. They won't miss you if you don't show up for your exercise class. They can't do much if you get hurt or sick. They're unable to help you plant a garden, or share a meal with you, or take in your mail when you're out of town. We're not suggesting you abandon your online connections, but they can never wholly replace a healthy local community.

STRUCTURE, SWEETNESS, AND SPACE

Having a strong and supportive community is like adding to your own resources the collective strengths and resources of those around you. Thus, community stands to play a major role as both *structure* and *sweetness* in your Well Life. A good community will hold you to your agreements and challenge you to bring everything to the table. Make *space* in your life for it.

Are Your Communities Intentional?

Intentional community creation isn't something we're usually taught, and for many people it doesn't feel natural. Most adults have a hodgepodge of friendships that developed organically through work, school, neighborhood, and other social groups. Perhaps you have a few left from high school, a couple of pals who lived in your college dorm, the girl you worked with at the Teriyaki Shack, and let's not forget the guy you shared a cell with after a particularly boisterous night on the town.

Now that you're grown up and you have a clearer sense of the extraordinary life you desire, the community you surround yourself with can be a tremendous asset, and it is worthwhile to think about what kind of community you'd *curate* for the greatest benefit to all involved. We're not advising you to dump your old friends, but the community you developed by circumstance may not necessarily be willing to engage in the quality of support, respect, and growth that would best serve the emerging You.

Imagine if your community were not only generous, kind, playful, and fun, but also included people who accept responsibility for their circumstances and feelings; who are honest; who take good care of themselves; who embrace and share their gifts; who enjoy helping, healing, and beautifying the world around them; who are able to have conversations of intellectual and spiritual depth; who keep their agreements; who pursue their dreams; who prioritize healthy *structure, sweetness,* and *space* in their lives.

It's worthwhile to think about what kind of community you'd *curate* for the greatest benefit to all involved.

Just consider how it might affect your life to be surrounded by individuals who are committed to the kinds of virtues you want to cultivate in yourself. Such saintly types might seem hard to come by, but we manage to find them wherever we go. These kinds of qualities naturally come up when you start letting your soul guide your life.

Take a look at our very scientific diagram. Human perspective ranges somewhere between the left end of the spectrum, where our Authentic Self (the Higher Self, our God-Nature—that part of us that yearns to evolve and awaken) is totally eclipsed by negative thoughts and toxic emotions, and the right end of the spectrum, where we're completely awake to this Authentic Self and we essentially let it run the show. Everyone varies a bit from day to day, of course, but we're suggesting that you may wish to deliberately invite into your community more folks who seem to be living toward the right end of the spectrum, and further, to endeavor to *be* that person in your community.

☹ ◄─────────────────────────────► ☺

"This sucks.   "Life is my playground.
Life isn't fair."   I choose my perspective."

Consider What Qualities Are Important to You

What other qualities would you choose if you were able to build your community consciously? While your natural inclination may be to seek out others who are as much like you as possible, your community may be richer, stronger, and more interesting if you incorporate diversity. Diversity can be a double-edged sword, actually. When there's a variance in people's basic *values* (especially in a population that's fearful and intolerant), diversity can push people apart. But when a community is composed of individuals with diverse roots, traditions, skills, and skin colors, yet similar values and vision, such diversity promotes evolution. Open-minded people, when challenged to connect with those who are different from them, end up discovering what's the same. And this sameness, well, it's the *sweetness* we've been talking about. So, make *space* to hold others' differences without fear or judgment, and watch what happens.

John McKnight, author of *The Abundant Community*, shares this wisdom on community building: "One way of thinking about how communities get built is by seeing that the principal resource people have for the task is their gifts, skills, talents, and capacities. . . . Building strong neighborhoods becomes a matter of everybody contributing as many of their gifts as they can to each other and to the whole." In the coming chapters, you'll identify these resources as you discover your gifts and values. Then, you'll take a big step toward becoming a contributing member of your community by identifying your life purpose.

Diagram Your Current Communities

We invite you to bring your attention to your various communities over the coming week. For instance, you have your local community — the people of your neighborhood, village, town, or city. Within this community, you probably have a tighter community of people you share your life with in a closer way. Perhaps you think of them more as your "tribe" or your extended family. You may have subtribes or separate groups that exist for specific purposes. Also, you probably have one or more online communities that may not overlap with any of your other circles.

If you're passionate about understanding the roles your various communities play in your life, you might enjoy using a pen and paper to graphically diagram these different worlds, their relationship to each other, the hierarchy of their priority to you, the ways they intersect, the terminology you use to distinguish them, etc. For example, you could use a circle to represent each group (people's names aren't required), with some circles overlapping, and certain circles entirely enclosing other circles. You might want to use colors to indicate the ways you're served by each group (e.g., spiritual connection, creative outlet, girl time/guy time, service, fitness) or the time and energy demand and return each circle holds.

This can be an especially valuable process if you have lots of connections and social obligations. Through this exercise, it will become apparent which groups are most nourishing to you, which respond positively to your contributions, and which may be worth divesting from. While we've primarily emphasized the value of *building* community in this section, we also advocate a broader, intelligent *restructuring* process, through which you'll probably decide to cut social connections that aren't serving you.

Even if you choose not to do this diagram exercise, it may still be useful for you to ponder the level of investment and participation you have in your different communities and to eventually consider how to work with them in a more intentional way. In the process of developing a clearer understanding of the functions of these communities, you may wish to use some of the following words (or make up new ones) to help differentiate them: family, tribe, group, folks, gathering, team, circle, congregation, collective, klatsch, and clan.

Shaping the Ideal Community for You

Get a piece of paper, open your journal, or start a blank document on your computer and answer these questions:

1. Describe the kind of community that would make you feel excited to participate.
2. If you could shape your community, what values would it have? Some ideas: mutual respect, creative expression, healthy living, education, helping, active participation, safety, tolerance of differences, honesty, integrity, fun, equality, inclusiveness, etc.
3. Write down the names of five people you value having in your life (they don't need to be local).
4. What skills and gifts could you share with your community?
5. What sorts of people would you like to invite into your community to make it more diverse?
6. What forums can you utilize to make these connections? One of the healthiest developments in social media is forums like Meetup for organizing real-life get-togethers.

This week, write cards to the five people you named in number three above. Not e-mails, not texts, not phone calls—actual written cards that you send in the mail. Tell them that you value them and explain how they enhance your life. Reflect on your answers to the other five questions and start working toward building a community that feels nourishing to your soul.

Your community is like your muscles. Both provide you support and strength. But they share another, less obvious quality: both will atrophy if they're not *used* and *nourished*. If you want to feel supported, inspired, and included by your community, use it and feed it.

HOW TO MINDFULLY BUILD YOUR COMMUNITY
- Ask people for help—whether it be in your garden, with your taxes, or finding a great preschool. Learn what gifts and wisdom those around you have and give them opportunities to share.
- Be involved. Go to local meetings. Participate. Know your community's plans for the future—and how you fit into them.
- Know the names of people you see often—the grocery cashier, the gas station attendant, the school principal, the guy who

takes the same bus as you every day. Allow them to be real people in your life.

- Make eye contact with the humans you pass on the street. Be the one who says "Hi!" first.
- Protect the green spaces.
- Fix something that's broken—a neighbor's fence, your niece's bike, the librarian's flat tire.
- Support local businesses—even if it costs a little more.
- Learn about others' traditions and celebrate together. Look for local festivals to attend, even if they're for an event you wouldn't normally observe.
- Stick up for someone—a disadvantaged person or population, someone being mistreated or disrespected, or someone who's unable to stand up for themselves.
- Be curious. Attend lectures at the library, senior center, or local university, check out a high school science fair, and—foremost—*learn what cool stuff people are up to in your town.* What are people building? What are they learning? Who can tell you about the history of this place?

⚜

Resource building isn't something we do once and then we're set up for life. It's an ongoing process, and it works best when you connect to the *sweetness*—the enjoyment in cultivating more life energy, in realizing your worth, in learning and developing your skills, in building trust in yourself, in becoming courageous, and in strengthening your community. Evaluate your resources, determine where to focus your efforts, and then check in again on a regular basis. Remember, you don't need to have your resources in perfect order before you can get started on your goals, but resource maintenance should be woven into your plan.

PART 3.

WHO ARE YOU AND WHAT DO YOU WANT?

When we live at a frantic pace, always on our devices, densely scheduled, bombarded by drama, and swept up in the Human Data Stream, it's easy to lose the instinct of inner listening and forget what really drives us. The good news is, it's never too late to change this habit! This chapter is about aligning yourself with what really matters to you.

Being in sync with a deeper sense of guidance, rather than constantly responding and reacting to the stimuli around you, brings you a feeling of peace and assurance that can be life-changing. It's not just an intangible satisfaction, either. Most people have specific, measurable goals they want to achieve, and we want this for you, too. There are likely to be a variety of obstacles along the way (and afterward, too!), and using the powers at your disposal can make all the difference in navigating around them.

CHAPTER 8.
DEFINE YOUR SUPERPOWERS

DISCOVER WHAT LIGHTS YOU UP

Find Your Light

Your goals are important. If more people were successful at bringing their potential into the world, our species would evolve in a profound way. Just think of how many gifted people you have known who, for whatever reason, ended up on a life path where their gifts were never really developed and shared. Even if your goals are quite modest, and even if you never reach them, if you're guided by your purpose and you use your gifts, life won't feel like a missed opportunity. More importantly, there's a qualitative difference to a life lived in this awareness. There may be minimal change to the *structure* but a fundamental shift in the access to *space* and infusion of *sweetness*.

We believe that the base state of every human's consciousness is Love. It could also be called Truth or Virtue. Most of us explored and experienced the world from this perspective as a baby. However, through socialization and traumatic events, we gradually accumulated a pile of beliefs and defense mechanisms that tend to override this natural state and impair our ability to experience life in an unob-structed, love-based manner.

This virtue is like *light*, and humans, when functioning at their healthiest, when doing what might be considered our "soul work," are like carriers of light into the world. When you meet someone with a really healthy soul, isn't it like encountering light? It's not a coincidence that we use expressions like "You brightened up my day," or "She's a shining star," or "Look on the bright side"—virtue feels illuminating. And when we say, "Shed some light on the matter," we mean that the truth, too, is like light. Sometimes one of these bright souls rings up our groceries, or takes our order at a restaurant, or teaches us an otherwise boring subject in school—and we feel posi-tively changed through the encounter, at least temporarily.

These folks transform the planet. They counteract the fear, stress, and bullshit of the world. They use their light to penetrate and heal the darkness and separation they encounter. There may be nothing conscious or spiritual about it—they're just being who they are and telling it like it is. They're simply people in whom virtue is relatively unobstructed. As more people bring more light to the world, the scale starts to tip—away from a history of ignorance, divisiveness, and brutality, and toward understanding, unification, and peace.

We want you to be one of these people. Earth will be better for everyone—including you and us—if you are.

We All Have Gunk

Your ability to be an emissary of light (virtue/love/truth) isn't like a switch that's either on or off; it's a range. The stuff that gets in the way—most of which is a product of your mind—impedes your abil-ity to be a vessel for light. If light were liquid and you were a pipe, the obstructing stuff could be understood as gunk (to use the technical term) in the pipe. Sometimes the gunk builds up and barely any light gets through. Other times, the gunk clears and more light pours out. Additionally, there's some variability in the force of the liquid (light).

If you're inspired, say, by another person who's really shining her light, your own light surges. In these moments, it manages to push past the gunk more effectively than usual.

Clearing Your Gunk

For the task of facilitating the expression of your virtue, holistic systems of medicine can offer some useful guidance. (By the way, "holistic" or "wholistic" simply means "addressing the *whole* being"—considering all facets of a person as one interconnected entity. It doesn't imply a particular modality of medicine; rather, any approach that attends to the big picture is a holistic one.) In our experience, the essence of holistic healing can be understood as consisting of two main divisions:

1. Clearing, releasing, transforming, or correcting whatever obstructs the expression of virtue through the individual (i.e., gunk), and,
2. Awakening or reinforcing one's virtue.

Gunk on one level, such as a bacterial infection affecting the physical body, could infringe on the expression of virtue on that same level—e.g., impairing vibrant physical health. Or it could affect the expression of virtue on another level—e.g., impairing vibrant psychological health. Therefore, in the process of gunk investigation, it's worthwhile to examine both the body and the mind. We have seen patients with depression and anxiety that cleared up entirely upon eliminating problematic foods from their diet. We have also seen patients with severe pain that cleared up entirely when a conflict was resolved or negative emotions were released.

If you try to awaken virtue without addressing the gunk—by, say, listening to an inspiring speech, taking a hike on a beautiful mountain, attending a ceremony in a holy temple, holding a newborn baby, or drinking a shot of wheatgrass juice—this usually results in you experiencing a transient feeling of energy, inspiration, or happiness, and then a return to your previous state. Unless the connection to virtue occurs through a *profoundly* powerful experience (and such experiences are almost impossible to manufacture), it's unlikely to "take" in a lasting way. The gunk is too deeply entrenched.

Perhaps counterintuitively, focusing *exclusively* on clearing the gunk doesn't really work either. Even if you get a colonic, go on a fast, break down all your negative beliefs, smudge yourself with sage smoke, or smash your cell phone, you usually just experience a transient feeling of energy or lightness and then a return to your previous state. Completely deprived of your gunk, you may feel vulnerable and lost and will quickly look for new gunk. Especially if you've been hyperfocused on gunk, there will always be more. Something needs to take the place of the gunk in order to stabilize the clearing process.

As you can guess, these processes work best in tandem: Clear your gunk and reinforce your virtues simultaneously. The cleanup work described in Chapter 3 and the inner critic work in Chapter 6 are a valuable start in gunk cleanup, while the self-care practices of Chapter 2, the integrity work of Chapter 4, and the self-worth recognition in Chapter 6 all support your connection to virtue.

STRUCTURE, SWEETNESS, AND SPACE

The difficulty in embodying your virtue points to a need for *structure, sweetness,* and *space* in order to be an effective vessel. You need *space* to perceive and access your inner light. *Sweetness* allows you to access virtue in the forms that are most palatable and lovable to you, and it makes your work enjoyable. Healthy *structure,* including the body itself, enables you to be a stable carrier of this high-level consciousness in the world—a world with plenty of conflict and doubt.

Now we'll focus on inviting the expression of your unique virtue by identifying the specific ways in which it shines though you: your superpowers, a.k.a. your core values, gifts, and purpose. Discovering these qualities imparts a subtle *structure* to your life that can revolutionize how you feel and operate. Further, this form of pragmatic self-awareness can help you navigate your new adventures with assurance and will make the challenging periods feel worthwhile.

Identify Your Core Values

There are many different human expressions of virtue, such as honesty, love, service, and courage. In this section, you're simply going to choose a few that are most important to you. Identifying your Core Values—your superpowers—gives you a personal code and internal compass that can guide and inspire your passage through life. Abiding by your Core Values guides you to healthy choices that nourish both yourself and the environment you live in. When you're faced with a decision you're uncertain about, you can start by asking whether it's in sync with your Core Values.

> Identifying your Core Values—your superpowers—gives you a personal code and internal compass that can guide and inspire your passage through life.

Grab a piece of paper or open a blank document on your computer and answer these five questions first:

1. What are your greatest accomplishments?
2. When have you been most productive?
3. When do you like yourself the most?
4. When have you acted in a way that made you proud of yourself?
5. What advice would you give someone based on what you've learned?

Finally, what Core Values prevailed over your conduct in the above instances? Here are some ideas:

○ Honesty
○ Kindness
○ Integrity
○ Purpose
○ Compassion
○ Love
○ Ambition
○ Expression
○ Individuality
○ Community
○ Service
○ Peace
○ Enjoyment
○ Ease
○ Trustworthiness
○ Beauty
○ Courage
○ Wisdom

○ Openness
○ Humility
○ Simplicity
○ Equality
○ Righteousness
○ Achievement
○ Lightness
○ Learning
○ Organization
○ Generosity
○ Devotion
○ Inclusivity
○ Optimism
○ Respectfulness
○ Vision
○ Truthfulness
○ Persistence
○ Connection

As you read through these values, check the ones that evoke a feeling in you. Also, feel free to come up with your own if you don't see what you're looking for on this list. Write down the top five (or fewer) that move you the most. Don't select them entirely on the basis of what *seems* most important intellectually. Which of these values actually *awakens* something in you and compels the gunk to make way for your light?

On many occasions, we have discussed important family decisions with respect to our core values. Once, we were exhausted from months of travel, living out of suitcases, eating foods that our bodies didn't love, and managing the erratic sleep schedule of a newborn baby. We had that raw, burnt-out feeling that can only be healed by *home*. But as soon as we collapsed on our own bed, we received news that Briana's beloved grandmother had died.

For the whole family to attend the funeral, it would have meant another week of travel, expensive plane tickets, more erratic sleep for the baby, missed school for our older daughter, and finding someone to care for our pets. But as we discussed the pros and cons, our shared core values of *connection* and *kindness* kept coming up. We *know* that showing up for others makes a difference, and as soon as the decision was made, we felt an affirming sense of purpose. Our energy came back, and the exhaustion abated. You'll experience this, too, when you make choices based on your Core Values.

What Are Your Gifts?

Everyone has gifts, but not everyone builds a life for themselves that allows them to use, hone, and share their gifts. By gifts we mean the talents or abilities that come naturally to you. When you identify your gifts and incorporate them into your Well Life, you feel an immediate sense of alignment, satisfaction, and fluency. It's like bringing your own *sweetness* with you.

Collect Feedback

Sometimes it helps to have outside opinions in determining your gifts. If you feel shy about asking others about your gifts, tell them we made you do it. Send an e-mail to a handful of friends and family members saying something like, "I have an assignment that requires me to ask others to identify what they believe are my top three gifts."

If you want more objective insights, consider taking the Clifton StrengthsFinder test. It's based on the book, *Now, Discover Your Strengths,* by Donald Clifton and Marcus Buckingham, which aims to help readers discover and better understand their strengths (gifts). If you buy the book, you have access to take the online test for free. Otherwise, you can purchase the test on its own at www.gallupstrengths center.com.

Clifton is considered the father of "strengths psychology"— essentially, the study of how people recognize and utilize their strengths.

A former professor of educational psychology, Clifton bought Gallup, the renowned research and polling company, in 1969. In developing the StrengthsFinder material, he utilized forty years' worth of Gallup's massive collection of research. The jewel of strengths psychology is this: People tend to experience greater success and happiness when they play to their strengths, rather than focusing on and attempting to correct their weaknesses.

While we feel that a more "organic" personal inquiry into your strengths reveals things a computer-based test cannot, we've found the StrengthsFinder test useful for our company. When our managers take it, they enjoy learning about the unique strengths they bring to the organization and how everyone's gifts work synergistically to create a powerful team. Besides Clifton's test, there are many other free online resources available if you simply do a web search using terms such as "find your gifts." We encourage you to get as many different perspectives as you like. It will only increase the likelihood of revealing congruities that will lead you to a clearer recognition of your gifts.

Conduct a Self-Assessment

After you receive responses to your e-mail, make some *space* for this gift-discovering exercise. Get a few pieces of paper or open a blank document on your computer. Entitle it *My Gifts*. Follow these directions:

1. Write down the answers your friends and family offered.
2. Write down any gifts revealed by tests or other gift-identifying resources.
3. Look again at your answers to the five questions in the Core Values section and comb through them for ideas of likely gifts.
4. Answer the following questions:

   - What did you love to do as a child?
   - What did the younger you want to be when he or she grew up?

- What activities are so engaging they cause you to lose track of time?
- If you had unlimited free time and resources, what sorts of projects would you take on?
- What kinds of things do people ask you for help with?
- What would be the ideal charity work for you?

5. Time for a mind dump! Write freely about your gifts for at least ten minutes. If nothing comes to you, just dump whatever your mind comes up with onto the page. Sometimes the gunk needs to come out before the light appears. Here are some questions to jog your inner Easter egg hunter:

- Are you good at helping others to feel heard?
- Do you have an ability to create art?
- Are you able to help people see their beauty?
- Are you gifted at teaching people complex ideas in a way they can easily understand?
- Are you skilled at connecting with children or animals?
- Are you good at figuring out what needs to happen in order to turn an idea into a reality?
- Is it easy for you to uplift people with humor or inspiring words?
- Do you have a talent for building and fixing things?
- Do you have a knack for helping people to resolve their conflicts?
- Are you brave? Curious? Open-minded? Supportive? Disciplined? Loyal? Optimistic?

6. Use a highlighter to mark the gifts revealed throughout the above sections.
7. Make a list of these gifts, refining the wording in the process.

Remember, this is not the time for modesty. Everyone is a healer. Everyone has the capacity to create beauty. *Everyone has gifts!*

Use Your Gifts

People who find ways to incorporate their gifts into their lives are happier, more satisfied, more confident, more creative, more engaged in their work, and learn faster. Don't *build your life* around your weaknesses, hoping that you'll improve. That's setting yourself up for a lot of work and continual reminders of the disparity between your current skill level and where you believe you should be. We're not saying you shouldn't try to improve your abilities—especially if these weaknesses detrimentally impact your relationships, health, or happiness. If you're a poor listener or unreliable, by all means, work to get better. But if you're bad at math, you should seriously reconsider a career in accounting.

Focusing on your weaknesses hurts you in two ways—it engages you in an ongoing struggle, and it deprives you and others of the expression of your gifts. When you focus instead on your gifts, you'll feel less tired and more motivated by the work you do. Even when employed in work that isn't explicitly based on your gifts, using your gifts in the workplace makes for greater satisfaction. Sharing your gifts is an excellent way to serve and build your community while doing something you're good at and enhancing your confidence. Plus, it encourages others to share *their* gifts.

Look at the list you made in step seven of the exercise. Now reduce this to a smaller list of about five of your most special gifts, and phrase them in clear, concise language. You don't need to give up the others; we just want to make it easy for you to *remember* your primary gifts by simplifying them. From time to time, you may wish to revisit this process, since your sense of your gifts, or which gifts need your attention, may change. We do the process at the beginning of each year as we're filling out our *Rituals for Living Dreambook* (you can find more information at www.dreambook.vision).

From now on, rather than shoving your gifts into the corner, bring them to the forefront of your life. Keep the list in a place where you'll see them regularly. Own your gifts. Accept that they are a permanent part of who you are. Be grateful for them and share them freely.

Don't Be Intimidated by a "Life Purpose"

Few people have the experience of consciously knowing their Life Purpose and accessing the clarity and drive that emerge from it. "Life Purpose" can sound so grand, so out of our hands. Often, people assume that it's some kind of revelation that's delivered through a dramatic or mystical experience. "Aha!" the chosen person cries as light pours down from the heavens, "I know what I'm meant to do with my life now!" Then they quit their job and maybe change their name to something that sounds Indian, but actually means "moldy pickle." Of course there's the more mundane version, too, that by sheer luck and an altruistic nature, a person ends up on the perfect path for them. After thirty years of rescuing orphans from the streets, they're sitting in the orphanage with sixteen happy children piled on top of them. They sigh contentedly and say, "Clearly, this is my life purpose!"

In actuality, with an open mind and an understanding of your Core Values and Gifts, you can discover your Life Purpose without difficulty through a combination of intuition and choice. Committing to your Life Purpose doesn't require changing your name, quitting your job, or ending your marriage. It's a way of knowing yourself better, knowing how you best share your gifts and how you can help the world. This last part is integral. As we see it, your Life Purpose is an expression of love, and it emanates from the recognition of your connection to the world.

> Committing to your Life Purpose doesn't require changing your name, quitting your job, or ending your marriage.

Your Purpose doesn't come with a mandate of commitment, but any moment you commit to your Purpose, including the moments of personal enjoyment and revelry, takes on a quality of significance and rightness. Choosing to be aligned with your Purpose is a choice to be guided by your Highest Self. It's always fulfilling. Also, as with your Gifts and Values, your Purpose serves as a valuable road map during difficult times.

The following exercises will guide you to discover your Life Purpose. We're presenting you with two very different ways of arriving at your Purpose. Remember, if you choose your Purpose with your heart, your choice will point you in the right direction, and over time you'll refine and evolve it. Don't worry about getting it perfect. Fifteen years ago, one of our teachers gave us ten minutes to come up with our Life Purpose statements. "Don't think about it too much!" he said. "Here's a pen and paper. Write it down. You already know what it is." And even though the wording has changed over the years, the core *sentiment* has always been the same. Your Purpose points you to virtue, and that's really all that matters.

STRUCTURE, SWEETNESS, AND SPACE

There are two routes to discovering your Purpose, which we call the *structure* approach and the *space* approach. In short, the *structure* approach is about figuring out your Purpose and the *space* approach is about making *space* in your consciousness for your Purpose to be revealed to you. Ultimately, the evolution of your Purpose requires making *space* for your broader awareness to trickle into your mind and body—you'll *know* it and *feel* it, rather than *thinking* it into being.

Find Your Life Purpose: The *Structure* Approach

We'll start with the more mechanical *structure* approach to get you in the ballpark, because most people are comfortable with mental analysis. With this method, you'll examine the structures of your life in the past and present, looking for clues and patterns. It's a somewhat intellectual approach to determining your purpose, but what you come up with will be a good starting point that can be revised based on your experience of *living* from this purpose. Get a piece of paper or open a new document on your computer. The heart of this method is to simply answer this question:

Considering who you are,
aligned as you are with your Core Values,
in possession of your special Gifts,
and moved by your inner Virtue to serve and share

with the world in your own way,
what is your Life Purpose?

Just sit with that for a minute or two and draft a preliminary Life Purpose statement. Here are some examples:

- My Life Purpose is to help children express themselves.
- My Life Purpose is to help people attain better health by educating them.
- My purpose is to make the world more beautiful.
- My purpose is to help preserve clean water on our planet.
- My purpose is to use my musical abilities to uplift people.
- My purpose is to empower women to learn and use their voices.
- My purpose is to inspire people to do what they love.

Consider the various service words in the above statements and others, such as: assist, inspire, motivate, improve, encourage, strengthen, help, nurture, produce, create, build, foster, teach, promote, facilitate, empower, guide, heal, communicate, master, educate, accomplish, give, integrate, uplift, organize, share, and understand.

If you still feel uncertain about what your life purpose is, here are some additional suggestions to help you come up with an answer. Consider these questions:

- Is there a population, a facet of the world, or a cause that you have a special affinity for? For example, children, women, veterans, elderly, refugees; water, rainforest, endangered species; education, preservation, medicine, peace, etc.
- What's the most deeply gratifying work you've ever done?
- What theme or pattern connects the fulfilling times of your life?
- How have you served the other inhabitants of the planet, or the earth itself, in a way that felt natural, exciting, or compelling to you?

- What sort of service makes you sit up and feel a sense of having a mission?
- What has brought meaning or peace to your life during challenging times?
- How have you used your gifts in ways that felt gratifying?
- What is the deepest reward you get from doing the things you love to do? When you think of something you enjoy doing, what is the most fundamental benefit to it?

Based on your responses to these questions, revise the statement you wrote previously. (Or, if you feel good about it, keep it as it is.) Now, evaluate your Purpose statement in light of the following guidelines:

1. Your Purpose statement should sit well with you. It should feel right.
2. Further, it should feel inspiring. It should awaken something in you.
3. Keep in mind that you may have adopted your ideas about purpose from societal ideals of success. If the Purpose statement you came up with revolves around worldly measures of achievement and wealth, it's worth questioning. There's nothing wrong with the pursuit of success and prosperity, but your Life Purpose is deeper than this. It's something you can fulfill regardless of your finances or accomplishments.
4. Your Life Purpose will generally be something you can do for the rest of your life and continue to feel gratified by it. Unlike worldly goals, there usually won't be an *endpoint*.
5. It's okay if your Purpose statement makes you feel vulnerable or uncomfortable, as long as it also feels right. Knowing your purpose and accepting the job may be a threat to many long-held beliefs.
6. However, if you feel heavy, burdened, or anxious when you think about the purpose you've come up with, chances are it's not your authentic purpose, but instead a product of your

social conditioning. Let it go. Find something deeper, aligned with Love, and closer to the truth of who you really are.

7. It doesn't need to be perfect. *Try living it.* See what happens. Return to your purpose statement and revise it if necessary.

In light of these considerations, make additional refinements to the wording of your Purpose statement, if necessary.

Find Your Life Purpose: The *Space* Approach

Regardless of where you landed with the *structure* approach, you'll get something more from trying the *space* approach as well. The essence of the *space* approach is to simply let your purpose come to you. What you arrive at may be completely different from the result of your *structure* process. If this is the case, it usually indicates a disparity between what you know in your heart—your expanded awareness—and the way you're operating in the world. As you proceed with living the heart-informed Life Purpose from the *space* approach, you'll notice that your *structured* interpretation of your Purpose will gradually shift to converge with this one.

In the process ahead, you'll be using meditation to tap into the vast *space* of your unrestricted consciousness, going beyond the confines of your everyday mind. Here, in the *space* that always holds you, you have access to a deep *knowing*—of your power, of your inseparable connection with the world, and of the love that illuminates all the darkness of human confusion.

Your connectedness to everyone and everything is an idea that's shared by many different spiritual and philosophical traditions, especially the "nondual" traditions, which hold that there's no real separation between all the countless things of the world. It's all part of the same Oneness. Love, like light and virtue, is unconditionally *inclusive.* And as your awareness opens to *include* every aspect of the world—which is, after all, *your* world—you'll find yourself recognizing ways that you can lovingly serve this world, as if caring for your own body. The more encompassing or unrestrictive your awareness, the more obvious it is that whatever you do for the world, you do for yourself.

You can go through this *space* approach either by reading the instructions here or by listening to our audio version, which you can download for free at www.welllifebook.com/resources. If you choose to guide yourself through it from the book, read the directions completely before you begin (including the notes that follow it) so that you'll only need to occasionally glance at the page to remind yourself of each step. As you proceed through the stages of "owning" an expanding sense of yourself, keep in mind that we don't mean this in a selfish or exclusive way, but an inclusive one. You'll know the difference, because the inclusiveness of love has an expansive and *sweet* feeling, rather than seeming contractive or exclusive.

This process consists of two sections:

1. The first is a meditation to facilitate the awareness of your oneness with the world.
2. The second is to repeatedly ask your expanded awareness, "What is my Life Purpose?" and write down whatever response comes through until you experience a powerful wave of emotion.

As you move through this second section, keep the following guidelines in mind:

- You might go through it 100 or more times before feeling that your purpose has arrived.
- Your mind may vomit out a lot of random or negative gunk. Facilitate the detox and keep the *space* open by writing it down and moving on. As in the mind dump for discovering your Gifts, sometimes the gunk has to clear out before the light can shine through. View the passage of gunk as an essential step to opening a *space* in your mind for the authentic answer to show up.
- If you get to a point at which *nothing* is coming to you, keep going. This is like the "dry heaves" part of the process. Your

mind isn't throwing anything up, but it's not yet in a receiving state. Write down *whatever* is there after you ask the question, and continue the process.

- You're likely to experience resistance. A mind that isn't accustomed to making *space* feels uncomfortable holding that emptiness and not being able to fill it with something. You might feel a powerful urge to clean, or stand up and move around, or get a snack. You might feel overwhelmingly tired, restless, or annoyed. You might think this is the stupidest exercise in the world. Don't give in. If your mind is becoming aggressive about disrupting the process, you're getting close to something good. We're telling you this now so you won't fall for your mind's tricks. Your mind's job now is to make a *space* for your expanded awareness to fill with the authentic answer to your question. Your unconscious mind already knows your purpose, or at least a starting point. The diagram below may help you conceptualize this process.

- If something sounds impressive but doesn't provoke a strong emotional reaction, you're not done yet. If you feel a small surge of energy, it may be worthwhile to quickly mark or highlight this answer. You can revisit these "on the right path" answers later.
- Trust that you'll know when your purpose has arrived.

Now, for the process. If you stick to it for an hour or more and feel that you absolutely must take a break, go ahead. Understand that you have made progress even if you don't have a complete Life Purpose statement yet. Some people need a couple of sessions before the good stuff starts flowing; just don't go more than twenty-four hours between these sessions.

1. Find a quiet room where you won't be disturbed for an hour or so. Have a pen and several sheets of paper next to you, or a computer with a blank document open.

2. Sit comfortably, close your eyes, and consciously relax your body from top to bottom. Put your attention on your head and let it relax. Put your attention on your neck and let it relax. Put your attention on your shoulders and let them relax. Keep going, part by part, all the way down to your feet. If you're able to relax quite readily, you can spend just a minute or two on this step. Otherwise, take your time with it.

3. Open the process. Make a statement to your Highest Self, God, Spirit, the Universe, or whatever name you choose to use for the bigger whole that you're contained in, asking to know your Life Purpose. Use words that feel good and comfortable to you. You might say something as simple as, "Dear Universe, I ask to now become aware of my Life Purpose," or you could choose more elaborate words.

4. Allow your awareness to encompass your whole body. In your mind's eye, see yourself sitting here. Let yourself feel the entirety of your body at once, from your center out to the periphery. Become aware of the outer boundaries of your body and feel the gentle expansion and contraction that occurs with your breath. Let yourself love the entirety of your body. As you let your love include and accept every atom of your body, say tenderly to yourself, "*My* body."

5. Now, allow your awareness to expand outward from your body by about three feet (one meter) in every direction. Imagine that

what is *you* now includes this three-foot layer of *space* that surrounds you. Your new boundary is the outer edge of this *space*. Hold the vision of this expanded *you* in your mind's eye, and allow yourself to *feel* the *space* that you now contain. Imagine that you can feel every atom within this *space*, and that these atoms are indistinguishable from those within your physical body. As you bring your awareness to your breath, feel how the *space* around you now expands and contracts with your body. Let yourself love and include the entirety of this *space*. Ask yourself, "Whose space is this?" And let yourself answer tenderly, "*My space.*"

6. Next, allow your awareness to expand outward from your body by ten feet (three meters) in every direction. This is the new, expanded *you*. Trace the edges of your new boundaries with your mind. Imagine that you can perceive all the atoms contained within both your physical body and this ten-foot *space* around you, and they are indistinguishable from each other. Hold the vision of this expanded you in your mind's eye, and allow yourself to *feel* the *space* that you now contain. Visualize this entire *space* expanding and contracting with your inhale and exhale. Let yourself love and include the entirety of this *space* and everything and everyone in it. Ask yourself, "Whose *space* is this?" And let yourself answer tenderly, "*My space.*" Give up any resistance to completely loving and accepting everything in this *space*.

7. Now, allow your awareness to expand outward from your body by one mile in every direction. Trace the edges of your new boundaries with your mind. Imagine that you can perceive all the atoms contained within both your physical body and this mile-thick *space* around you, and they are indistinguishable from each other. The whole sphere is you. Hold the vision of this expanded you in your mind's eye, and allow yourself to *feel* the *space* that you now contain. Visualize this entire *space* expanding and contracting with your inhale and exhale. Let

yourself love and include the entirety of this *space* and everything and everyone in it. Ask yourself, "Whose *space* is this?" And let yourself answer, "*My space.*" If there are people within this *space*, ask yourself, "Whose people are these?" And let yourself answer tenderly, "*My* people." You can ask yourself the same about any buildings, plants, and animals within this *space* if you like. Give up any resistance to completely loving and accepting everything in and about this *space*.

8. Next, allow your awareness to expand outward from your body to encompass the entire Earth. Trace the edges of your new boundaries with your mind. Imagine that you can perceive all the atoms contained within both your physical body and the whole planet around you, and they are indistinguishable from each other. The whole planet is you. Hold the vision of this expanded you in your mind's eye, and allow yourself to *feel* the *space* that you now contain. Visualize the whole Earth expanding and contracting with your inhale and exhale. Breathe the planet. Imagine that you're drawing the entirety of it into yourself with your inhale, collecting and accepting it all as yourself, and then, with your exhale, letting it all relax, feeling out to the farthest reaches of your borders and including everything in your love. All the people, land, water, structures, plants, animals, and air. Ask yourself, "Whose planet is this?" And let yourself answer tenderly, "*My* planet." Give up any resistance to completely loving and accepting everything in, on, and about this planet.

9. Finally, allow your awareness to expand outward from your body to encompass the whole universe, as far as you can fathom, and imagine that all of it is you. See yourself in your mind's eye, growing to include all the stars, planets, moons, and galaxies. Imagine that you can perceive all the atoms in the universe and they are indistinguishable from the atoms within your physical body. All of it is you. Allow yourself to *feel* the *space* that you now contain, which is everything. Nothing is outside of you.

Nothing is *not* you. Visualize this entire universe expanding and contracting with your inhale and exhale. Breathe the whole universe into yourself with each inhale. And release the whole universe with every exhale, as if you're the Big Bang, and the universe expands outward from your own physical body. As you inhale the universe, include all of it in your love. As you exhale the universe, forgive it and all its inhabitants for anything and everything. Ask yourself, "Whose universe is this?" And let yourself answer tenderly, "*My* universe. This universe is *me.*" You can also ask yourself the same about the stars, the sun and moon, the people, or anything else that comes to mind. It's all within you. Give up any resistance to completely loving and accepting everything in and about this universe.

10. Take a few moments to feel this unlimited awareness of You.

11. Now, ask yourself, "What is my Life Purpose?" and simply allow the answer to come to you.

12. Open your eyes gently and write down *whatever* comes to mind.

13. Close your eyes again and repeat steps eleven and twelve until you come up with the answer that makes you cry.

14. Close the process. Make a statement to your Highest Self (or whatever name you use) expressing gratitude for this process—even if you didn't get exactly what you wanted out of it. You might say something like, "Dear Highest Self, thank you for revealing my purpose to me. Please, help me live my purpose to the best of my ability." Or, if you plan to continue the process later, perhaps a statement such as, "Thank you, God, for holding me in this *space*. I ask for your continued guidance to clearly understand my purpose."

* Steps eleven, twelve, and thirteen of this method are based on the bare-bones technique developed by Steve Pavlina, who has written extensively and brilliantly on personal development. We encourage you to check out his articles for more insights on Life Purpose.

Integrating Your Purpose with Your Life

Once you have come up with a workable Life Purpose statement, remember that you'll have the rest of your life to work with it and refine it. Even if you sincerely endeavor to remember and follow the guidance of this Purpose, it's quite possible that there will be days, weeks, or even months when you'll forget about it completely. You'll get immersed in life. This doesn't mean you're not *on Purpose* during these times, though — especially if you have made a conscious choice to give yourself to your Purpose. Consider a brief meditation to express this intention, such as simply relaxing your body, quieting your mind, allowing yourself to expand into a sense of oneness with the universe, and stating, "I offer my life to my Purpose of (insert purpose here)." If that sounds too big, or you have a fear of commitment, try offering a single day to your purpose. When you wake up in the morning, you could make an intention statement such as, "I give this day to the full expression of my Life Purpose of (insert purpose here)."

By "giving yourself to your Purpose," again, we don't mean that you have to completely overhaul your life. Depending on your current circumstances, it may be entirely possible to live your Purpose without changing much except your intention. There are so many ways to fulfill your Purpose; think creatively. Going out on a date or watching a movie may be completely "on Purpose" for you. For instance, it may help you connect to others, experience more love, or better understand your species.

On the other hand, if your current situation presents significant obstacles to living your Purpose, perhaps some change is warranted. Even if these changes are difficult to face, you will grow and heal through the process. When you consciously live through your Purpose, you get to experience success in a way that's very different from typical achievements — you'll feel it as an ongoing sense of fulfillment. Moreover, when you align the real-world elements of your life (such as your career and relationships) with your Purpose, it becomes easier to achieve balance and success in these areas. Everything you're doing comes to feel like a contribution toward the big picture. It's empowering and energizing, and it facilitates a sense of trust in the trajectory of your life.

From now on, you have this compass. When in doubt, let your Life Purpose guide you. Your Purpose, along with your Gifts and Values, will help clarify your priorities and elucidate difficult choices. You can always ask yourself:

- Is this aligned with my Core Values?
- *Or,* If I were to approach this while embodying my Core Values, how would I act?
- Does this allow me to share my Gifts?
- *Or,* If I honored and utilized my Gifts to my fullest potential, how would I act?
- Given my Life Purpose of . . . is this "on purpose" for me?
- *Or,* If I were living in accordance with my Life Purpose of . . . how would I act?

You may not be successful at always staying aware and reverent of your Values, Gifts, and Purpose, but when you begin to consciously do this more and more, it starts to become a habit. You'll experience a sense of *alignment*—a *knowing* that you're on the right track—and there's both peace and power in this.

Bring Your Own Bliss

Joseph Campbell's famous nutshell philosophy, "Follow your bliss," has become a popular quote in the personal-growth world, and it's easy to understand why: Who doesn't want bliss? Unfortunately, Campbell's words are often taken to mean, "Don't do anything you don't like." The way most people live this credo is essentially animal-istic—the seeking of pleasure and the avoidance of pain. It's a form of bypass that leads us to chase good feelings and avoid discomfort, mis-takenly believing we'll achieve genuine, long-term happiness this way.

The avoidance of discomfort is shortsighted at best, and it trans-lates to lots of closed doors. Feeling uncomfortable isn't necessarily an indication that you're engaged in something that your soul doesn't want; usually, it indicates only that you're resisting your experience. Campbell actually felt that as long as someone is following their passion (and we'd add, their Life Purpose), they could know for *certain* that any difficulty or hard work they encountered along the way was *absolutely* meant to be part of their journey. He later remarked, "I wish I had said, 'Follow your blisters!'"

We had never seen the misunderstood side of Campbell's quote so much until becoming employers. The great majority of the good folks who have worked for us are truly high-quality human beings, many of whom we're honored to call friends. But we've also been on the short end of the stick with employees who didn't show up to work due to pleasure-seeking and pain-avoiding behaviors. Those who were *compelled* by their bliss would say things like, "I know I had a shift, but I was feeling called to get a tattoo on my heart chakra that day." And those who were convinced that discomfort is God's way of telling you to avoid something would say things like, "I know I had a shift, but I was out late last night. Then when I got up this morning, I had this bad feeling, like, 'Going to work would not be right for my soul today (we call that feeling a hangover), and I'm really trying to honor my boundaries these days."

> Feeling uncomfortable isn't necessarily an indication that you're engaged in something that your soul doesn't want; usually, it indicates only that you're resisting your experience.

We're not opposed to impulsive behavior. We just haven't seen the chasing of bliss or the fleeing of discomfort produce sustainable happiness. Seeing happiness as something that must be pursued reflects a belief that it comes from outside of you and that you're fundamentally inadequate. If that's the case, you'll always be looking for the right external circumstances—the right job, possessions, partner, or approval—as if you're a toy monkey who can only play your cymbals if the world winds you up. But the world can't give you something that's borne inside you.

Revising the Philosophy

We believe there's brilliance in Campbell's words; people just get hung up on two words—*follow* and *bliss*. The *your* part is pretty straightforward.

First, *bliss* is a bit of a holy grail. Most people have had just a few moments that approach something they'd call bliss. As such, it lends itself to never-ending pursuit. We could replace it with any of these synonymous terms to give it better context with the language of this book and this particular chapter, such as:

- Follow your *sweetness.*
- Follow your Virtue.
- Follow your Truth.
- Follow your Light.

How do we bring *sweetness*/Virtue/Truth/Light into our lives? We make *space* for them. In the same way that insight enters the mind, as we showed in our earlier diagram, Light needs *space* to come in.

How do you make *space*? One way is through the deliberate invitation for your Values, Gifts, and Purpose to guide you. This opens you, Light comes in, and it leads the way.

So, here we come to the second tricky word—*follow*. It's natural that one would think of following something *outside* of themselves, but that's not the case here. The Light you're meant to follow emanates from inside you; it's the light of your own Virtue, illuminating the path in front of you.

⬥

It's time to stop treating life like a temperamental slot machine—you're not at the mercy of an unconscious thing that delivers a series of random outcomes, determined only by luck. You have a tremendous influence on the shape of your life. You know what your Values are. You know what your Gifts are. You know what your Purpose is. And in the forthcoming chapters, you'll strengthen your connection to your Highest Self, and you'll learn how to shape your life. Instead of relating to the world as if *it's* the slot machine and you're the inebriated player, you'll realize *you're* the slot machine. It's all you. The cherries are inside you, and you can bring them up over and over again. Or maybe it's a liberty bell day today—that's fun too. Plus, there's an endless supply of quarters in you, and you can spill them out into the world—emanating your happiness—without any concern that you'll ever run out. It's a game we call BYOB—Bring Your Own Bliss. With practice, you can brighten up the darkest, most uncomfortable places.

Make *space*.

Choose *sweetness*.

Be the Light.

CHAPTER 9.
CHOOSE YOUR PRIZES

DEFINING YOUR WELL LIFE

What Is Your Dream Life?

Having identified your Core Values, Gifts, and a Life Purpose, it's time to make some choices. What "prizes" would you like for choosing a life as a human being? These are the goals that will make your dream life a reality. A loving and supportive relationship? Enjoyable work that provides a great income? You get to stand at a vast counter, look over an endless array of exhilarating choices, and make your selections. This chapter is all about identifying the particular expressions of *sweetness* you want in your life. You'll be opening *space* to get past the more superficial, conditioned desires of your mind in order to tap into what your soul *really, really* wants for you.

You can be happy regardless of your external circumstances, regardless of your possessions and accomplishments. This is especially true if you *follow your light*, as we explained in the previous chapter.

But we recognize that while this ideal is possible, most people aren't entirely there. Early in our training, we encountered a similar idea: "Nobody can make you feel a certain way. You're responsible for your own feelings." The hope was that, once you realized this, noth-ing anyone said or did would bother you. Yet it just didn't have the instant-enlightenment effect we hoped for. People affect each other; it's almost unavoidable. As clearheaded and peaceful as we might get, very few humans are immune to the influence of their planet-mates.

So, rather than trying to convince you that you should be happy and peaceful, even if you can't afford groceries and your dog just died, we need to strike a balance. You're going to continue to want things and to pursue success in your own way. The best we can do is to teach you ways to be most effective at this, remind you that lightness and peace are always available, urge you not to get attached to the mate-rial stuff, point you to the deeper, intangible outcomes that your soul *really* wants, and guide you to heal and grow in the process.

All Prizes Are Fair Game!

We feel it's important to stress that we don't have any problem with someone wanting to be phenomenally wealthy, or to have a gorgeous house, a fancy car, beautiful clothes, hot sex, lots of fun, plenty of free time for travel, and pretty much any other nonexploitative desire. We want you to *revel* in these prizes of life as a human! The key, for us, is to encourage you to have and pursue these goals *consciously:*

- In alignment with your Core Values and Purpose, and through the expression of your Gifts.
- Seeing the big picture of how you relate to the world and yourself.
- Admiring the material stuff without confusing it as the source of true happiness.
- Making lifestyle choices with minimal negative impact (if any) on the planet and its inhabitants.
- Recognizing your unbelievably good fortune.

Everyone, even the most enlightened being, has preferences. There's nothing unevolved about wanting your life to look a certain way—only in the inability to make the most of it when it *doesn't* look that way.

After saying to the universe, "I am *thoroughly* grateful to be alive, to be healthy (to whatever extent you are), to have my needs met (to whatever extent they are)," it's completely reasonable to say, "And *also*, my preference would be (to have more money, to be healthier, to be in a happy and loving relationship, to have a peaceful mind, to have a job that allows me to use my gifts and earn a good income, to have more time for play and sheer enjoyment, etc.)."

Just Choose and Trust

Many of our clients and *Dreambook* users have told us it's difficult for them to choose their prizes, so they get stuck in this stage. The most fundamental reason why it's hard to choose is a fear of regret. You think you'll make the wrong choice or that you'll miss out on what you didn't choose. From this perspective, choosing may feel like a trap. Keeping many options open—by not choosing, or having one foot out the door—appears to protect your freedom and ensure a greater chance of success, since you'll be available if something better comes along. But, if anything, the opposite is true.

When you avoid making a decision, you limit your success, because not choosing is, of course, a choice—a choice of avoidance and stagnation. Until you choose, you're resisting the flow of life and impeding growth and progress. You may believe that if you keep thinking about it, you'll eventually arrive at the perfect answer, but this state of analysis paralysis keeps you mired in rumination without action, and your fear of missing the best opportunity may *cause* you to miss the best opportunity. The perfect choice you're holding out for may never come, and even if it does, you can still feel trapped and afraid of regret.

Action Creates Clarity

Within the fear of making the wrong choice is the belief that choosing one path will cause all the other options to disappear, but it's simply not true. Besides, as long as you avoid choosing, these options aren't even *real*. All paths are theoretical until you choose one and start walking down it. Imagine you're standing at a crossroads. The roads extend only a few bricks in each direction because they represent options that haven't yet been taken. A team of masons awaits your decision and will continue paving the road that you select, always a few feet in front of you.

You may believe that the right path should be more obvious. From this vantage point, no path may seem to lead to your desired destination, but the truth may be that you simply can't see that far ahead. Perhaps the path curves around some bushes and disappears. All you can do is follow the signs, trust yourself, and start walking. The moment you choose, you initiate *movement*—the cure for stagnation. The path materializes in front of you, new choices appear, and, if you pay attention, you'll be shown the next steps. The magic doesn't happen until you really, wholeheartedly *choose*.

Making and committing to a choice can be tremendously relieving, even if you're not sure it's the perfect choice. As the saying goes, the journey matters more than the destination, but *choosing* a destination (or many destinations—i.e., your prizes) is of vital importance. What kind of person do you want to be? How do you want your life to look? What do you want to share with the world? When you consciously choose, you invoke a magnetism that brings a multitude of positive qualities with it, such as curiosity, amusement, fascination, momentum, challenge, and determination. These alone are worth the price of admission, but where these qualities will take you is even better.

Vision

Choosing your destinations wisely—and making them a reality—requires good vision. The vision we're talking about here is the ability to project yourself beyond your current circumstances, to *see* yourself in the actualization of your potential. To dream. If you're sick, it's the ability to see yourself healthy. If you feel broken, it's the ability to see yourself whole. If you're in the dark, it's the ability to see yourself in the light. If you're dissatisfied with life, it's the ability to see yourself at peace. Your inner vision comes from the true, authentic, unmanipulated You. While your physical sight and the predictive abilities of your analytical mind may help you see a few steps ahead, your inner vision will take you further. And, what you choose to focus your inner vision on is ultimately of much greater importance than the outward choices you make.

What (or Who) Has Shaped Your Vision?

This sight is always within you, but it can sometimes be tricky to access, especially if you're severely worn out, or if you've been living under an imposing belief system. Someone who's exhausted (and has perhaps been ill and medicated for a long time) may barely have the energy to open their inner "eyes." For this reason, we'll remind you again of the value of the self-care practices outlined in Chapter 2. The better your physical and spiritual health, the easier it will be to *see* clearly.

As for imposing beliefs, they may present a challenge even more formidable than physical and mental exhaustion. We can be deeply programmed—by ourselves, our partner, our family, our community, our politics, our religion—as to how we should look, act, feel, and think, and what we should value. Our programming can override who and what we really are, so much so that our own, authentic vision and expression are eclipsed. We lose sight of who we really are and what we really want. In certain forms of Eastern medicine, this is referred to as *possession*. It's not the head-spinning, green-projectile-vomit kind of possession. If you have that, we encourage you to put this book down immediately and find an exorcist (preferably one who makes house calls—you don't want to go out in public like that). It's more simply a case of allowing something other than our soul to lead the way, or what the Russian philosopher G.I. Gurdjieff would have explained as *the personality obscuring the essence*.

"Essence in man," Gurdjieff wrote, "is what is his own. Personality in man is what is not his own. 'Not his own' means what has come from outside, what he has learned, or reflects." This is a bit different from the life essence (*jing* or *ojas*) that we described in Chapter 5. Gurdjieff goes on to explain that a small child has no personality yet; she is only essence. Her feelings, desires, and tastes are all her own. Later, her personality begins to grow—through the intentional influences of others, through her imitation of what she sees, through her resistance against what she sees, and through her attempts to conceal from others what is *her own* or *real*.

See Your Essence

As you proceed with identifying what you'd like to bring into your life, we invite you to tap into your own essence. What is real in you that may be buried or concealed? Use your inner vision to see yourself as the most radiant expression of this potential. There's a feeling of "rightness," of being *home* in yourself when you're in touch with your essence—even while there may also be some apprehension around the notion of sharing it with others.

What Do You *Really* Want?

Now, it's time to dream. You'll need at least an hour for this process. You can split it up into multiple sessions, if you wish. If you prefer to write, get a notebook, a journal, or several sheets of paper. If you're able to type and still feel "tuned in," open a new document on your computer. You can also download a printable PDF version of these inquiries at www.thewelllifebook.com/resources. You'll be answering an extensive series of questions, derived from our *Rituals for Living Dreambook*, to get clear on what you really, *really* want.

As you consider these questions, tap into that essential you—the presence that was there when you were a small child and has never left (though has possibly been stifled). This is only for you, so there's no reason to hold back from answering as honestly as possible. Answer as if you, your parents, your friends, your community, and everyone you admire would thoroughly accept and approve of you no matter what you decide. As you present these questions to yourself, we encourage you to also discover and let go of goals you're pursuing (perhaps subconsciously) that *don't* reflect what your soul wants, or that no longer match who you've turned out to be.

Before you begin, find a tranquil place, light a candle or do something else to set this ritual apart from the rest of the day. Close your eyes, take a few deep breaths, and take a few minutes to relax your body, part by part, from your head to your feet. Put aside your stresses. Imagine placing them in a container, and tell your mind it's allowed to take a break from chewing on these things for a while. Set an intention, either silently or aloud, such as, "I hereby give my inner essence an opportunity to be seen and heard. I welcome the deepest desires of my soul to come to the surface and be recorded in this process."

Answer as if you, your parents, your friends, your community, and everyone you admire would thoroughly accept and approve of you no matter what you decide.

Now, look inside yourself and imagine a light in your heart. This is that awareness, that essence, that has been here, unchanging, since your childhood. Visualize a stream of light that runs upward from your heart and then splits into two branches that extend out through your arms to your hands and the tips of your fingers. As you quiet your mind and write freely, allow the words to emanate from your heart to be expressed directly through this pathway onto the paper or screen. Each set of questions addresses a different area of your life.

Your True Desires

1. What are you longing for most in life?
2. When you're at the end of life, what do you want to have accomplished?
3. If you knew you had one year left to live, would there be anything you'd want to fix or clean up?
4. What are you ready to let go of—habits, attitudes, obligations, beliefs, outdated goals, etc.—that is not serving you?
5. What do you want to explore more deeply?

6. What would make life feel ridiculously fun?
7. What feels really nourishing in your life?
8. Of all the things you've done or accomplished in your life, what has given you the deepest sense of fulfillment? When have you been most proud of yourself?
9. Where do you find yourself not being fully "present" in your life, or not participating fully?

Now, it's time to use your ability to *project* with your inner vision. In the question sections that follow, you'll be sending yourself three years into the future. Become the ideal You in your ideal circumstances. Take a few minutes to tune in before beginning each section. See yourself in your mind's eye as the happy, peaceful, confident, and wise person who has always been waiting to emerge and claim your life.

Livelihood, Career, and Influence

Projecting three years into the future of your most powerful dreams, consider these details about how you earn money, the work you do, and the nature of your influence on the world. Answer all the questions from this perspective.

1. What does your business/career look and feel like?
2. How much money do you make? What other benefits do you get?
3. How do you feel when you get up in the morning to start your workday (even if this work isn't how you earn money)?
4. What do people say about what you do? How is your reputation?
5. Who (what kinds of people) do you work with?
6. What is your ultimate vision for the financial life you're headed toward (income, investments, savings, etc.)?

7. What sort of influence do you have on your community? What value do you bring to the world?
8. How do you feel about paying bills, taxes, or unforeseen expenses?
9. How do you feel when you check your bank account?
10. How do you spend your money in ways that make you feel you're having a positive impact?

Relationship and Family

Projecting three years into the future of your happiest dreams, consider these details about how you want your love relationship and family life to be. Answer all the questions from this perspective—as if you have already attained this.

1. Describe your primary love relationship.
2. In this ideal relationship, what do you give, receive, create, and experience together? Consider all the realms of your relationship, including love, intimacy, friendship, support, play, etc.
3. How do you feel when you're talking with your partner? When you're expressing something that matters to you or makes you feel vulnerable?
4. How do you grow through being in this relationship?
5. In your ideal family life, how does it feel when everyone is home together?
6. What do you and your family members do together?
7. What are family conversations like? How does your family respond when you speak from your heart about something that is very important to you?
8. How does the family respond if someone has a problem?
9. What are holidays like together?

Community Connection

Projecting three years into the future of you at your most engaged, consider these details about how you want your community to be. Answer all the questions from this perspective—as if you have already attained this.

1. What are your friendships like? What do you do together?
2. How prominently do your friends figure into your everyday life? How often do you get together?
3. How are your conversations? Are you able to share on all matters that concern you?
4. How do your friends respond when you're having a difficult time?
5. How do you and your friends support each other?
6. What needs of yours are met by your friendships?
7. Describe your community, including how you engage with it, what value you bring to it, and how you're nourished and supported by it.

Physical Wellness

Projecting three years into the future of your most healthy and vibrant self, consider these details about how you want your body, energy, and overall health to be. Answer all the questions from this perspective—as if you have already attained this.

1. Describe your beautiful body.
2. How do you feel in your body when you wake up in the morning?
3. How do you feel in your body at the end of a long day?
4. How is your relationship with exercise, and what do you do to keep your body in good shape?
5. How do you feed your body? What do you eat and how do you eat?

6. How is your energy?
7. How is your sleep?
8. How does it feel when you take a deep breath?
9. How are your strength and flexibility?
10. How do you feel about aging?
11. If you used to have any health problems, what has happened with these?

Creation, Exploration, and Play

Projecting three years into the future of your most fun and fascinating dreams, consider these details about how you want to be engaging and expressing yourself creatively, intellectually, and playfully. Answer all the questions from this perspective—as if you have already attained this.

1. What percent of your life is reserved for playing, exploring, and creating?
2. How much do you travel and to where?
3. What forms of creative expression do you engage in (painting, drawing, sculpting, gardening, singing, playing an instrument, writing, acting, photography, dancing, building, sewing, etc.)?
4. How is your life affected by prioritizing creative expression, exploration, and play?
5. What forms of play and exploration do you engage in, and how often?
6. Who else do you involve in your creative and playful endeavors and what role do they play?
7. Do you have a space just for doing your creative thing? What's it like?
8. What forums do you have for exploring the topics you're passionate about with others?
9. What fascinates you?
10. In what ways is your life beautiful, and how do you live it in a beautiful way?

Psychological and Spiritual Health

Projecting three years into the future of your most lucid and uplifting dreams, consider these details about how you want to be thinking, feeling, and connecting. Answer all the questions from this perspective—as if you have already attained this.

1. For what percentage of your waking life do you feel happy?
2. Describe your outlook on life and the quality of your thoughts.
3. What percentage of your communications come from a place of truth and love? And how does this affect you and others in your life?
4. How do you feel and respond during challenging times?
5. Do you trust yourself to manage whatever might happen?
6. What percentage of your life is spent in a peaceful state?
7. In what ways do you express love to others, to the world, to your higher power?
8. How is your life affected by your cultivating a more peaceful and loving experience?
9. How do you connect to your Higher Self, God, or the Universe? And what does it feel like?
10. How do you feel about the state of the world and your place in it?
11. How is your self-esteem?
12. How do you feel about the new day when you wake up in the morning?
13. How do you feel about dying?

Close the Process

When you complete all the questions, close the ritual in a way that feels meaningful to you. For instance, you could express your gratitude for the clarity to have given a voice to your essence, or you could state an intention, such as, "May I abide by the guidance of my Highest Self and make these dreams a reality."

A Prize-Winning Life

Simply having stoked this mature vision of your future self and given words to what you intend to create, you'll find your path shifting toward the life you've just described. Of course, a lot can happen in three years. You could probably attain many of the circumstances you chose in much less time.

STRUCTURE, SWEETNESS, AND SPACE

Choosing the sweetest forms of *sweetness* to bring into your life is a gigantic gift to yourself. Integral to the achievement of these goals is opening *space* to regularly tune in to your vision of the destination; *space* to receive this *sweetness*; *space* to access nonphysical avenues of manifestation; and *space* to allow for the growth that's going to be required to get there. This process will also naturally prompt the refinement of your life *structure*. Not only will your *structure* evolve for the attainment of these prizes, but you're also likely to learn new "architectural techniques" along the way. When the prizes start showing up and you reflect on the remarkable way they got there, you'll understand how to build increasingly light and efficient structures for an ever-evolving life.

However, we'd be lying if we even suggested that this is a guarantee. We like talking about "tuning in" and "connecting with your essence" and other things that may sound woo-woo or New Agey, because, even though the language may be imperfect or cliché, it brings us closer to the truth, and we hope you know what we're getting at. But believing in virtue and truth doesn't make us blind to the fact that sometimes life just sucks. That's why the remainder of this chapter and the ones that follow are about how to turn this vision into an intention, and how to carry it with you and feed it.

Unearth the Feelings Behind Your Dreams

The first thing you need to remember is that what's most important is *the quality of your experience* that these goals represent. When you envisioned yourself in the attainment of your dream life, what *feelings* went along with those circumstances? Peace? Joy? Awe? Admiration? Love? These states are your ultimate goal. If you were deeply happy and peaceful, would you care if your circumstances weren't the way you once envisioned them? Of course not! You'd be deeply happy and peaceful!

There's nothing wrong with defining the specific conditions that you'd prefer. In fact, most people need these details in order to elicit the feeling that becomes the ultimate goal. For instance, what if your office manager announced, "Hey, everyone, we're going to have a little contest to see who can sell the most dental floss in April. The winner gets to experience a deep sense of ease and trust around money!" Would that motivate you? Chances are, you hadn't considered that a deep sense of ease and trust around money is what you *really* want when you chase money. (You might also be doubtful about the office manager's ability to *produce* that deep sense of ease and trust in you after you won.) But what if she said, "The winner will receive ten million dollars a year for the rest of your life!" Would that do the trick for you?

Revisit Your Goals Periodically

Use the details to elicit the feeling, with the understanding that the feeling is the most powerful part—and, it's something you can begin cultivating immediately. Keep your answers to the questions in this process handy. Reread them at least once a month and let that stoke your enthusiasm. If you find yourself getting rigid about the specifics, loosen up. Remember, as long as you get the feeling that you believed the specifics would produce, you still win.

Using Intention Statements

We know that your answers revealed many things you want to bring into your life. For now, choose just *one* desire to use as an intention in the upcoming exercises. Your goal is to think about how you would phrase that desire into an intention statement.

WRITING EFFECTIVE INTENTION STATEMENTS

1. **Stay positive.** Intention statements should always be phrased in the positive—i.e., in terms of what you *do* want, not in terms of what you *don't* want. Look for indicators of negative phrasing, such as the words no, not, don't, won't, can't, stop, quit, never, etc. Rather than saying, *I want to stop smoking,* you might say: *I will overcome my addiction to cigarettes.* Even a statement such as *I will be more focused at work* is less than ideal since it apparently refers to an unsatisfactory situation. When you think, *more focused,* the mind naturally continues with *than (something else).* Instead, go for a purely positive statement, such as *I am focused and efficient at work.*

2. **Don't use trigger words.** If you want to avoid something, you may be more successful with an intention statement that doesn't specifically name the substance or behavior you want to avoid. While, *I will overcome my addiction to cigarettes* is okay, whenever you think or say this phrase, your mind is reminded of cigarettes and this may trigger the addiction. Alternatively, you might find that a phrase such as, *I breathe only pure air into my clean, healthy lungs,* succeeds at bringing you to your goal, but without using triggers such as "smoking" or "cigarettes." Instead of, *I want to get over this depression,* consider, *I allow myself to feel light and happy.* Instead of, *I want to be out of pain,* consider *I choose to feel comfortable and at ease in my body.*

3. **Keep *want* out of it.** A statement such as, *I want to weigh 150 pounds* or *I want to make $200,000 a year* doesn't feel

especially compelling. The word *want* reminds us that we don't *have* this goal and it promotes a feeling of lack. Instead, use a statement such as, *I intend to weigh 150 pounds* or *I allow myself to weigh 150 pounds* or *I choose to weigh 150 pounds.*

4. **Use wording that your mind can accept.** Some people prefer phrasing intention statements as if they are true in the present, such as, *I am 150 pounds* or *I have a slim and muscular body.* The idea with this approach is to avoid putting the goal "out there" in the future. You can use this form of wording if it works for you, but we find that sometimes the mind simply rejects such statements because they aren't actually true in this moment. If you tell yourself *I have a million dollars in my bank account* and the truth is that you currently have seven dollars, your mind may ignore it—not only because of the present-tense phrasing, but also because of the huge disparity between the goal and the present circumstances. For this reason, we prefer words such as *choose* or *allow* (*I allow myself to have a million dollars*), and/or building time into the statement. You can build time into the statement by combining *choose* or *allow,* or even present-tense language, with a date. For example, *I am in a happy romantic relationship by April 30,* or *I have a thousand dollars in my bank account on Friday.*

5. **Be reasonable, but also make it a challenge.** If you have never had more than a hundred dollars to your name, an intention statement such as *I allow myself to have a million dollars* may be setting the bar a bit high. It's not impossible, but your mind may invalidate it as unrealistic, and you may simply need more practice at attaining easier goals. On the other hand, if you make your goal too easy, you won't grow.

6. **Be specific—but not *too* specific.** While it's best to avoid getting *attached* to the specifics, being specific in your intention statement often makes it more focused and powerful. For instance, *I intend to find a higher paying job* could be *I intend to be making $5,000 a month doing work I enjoy by March 1.*

You can also add language to allow for an even better outcome if you're concerned that the specificity of your wording could be limiting. For example: *I make an income of $5,000* **or more** *every month*. If you get *too* specific, such as *I allow myself to be in a happy and fulfilling love relationship with a black-smith who's 5'3" with a third nipple, a long nose, and a curly mustache*, the universe may have some difficulty fulfilling your order. Especially when it comes to intentions that involve the behavior of other people, you need to be flexible.

7. **Keep it about you.** Don't make an intention statement about other people getting healthy, other people falling in love with you, or other people "accidentally" falling down the stairs and leaving their fortune to you. This is about *you*. If you can't stop thinking about the other person, consider an intention statement, such as *I allow myself to trust that the right relationship is coming to me*, or *I allow myself to be at peace with Ben's health*.

Release Your Resistance

Once you have chosen an intention statement, and before we get into activating and amplifying that intention, it's important to clear your resistance to it. Otherwise, it would be like driving with the parking brake on—the car may still move, but you can feel that something's slowing you down. "But what resistance could I possibly have to being wealthy?" you may ask. Well, lots.

Maybe you think rich people are shallow jerks, and that you'd therefore become one—or have to hang out with them—if you had more money. Maybe you feel a sense of solidarity with people who don't have enough money, and you don't want to "betray" them. Maybe you secretly enjoy the thrill of scraping together enough money to pay your bills at the last minute. Maybe you believe there would be a lot of pressure associated with managing your wealth. Maybe you're attached to the story that life never gives you a break. All of these ideas are known as *counter-intentions*. A counter-intention is any intention, desire, or belief, whether conscious or hidden, that goes against or impedes your intention. And now, it's time to let yours go.

This three-part process will help you release resistance on numerous levels. We believe the second part of the process works best with the help of a partner—someone you feel super comfortable with. You could meet in person or connect over the phone, Skype, or FaceTime. Tell them it will probably take twenty minutes or less. You can explain the meaning of intentions and counter-intentions to your friend, and tell them how the process will go. Instruct them that their role is just to prompt you to state your intention and counter-intentions. They are *not* there to *process* the counter-intentions with you. It's okay if they want to offer a reassuring touch now and then, or to remind you to let go of whatever is coming up, but it's most helpful for them to simply keep the process moving. Although you can do the process on your own, without a facilitator it's easy to get sidetracked by analyzing your counter-intentions. Having someone prompt you makes it easier to stay engaged with what's arising in the presence of this intention.

> A counter-intention is any intention, desire, or belief, whether conscious or hidden, that goes against or impedes your intention.

If you don't have someone in your life who's available and qualifies, you can do the process alone. You'll probably get the most out of these processes by doing them all in one session (about thirty to sixty minutes), but you're also welcome to do them individually.

Part One: Body-Centered Releasing

First, you'll release the resistance that arises in your body in connection with your intention statement. We see the body, emotions, and thoughts as one interconnected continuum. When you experience conflict or resistance around a thought, this conflict or resistance is also perceptible on an emotional level (as an unpleasant emotion), and on a physical level (usually as a subtle tension that you likely ignore). When releasing such an issue, we prefer to start on the physical level because it's simpler than using the mind to revise itself. In this exercise, you'll tune in to the physical experience of resistance that arises in connection with your intention statement so that you can release it.

Begin by finding a quiet, comfortable spot where you won't be disturbed. Light a candle, set out a dish of water, or bring in some other natural object of beauty. Sit down. Take a few deep breaths. Relax your body from your head down to your feet. State an opening intention for the process. This could be something like: "My purpose in this ritual is to release any resistance, blockages, or counter-intentions to my intention of (state your intention). I ask my Highest Self to allow me access to all the parts of my body and mind where I may be holding resistance against this intention, and I ask for these impediments to leave me, with grace and ease."

1. Close your eyes and say your intention statement.
2. Feel what comes up in your body.
3. Whatever you feel (there may be a tightness somewhere, muscle clenching, irritability, jitteriness, a blocked feeling, or something else), don't fight it.
4. Feel whatever arises as willingly as possible. Don't resist it. Let it open up. Experience it with your whole being.
5. Inhale, and as you exhale, let it go. Imagine you're opening yourself and allowing this feeling to leave.
6. Repeat from step one until you can state your intention and feel peaceful and at ease in your body.

As you move through this process, you may feel sensations come and go or move from place to place in your body. If it's difficult to tune in to what's happening in your body and figure out if it's changing, you may find this easier—after stating your intention, take a breath and let it out. Get a sense of how free, deep, and unrestricted it feels. As you repeat the intention and continue to breathe, notice when your breathing becomes easier and deeper, and continue until it feels totally unrestricted.

Part Two: Clearing Your Counter-Intentions

This simple but powerful process is based on the teachings of our most influential mentor, Matt Garrigan. If you'll be assisted by a friend, now is the time to invite them in or call them. Try to remain in the meditative state you established in the first process.

1. If you're working with a friend, they'll prompt you with, "What is your intention?" Or, if you're doing this alone, you'll ask yourself, "What is my intention?"
2. State your intention. Feel it as you say it. Believe it. For example, "I allow myself to earn $10,000 every month."
3. Immediately, your friend will prompt you with, "What counter-intention is coming up?" Or, if you're doing this alone, you'll ask yourself, "What counter-intention is coming up?"
4. Voice *whatever* comes up in opposition to your intention. It might be a clear counter-intention, such as, "I don't want my friends to think I'm different." It might be a protest, such as, "How is that going to happen?" It might feel like a complaint from your inner child. Bring it to the surface; amplify it. You may feel like voicing in the way you're experiencing it, as a whine or a shout or with tears. You might just yell, "I don't want to be poor, but it's too hard to change my life!" You might just come up with some sound, like, "Blaaaaarrrrrrghhhh!" The counter-intention might take the form of discomfort or sabotage, like "I hate this!" or "This is ridiculous!" Whatever comes up, let it out and let it go. Your friend is there only to prompt you, not to discuss what comes up or validate your counter-intentions.
5. Go back to step one and repeat the process until no more counter-intentions come up.

The process moves fairly quickly and should feel spontaneous. Each round will usually take about ten to fifteen seconds, and you may do this fifty times before you feel like nothing more is coming out—there are no more protests, excuses, or other expressions of counter-intention.

We have used this process for over fifteen years and have often been amazed by the results. When you release everything within you that's obstructing your own success, you can embody your intention in a powerful, unconflicted way, and this enables you to more easily make it a reality. A single session (to the point of feeling complete) is often enough for a *clean launch* of an intention. However, if you feel that some of your counter-intentions were especially reluctant to go, you may benefit from repeating the process. You could do a complete session every day until these persistent counter-intentions stop coming up. Alternatively, you could prompt yourself through a handful of rounds a few times throughout each day. For especially stubborn counter-intention statements, write them down and spend some time doing body-centered releasing with each statement (as in Part One, but repeating the counter-intention statement instead of your intention statement).

Part Three: Relinquishing Your Resistance to Failure

The last step is to *get okay* with the idea of *not* achieving your intention. If you strongly desire something, you're often strongly *opposed* to or fearful of the alternative. If you strongly desire more money, you're often strongly opposed to being poor. If you strongly desire a relationship, you're often strongly opposed to being alone. If you strongly desire being thin, you're often strongly opposed to being fat. Dropping the opposition isn't the same as asking to fail.

The thing is, the fear of being poor isn't what makes someone rich, and the fear of being fat isn't what makes someone thin. Aversion may motivate us, but it doesn't produce healthy, lasting, sustainable change. Our opposition to the result we *don't* want keeps us in relationship with it. If all day we're thinking, *I hate being fat . . . I don't want to be fat . . . Fat is ugly . . . If I eat this it might make me fat,* we have a very strong relationship with *fat.* It's an obsession! And this acts as a counter-intention to letting go of *fat.*

This process is similar to Part One, except that you'll be doing body-centered releasing around the idea of *not* achieving your intention.

1. Close your eyes and say to yourself, "What if I don't achieve my intention?" (You may also say, " . . . my intention of (having a slender body, making $10,000 a month, etc.)."
2. Feel what comes up in your body.
3. Whatever you feel (there may be a tightness somewhere, muscle clenching, irritability, jitteriness, a blocked feeling, or something else), don't fight it.
4. Feel whatever arises as willingly as possible. Don't resist it. Let it open up. Experience it with your whole being.
5. Inhale, and as you exhale, let it go. Imagine you're opening yourself and allowing this feeling to leave.
6. State your intention or "what ifs."
7. Go back to step one and repeat the process until you can make the statement in step one and feel at peace in your body and okay about yourself. Besides the question, "What if I don't achieve my intention?" in step one, also try any other "what ifs" that come up around not achieving your intention. For instance, if your intention is to make more money, you might try saying, "What if I end up poor and lose my house?" "What if I can't pay my bills?" "What if I have to take a job I don't like?"

At this point, you've probably cleared much, if not all, of your own resistance to achieving your intention. You should feel light and confident when you say your intention statement. To finish this process, make a closing statement and consider expressing gratitude for having released your internal obstacles. For example: "I am grateful to my Highest Self for the clarity to see my blockages and for the courage to release them. I hereby seal and stabilize this work and intend that it serve the highest good of everyone involved."

In the future, you can have multiple intentions working for you simultaneously. For now, however, focus on just this one intention. In the following chapters, we'll teach you how to strengthen this intention, how to integrate it into your life, how to ensure that it serves your highest good, how to take meaningful action in support of it, and how to open yourself to receive its fruits. As you experience success with the process, you'll gain clarity on which intentions are worth launching, and how to do so with ever greater efficiency, grace, and trust.

CHAPTER 10.
OPEN UP YOUR LIFE

You Need Space to Live Your Well Life

Now that you've clarified your life purpose and have chosen specific goals, it's time to bolster these choices through *structure, sweetness,* and *space*. These three elements will help make your Well Life easier to attain because they'll help you weave your goals and purpose into the fabric of every day. In this chapter, we'll show you how to access *space* in order to connect with your Highest Self, to enrich your experience, to empower your goals, to embody the future you desire, to let go of anything that's getting in your way, and to receive the success that comes to you.

Overview of Space

Let's review some of the attributes of *space*. *Space* gives you the capacity to understand who you really are. It allows you to receive and grow. It enables you to reflect, refine, and heal. It lets you listen, feel, and see. It offers you access to universal wisdom, creativity, and insight. And it's the openness to allow life to just *be*—without the need to resist it, to cling to it, or to change it.

Space is the hardest thing for most people to cultivate and the trickiest to understand. There's an unfathomable awareness being expressed through you; your body and personality are but one narrow expression of that totality, but it's all accessible to you. Your Higher Self empowers you, breathes through you, inspires you, holds you, and gives perspective to all the stuff your life revolves around.

All the challenges of the physical world are manageable when you're connected to the vastness that you are. You can call this God, Goddess, Spirit, Awareness, Highest Self, or whatever feels good to you. For the sake of simplicity, we'll mostly use the word Spirit in this discussion because it feels pretty neutral, but we'll switch it up a bit to emphasize that they're all names for the *same thing*. The point is, whatever you call it, you must make *space* to fortify this connection and access the wellspring of power and clarity within.

Incorporating Space Into Your Life

Because you're bringing this *space* into the structured real-life world, it's important to integrate it into the *structure* of your days in order for it to fully imbue your life with its significance and magic. Many people start with a spiritual practice—such as yoga or meditation—that entails the deliberate opening of *space* to connect with Spirit for a few minutes here or there. While it's absolutely worthwhile to have times of pure *space*, such a practice can give you a *compartmentalized* sense of the spiritual realm—as if you have to stop everything to connect to it.

Eventually, a compartmentalized spiritual practice may start to spill over into the rest of your life, but we prefer to *invite* this specialness and the sense of trust that comes from it into the everyday, which means working it into your life *structure*. If the goal is a more spiritually charged life, small, frequent doses of *space* are likely to accomplish this more effectively than big, infrequent ones. In Chapter 12, we'll explain how and why to create rituals. You'll find this an excellent way of utilizing *structure* for this purpose.

Physical and Nonphysical Realms

We want you to bring your potential into the world, to achieve your goals, and to relish life to the fullest. There are two main routes through which to pursue such a Well Life:

1. The physical realm (other words for this include tangible, worldly, visible, temporal, mundane, earthly, or material). Physical means include, for example, planning, working, communicating, building, and networking.
2. The nonphysical realm (other words for this include unseen, spiritual, intentional, mystical, metaphysical, or immaterial). Nonphysical means include, for example, setting an intention, praying, *Qi Gong*, altering our thoughts, and believing.

Most people seem to have a bias toward one of these routes. For maximum effectiveness and greatest experience, however, it's important to utilize both. The physical realm, after all, is not unspiritual or unevolved. And the nonphysical isn't as inaccessible and "woo-woo" as some might think.

Expand Your Understanding of How to Succeed

Most of us grew up thinking of achievement as resulting entirely from physical efforts—a perspective that looks something like this: *If you want something, it's going to take work—perhaps lots of work—but there's no way around it. Also, there are people, circumstances, and obstacles that you may need to influence or manipulate in order to succeed. Except in rare cases of luck and talent, successful people work very hard, sleep very little, have tremendous energy, are extremely tenacious, and make big sacrifices.*

Such a viewpoint often involves coming up against your own physical limitations, the role of other people's wills, and worldly factors you can't directly control, such as weather and financial markets. However, for the most part, you already understand the basics of how to achieve something through such means. If you want to make more money, you can learn how to perform a certain job that pays better, you can do your best, you can participate enthusiastically, and you can ask for a raise. If you want to lose weight, you can restrict calories and work out more. There's nothing wrong with hard work—we're big fans of it. In most cases, there is indeed a way to triumph that involves lots of willpower and zero mysticism. The limitation is that it can feel like a lot of brute force. For someone who has a sticky metabolic set point and a body that likes to hold onto its reserves, the physical path to weight loss may mean a *lot* of exercise and *very* few calories, and therefore nearly heroic discipline and determination. It's a high bar for most folks.

Furthermore, sometimes you don't *want* to take the usual route. You know, for instance, that you could make more money by training to be a lawyer and working your ass off at a prestigious firm. But what if you want to do work that feels more meaningful to you and *still* make a good income? And what if there isn't really a clearly established route to get there? There are two ways we'll help you with such tasks.

1. The first is to give you tools to manage the physical path more effectively (the next chapter is all about this).
2. The second is to give you tools for working more effectively through the nonphysical. In cases such as this (and really, in all cases), it's worth enabling the unseen mechanisms for achievement, or what's often referred to as "manifestation."

What Is Manifestation?

These days, many people are familiar with the concept of manifesting and its popular tenet, the Law of Attraction. This idea grew primarily out of the New Thought movement that began in the United States in the nineteenth century. These writers and philosophers affected the way we think today much more than most people know. New Thought philosophers ranged from the mystical to the pragmatic, though all shared a central belief: Our thoughts affect our reality. They also shared a belief in God as a form of infinite intelligence that is everything and everywhere and that dwells in and is accessible to all people. These ideas were first articulated long before the modern self-help, New Age, and "spiritual, not religious" trends of the late 1900s.

A Brief History of New Thought

The notion that we're able to affect reality with our thoughts is both the most special and the most troublesome feature of New Thought. Most New Thinkers, especially the early ones, applied this concept specifically to health, with the fundamental belief that all disease begins in the mind. Phineas Quimby (1802–66), a New Thought forefather (and the doctor of Mary Baker Eddy, who founded Christian Science), asserted that illness always arises from negative or erroneous beliefs, and that changing the mind—specifi-cally, making it "open to God's wisdom"—could initiate the cure of any disease. Later New Thinkers broadened the idea into the Law of Attraction, which states that we draw to ourselves a life that matches the quality of our thoughts. Napoleon Hill's 1937 book, *Think and Grow Rich*, was one of the earliest pragmatic expressions of the con-cept, a perennial bestseller on using nonphysical means to attract wealth.

Just as with teachings on achievement through mundane means, there are both uplifting and harmful perspectives on achievement through nonphysical means. We know people who are so capable at engaging these mechanisms that they seem to float through life with an almost magical ease—even when "bad" things happen. We've also encountered many friends and clients who, whether due to their own misunderstanding or through confused teachers, have gotten stuck in philosophical potholes around the Law of Attraction and related ideas. So, besides sharing the strengths of nonphysical approaches, we'll discuss the damaging beliefs associated with them so you can steer clear.

The Power of Positive Thinking

Much of the value of the Law of Attraction can be attributed to positive thinking. The quality of our thoughts profoundly affects the quality of our life. If you consistently had positive thoughts about your life, do you know what would happen? Your experience of life would feel consistently positive. And that pretty much constitutes a good life, doesn't it? If you believe life is good, then it *is* good—to you, anyway—regardless of the material circumstances of it or any objective measures. Your perspective is more important than your circumstances. Would you rather be poor and happy or rich and miserable? If you're happy, you're happy.

But we're not trying to enroll you in a mind trick where you fool yourself into being thrilled by a pathetic life. As you make a habit of changing your thinking around what is possible for you, *you become a different person*, and then the objective circumstances of your life change. Have you ever met someone who is really successful and also super positive? Which do you think came first? We'd bet that 100 out of 100 times, the positive thinking came first. They saw themselves as the kind of person who had the kind of life they wanted, and they became comfortable with that and willing and able to receive it. Not only does a positive mindset favorably color the lens through which you view your life, it makes you alert for opportunities for *sweetness* and the advancement of your goals.

The tricky part of positive thinking—or so it seems to a mind that loves complication—is remembering to do it. Many people feel it's not in their nature to be positive, or that life circumstances have made it difficult to be an optimist. But the truth is that they have just made a habit of focusing on and emphasizing negative viewpoints. It's an indulgence that people are often masochistically attached to. Have you ever been brooding about something and you catch yourself going back to it over and over and over, even though it feels bad? You're addicted to the fight, even if it's all in your own mind. Furthermore, your own negative tendencies may be reinforced by the company you keep. Complaining and critiquing are popular social activities, and many people seem to believe that the ability to point out flaws is a demonstration of intelligence.

Invite Positivity Into Your Life

Here are eight strategies to keep you on track:

1. **Follow the good.** Look and listen for good signs, positive news, beauty, and fascinating things, and then *latch onto them*, talk about them, share them, savor them, amplify them, and run with them. Imagine you just tapped into a vein of gold in the earth, and now you want to follow that vein. Jump from one good thing to the next. Make a game out of it.
2. **Generate more positivity in the world.** This is especially important if you find it hard to generate your own optimism. Point the people around you toward the positive, even if you feel dark inside. *Create* the vein of gold that you can then follow by asking people about their lives, their kids, their dreams. You will ignite a light in someone else that will lead you in the right direction. Then keep doing it. Deliver genuine compliments. Help others to see the bright side of whatever they're grappling with. It's often easier to do for others than for yourself.
3. **Get out of the dirt.** Following the gold vein is as much a matter of *not choosing to veer into the dirt* as it is a choice to follow the gold. Catch yourself choosing to indulge in negativity and be disciplined about shifting your attention to something else. It's like breaking an addiction. Notice which of your friends or family members have a "this sucks" mentality and (A) hang out with them less (this is especially important if you feel incapable of staying upbeat in their presence); (B) find the humor in their perennial negativity, like Eeyore in Winnie-the-Pooh, and laugh inside; (C) don't let them enroll you or throw you off your gold vein. Also, choose your media consciously. Stop watching "feel bad" videos and avoid tragic news unless it truly serves a purpose.

4. **Tweet, post, and comment responsibly.** The stories and opinions you choose to share shape who you are in the world—plus who and what you attract. Are you a positive influence on your environment or a negative one? Before you click "Post," look at what you've written. If it's snarky or amounts to "Doesn't this suck?" just delete it. You won't feel any regret.

5. **Respond with humor to situations that would otherwise make you angry, irritated, or anxious.** It can be hard, but if your habit is to relinquish the whole gold vein just because of some stupid situation, then you simply cannot engage with it in an adversarial way. Be imperturbable. Go on a drama fast. Stay committed to your positivity.

6. **Stop looking for the problems.** Lose the belief that finding problems and errors makes you smart or likable. People who enjoy finding what's wrong with everything rarely care much about looking for solutions.

7. **Know what you want.** Most of us spend so much time thinking about our current problems and the undesired future situations we hope to avoid that we have a clearer sense of what we *don't want* than what we *do want*. Know with laser-like precision what kind of life you want and replace the habit of dwelling on what you don't want with savoring what you have and eagerly anticipating the great things that are coming.

8. **Don't expect yourself to be happy all the time.** If you're in a funk, focusing on the disparity between how you're feeling and how you think you *should* be feeling will usually make you feel worse. If, on a theoretical scale of happiness from one to ten, you're feeling like a two, don't shoot for immediately feeling like a ten. Shoot for feeling like a three first. Usually, this can be accomplished by simply ceasing to *fight* what you're experiencing. Accept it. Breathe. Stop making it wrong. Tell yourself, "This is just what I'm feeling in this moment. I'm open to the possibility of feeling a little bit better." If you make it to a three, aim next for a four. Then review the previous seven recommendations. See if there's some beauty you

can appreciate. See if there's some negativity you can let go of, even if just for a moment. See if there's someone else you can turn your attention to, instead of yourself. The gold vein may feel at times like a very fine gold thread, but you'll find it again.

Positivity Improves Your Health

Becoming more deliberate about the quality of our thinking affects us beyond our own perception. It can actually change our body. Research shows that positive thinking is associated with a faster rate of recovery after surgery, better chances of surviving certain cancers, slower progression of HIV and atherosclerosis, lower risk of heart failure, lower blood pressure, and less pain. These beneficial effects probably apply to a certain extent in nearly all illness.

There's been a general recognition of the advantages of positive thinking on health for a few decades, and this connection isn't a stretch for most people. What's emerging in new research is a bit more mind-blowing: Beyond the resilience that optimism confers on us, specific kinds of thinking can act like *training*, producing the same kinds of responses in the body that physical activity would.

Multiple studies have shown that when people imagine exercising, the same nerve cells are activated as when the exercise is actually performed, and imagined exercise even causes significant gains in muscle strength. A similar phenomenon was demonstrated in a study on piano playing. Participants who imagined practicing piano learned a song almost as well as those who actually practiced. Clearly, the mind is a powerful tool.

See It Happen

These impacts on mood, outlook, health, and performance may translate into better outcomes in a variety of circumstances. Peter is a longtime woodworker, and several years ago, while browsing in a bookstore in British Columbia, we came across a book on woodworking that seemed to treat the subject in an especially loving way. It turned out to be well written, with lots of gorgeous photos. But what really stood out about it was the *sweetness* with which the author regarded the craft and the emphasis on old-fashioned techniques for shaping and joining wood. Looking at it together over afternoon tea, we noticed a curious piece of advice in the section on sawing: "Think the saw down the line."

Sure, the book discussed examining the teeth of the saw, holding it at the right angle, keeping your elbow in close to your side, and other practical tips. But here was an oddly esoteric recommendation in a book on—of all things—wood. It got our attention. The writer went on to explain that generations of woodworkers have done this, and that he was passing it on because it just plain works. The idea is that, rather than focusing on what you're *doing* with the saw, you put your attention on *the line you're following*, and intend the saw to go there. There's a certain elegance to it.

Nowadays, you hear about athletes utilizing positive visualization in virtually every sport, from archery to foosball. People who might be skeptics in every other area of their lives are watching mental movies of themselves succeeding at sports and seeing their performance improve. There are probably thousands, if not millions, of athletes who would attest to the value of this form of "training." Beyond the positive thinking mechanisms we've discussed, the deliberate mental rehearsal of the state you desire (peace, happiness, abundance, etc.) builds your confidence, as we discussed in Chapter 6. This confidence translates into relaxation and better physical control during the performance and a willingness to pursue opportunities that arise.

If it works on balls and saws, why not use it for getting a new house or being in a fulfilling relationship? Here we come to the great leap of faith, and the main stumbling block around the Law of Attraction for so many: Can you affect things *out there* without interacting with them directly on the physical plane? We've established that thinking positively and intentionally can enhance your point of view for a better experience of life, it can make you alert for chances to grow and advance your goals, it's good for your health, it can promote positive changes in your body, and can enhance learning and physical performance. But can it draw money to you? In our experience, the answer is yes.

Utilizing whatever nonphysical means you can to compound your physical efforts is likely to benefit your life. Even if it *isn't* true that positive intention alone can affect what the universe delivers to you, we've already established that it's going to do all sorts of other good things for you. You have nothing to lose except your outdated perspective.

Your Intentions Are Like Stars

Although we're not going to attempt to validate the Law of Attraction through science, we're actually quite fond of science, and there's a scientific phenomenon that makes a good metaphor to help explain our method for conceptualizing this process: gravity. Gravity can be thought of as a force that bends space-time toward itself. The more massive an object, the stronger its gravity and the greater its effect on the world around it.

This figure (which appears in a similar form in most basic astronomy and physics textbooks) is meant to depict the effect of a celestial body on the fabric of space-time around it. It's as if a lead ball were dropped onto a sheet of stretchy cloth: Both space and time are bent toward it. As you can see in the diagram, if you were flying past this object in a straight line, your path would become curved toward it due to the pull of its gravity. Time would even be slowed down within its gravitational field. With their tremendous mass, stars like our sun have such powerful gravity that they are able to hold onto all the planets that orbit around them. This is what keeps the planets from flying off into space. Pluto is almost *four billion miles* away from the sun, yet it's still within the sun's gravitational grasp!

Think of your desires like stars—dense ideas that bend reality toward themselves. To begin with, they're just tiny stars with minimal gravity, but over time, your held intention, potentiated through the approaches we describe in this book, causes them to grow and acquire more and more gravity. Another way in which your desires are like stars, especially when aligned with your Spirit, is that they become a source of light that leads the way and encourages growth. Just as every plant grows toward the sun, so does your life grow toward your clear intentions.

The groundwork we've already covered makes a difference. The initial gravity of a "star" born to someone who is physically healthy, who is very clear about what they want, who keeps their agreements, who uses their gifts, who has minimal baggage, etc., tends to be significantly greater than that of a star birthed by someone who is fatigued, conflicted about what they want, and who rarely follows through on their agreements. Also, as we explained earlier, few people have much experience with consciously shaping their life through intention. But we all get more effective at it with practice.

You don't have to be an expert on everything we've covered so far in order to do effective work through the nonphysical realm, but as you make progress on these items your power will grow. You'll also become more aligned with what your Highest Self really wants for you. In addition, we'll share more techniques in this chapter that will enhance your effectiveness.

Pitfalls to Avoid

Now for two major pitfalls that we'd like to help you avoid.

Your Thoughts Aren't *Everything*

First, we often encounter folks who have taken the idea that thoughts affect reality to mean that *everything that happens is due to our thoughts*. Since most of us grew up believing that our lives are shaped mostly by objective mechanisms—the things we say and do and the environment we live in—it can be exciting to have that first real sense of *knowing* that you can influence your life through your thoughts. It's like discovering you have a muscle you were unaware of. But in our opinion, it's as erroneous to believe that what happens to you is *entirely* due to your thoughts as it is to say that it's all determined by physical forces and outward actions. Don't put all your eggs in either basket.

Thoughts can be powerful, but they aren't the only form of energy in the universe. When a person suspends thought for a moment (and this is indeed a special thing), the world does not cease to exist. In health, countless other influences play a role, including genetics, nutrition, weather, toxins, trauma, and more. In the world at large, our thoughts typically have only a subtle impact on other people, because everyone else has their own free will. And, because almost no one has deliberately practiced using thought to affect objective reality, and even fewer have received instruction from a qualified teacher or used a time-tested methodology, we really can't say your thoughts are the *only* effector of events.

Aside from whatever reasons we can offer as to why it's not true that your thoughts are the sole cause of what happens in your life, we encourage you to simply inquire within—beyond your mind—and ask, if this *feels* true. Does it feel true that this device, your mind, which was essentially nonexistent in babyhood, which you built and gave power to over the years, which rambles continuously and recycles the same observations, worries, and criticisms over and over and over, is the real Source of everything that happens in the universe?

Thinking Negatively Doesn't Make Bad Things Happen

The second damaging interpretation of the relationship between thoughts and objective reality is that thinking negative thoughts will cause bad things to happen to you. We usually encounter this idea in discussions on the Law of Attraction, and it's presented in a way that seems logical: If positive thoughts bring you good things, then negative thoughts must bring you bad things. There's even a cute saying to reinforce this fallacious curse: "Worrying is like praying for what you don't want." Unfortunately, we both fell for this idea when we first encountered it. What a recipe for paranoia and guilt!

Let's back up a bit, though. There's a certain amount of truth in the idea that negative thoughts degrade your life. As we discussed in the section on positive thinking, the quality of the lens you see life through is arguably a more significant determinant of your quality of life than your actual circumstances are. A person with good food, warm clothes, a healthy body, beautiful surroundings, and people who love him could nonetheless have an experience of misery if his mind believes something is wrong. A negative mind can imprison you. And because negative thoughts and the emotions associated with them cause *stress*, they can contribute to illness and pain. These impacts on your body and especially your mind can be *huge*. But it's quite a different thing to believe that your worries and fears are going to *cause* bad circumstances.

If the formula for manifesting is to hold something intensely in the mind, then many of us do this all the time when we're anxious, sad, or angry. In fact, it's usually easier to focus relentlessly on something we're upset about than on a goal we desire. Just consider the many, many times you have worried long and intensely about something and it didn't happen. If it were true that thinking negatively caused bad things to happen, worried parents would unwittingly cause their children to die or get kidnapped. People with phobias would inevitably end up the victim of whatever they fear (there would be many more cases of attacks by mobs of spiders and snakes). And hypochondriacs would always have short lives.

We've had many clients who believe they brought a tragic event upon themselves through their bad thoughts, and this belief serves to add an element of self-blame to the pain they're already experiencing. We've also had clients who are experiencing anxiety or depression, and it's compounded by their fear that the negative thoughts they feel powerless to stop are going to eventually cause something terrible to happen. It's a poisonous notion.

There are three main reasons why you shouldn't worry that your bad thoughts will cause bad things to happen:

1. **It's pointless.** If you believe it's not okay to have a bad thought, this causes you to resist your bad thoughts. Then, instead of a bad thought simply flowing through the mind, you latch onto it and engage in a struggle with it, which just prolongs your immersion in negativity.

2. **Your Spirit can distinguish between intentions and worries.** Now, let's look at the mechanics of the idea that negative thoughts will make bad things happen. It makes sense on the surface, if we relate to Spirit as if it's a computer: Think positive thoughts, good things come out; think negative thoughts, bad things come out. But we've completely removed *intelligence* from the equation! So, the second reason is this: There's a qualitative difference between an intention and a worry, and Spirit is intelligent enough to know the difference. We *want* our positive thoughts to come true, whereas our negative thoughts are mostly just anxious mental noise with lots of resistance around them. Resistance begets stagnation, and stagnation doesn't make things happen.

3. **Thoughts that are aligned with the Truth are much more powerful in their ability to affect the trajectory of your life than are thoughts that aren't aligned with the Truth.** Generally speaking, positive thoughts are aligned with a greater Truth and negative thoughts are not. When you hold the Truth in your mind, you connect yourself to what is *real*, and when you hold a non-truth in mind, you connect yourself to *nothing*

except illusion. Because Truth is real, it lends potency to those thoughts and ambitions that are aligned with it. Thus, attunement with the Truth (which is synonymous with Love) is a relatively fortifying act, while attunement with non-truth, as a mere thought, is weak in its ability to affect objective reality. If we regarded Truth and non-truth as a binary system — zero and one — Truth would be one. It exists, it's real. Non-truth would be zero. It's empty. It's nothing but a mental construct, so it's weak in its ability to affect objective reality.

Of course, there have been massive fear-based movements in human history, and we can become enrolled in fear due to the power generated by the participation of millions of other minds. When we hold a fear-based thought, such as, "We need to keep foreigners out of our country; they will take all the jobs!" there's a certain power to it due to the sheer number of people who subscribe to it and who perpetuate it through conversation and media. Such power can cause people to start wars and commit other atrocities. Yet this power is limited to exerting its influence over human consciousness and emotions. So, while we urge you to stay positive, to avoid getting swept up in mass emotional tides, and to stand for the Truth, even when everyone around you is wrapped up in fear, remember that these negative thoughts are empty in the spiritual realm, because they are disconnected from Truth, i.e., Love. They won't cause tsunamis or epidemic diseases.

If you say to yourself, "I am in a fulfilling love relationship," this is fundamentally aligned with your deepest Truth. Even if this thought is not currently true (you're single, for instance), there's something intrinsically truthful and fortifying about it, as is any aspiration toward happiness, love, abundance, generosity, freedom, gratitude, peace, forgiveness, connection, inspiration, acceptance, and health. These qualities are your native state — what you *are* beneath all the stuff that's been piled on over the years. Love is available to everyone, so an expression of desire for a relationship in which to experience Love is something that will serve you. It stands to support you to come into your power, to share your gifts, and to grow. Such a thought has substance because of the Truth—Love—Reality that it's aligned with, and therefore it has "gravity" to shape the world.

But if you say to yourself, "I'll be poor forever," or "Nobody loves me," or "My daughter is late; I bet she got into a car accident," these fear thoughts are disconnected from your fundamental Truth. Because they don't have the substance of Truth or Love behind them, they are illusory and impotent in comparison. They aren't going to produce these circumstances on their own. Remember your math: Anything times zero is zero. *Fearful thought* x *zero* (non-truth) = *zero*. So, while we strongly encourage you to cultivate positive thoughts— they're like medicine—don't obsess that your negative thoughts are going to bring you catastrophe.

❖

Your nonphysical resources are significant, and the process of discovering how to access them can be tremendously fun. It's like discovering that the world really is as magical as you once believed.

CHAPTER 11.
CONNECT TO SPIRIT

Connection to Spirit Can Help You
Fulfill Your Intentions

In addition to providing you with perspective, clarity, peace, and lightness, your connection with Spirit can be powerful fuel for your intentions. You're so much more than the flesh-and-blood vehicle you reside in; awakening this connection helps you reside closer to the conscious source of your life.

Our childhood experiences of organized religion—Judaism for Peter, and Christianity for Briana—didn't involve much inspiration or connection. Consequently, we both spent many years without any spiritual practice, religious or otherwise. Later, we each felt drawn to revisit this realm. We explored with open minds the spiritual traditions of many cultures and forged some of our own. And, we both had powerful experiences that revealed to us something we couldn't forget.

We've both had times when we almost threw the baby out with the spiritual bathwater due to our interactions with proselytizers who insisted, "You need *this* religion; this is the *only way* to God."

Such experiences have made us keenly aware of what a sensitive topic this can be, and we're determined not to foist our views on you. The fact is, you don't *need* spirituality. There are many happy people who never think about spirituality. But if you're open to an innocent and humble examination of your relationship to Spirit—without any rules, dogma, or preconceptions—we believe that you'll find something both challenging and rewarding there. So, we're going to proceed with the assumption that you're onboard, and that you'll do this on your own terms, in a way that feels authentic and meaningful to you. We're going to address three basic questions: What are we connecting with? How do we connect? And, with regard to the desire for positive change in our lives, what do we do with this connection?

What Are We Connecting To?

It's important to have a term that feels comfortable to your mind. *God* is easy for most people, but too loaded for some. If you're uncertain, here are some ideas.

- There are religion-specific equivalents of the word *God*, such as: Allah, Jah, Yahweh, Elohim, etc.
- In many traditions, the primary conception of God is in male form, such as: Divine or Heavenly Father, Lord, Shiva, Father Sky, etc.
- Other traditions focus on the female form: Goddess, Divine Mother, Shakti, Ma, Guanyin (Kwan Yin), Mother Earth, etc.
- Frequently, people relate best to the holy human or avatar form of God: Jesus, Mohammad, Krishna, Rama, Buddha, etc.
- If you shy away from anthropomorphic notions of God, there are more abstract terms, like: Spirit, Almighty, Dao (Tao), Guru, Holy Spirit, the Divine, the One, Divine Light, the Absolute, the Force, Infinite One, and Source.
- As an expression of the idea that God is our identity, there are names such as: Higher or Highest Self, Great Self, Universal

Self, Divine Self, Buddha Self, I Am, Supreme Consciousness, and Awareness.

- There is the understanding of God as our World, with names such as: Nature, Universe, Cosmic Oneness, Ultimate Reality, and Totality.

- Finally, if all of these words feel too grand to you, you may wish to choose a simple term such as *prana*, qi (chi), love, light, truth, or life force.

Choose a way of relating to Spirit that feels the least threatening or complicated. Just as importantly, go with the way that feels most awe-inspiring, most all-encompassing, most benevolent, most peaceful, most intelligent, and most lovable.

How Do We Connect?

In truth, you are already connected. You're sitting in the lap of Spirit. Spirit moves through you. Though, if you're like the rest of us, you're usually unaware of it. As many spiritual traditions explain, this is one of the trappings of being surrounded by the stuff of the material world. We can get so wrapped up in our bodies and possessions, in our relationships and drama, that we lose sight of the most fundamental quality that is always here and has always been here—a deep sense of belonging to the oneness that encompasses everything.

In Hinduism and Buddhism, this hurdle is called *maya*—literally, "illusion"—that which veils the true nature of reality. It's not that the stuff of the world isn't real or that it doesn't belong to Spirit, but our tendency is to relate to these things only as deep as their labels take us, not seeing them as expressions of the Totality. When we see a cup, we think the word *cup*, we equate this object with "a thing that holds a drink," and that's as deep as we go with it. These labels are functional, of course, and necessary for operating in the human world, but they also cause us, from a very early age, to engage with our surroundings in a shallow way.

That's how, rather than seeing ourselves as surrounded by many fascinating expressions of Spirit, we look around and see just a bunch of items with certain names and mundane purposes. There's a bit of arrogance to it that inhibits us from diving in. "I *know* these things already," we think. "That's a flower. I've seen lots of flowers. That's a person. I know people." And so this flower is put in a category with all the other flowers, and this person is put in a category with all the other people. And an opportunity is missed for deeper connection. Luckily, each moment presents us with a new opportunity.

Here are thirteen approaches to connecting with your Highest Self. Hopefully, you'll resonate with at least a few of them. Try several and then make a practice of the ones that feel the best.

THIRTEEN WAYS TO CONNECT WITH YOUR HIGHEST SELF

1. **Approach life with innocence and humility.** Don't assume that you know what a situation holds in store for you. Pretend you're a baby or a traveler in a foreign land. Be willing to go deep. Dive in with something or someone you might otherwise skim over.

2. **Connect to what inspires you.** Whatever it is—art, music, writing, healing, gardening—that stirs something in you, make it an integral part of your life. Make it your religion. And when you feel this stirring, ask it where it comes from, what it has to say, and how it wants to move you.

3. **Be in nature.** Let yourself experience awe in the splendor and power of the elements. Put your feet on the earth. Get among trees. Venture high up a mountain. Feel the expansiveness of the desert. Experience the rush of a river, the glassy reflectiveness of a tranquil lake, and the push and pull of the ocean. Let the rain pour over you. Let the snow land in your hair. Hold your face up to the sun. Look at the stars and moon. Feel the wind. Light a fire. Examine grains of sand under a magnifying glass. Admire crystals, plants, and animals. This isn't just scenery; it's an extension of You. Awaken the connection.

4. **Meditate.** Make *space* without anything else to occupy your attention. *Space* for the sake of *space*. *Space* for an *unmanipulated experience*.

5. **Pray.** If you have a way of praying that works for you, keep it up. Some people feel drawn to the traditional supplication form of prayer—making a humble request to a higher power. Others prefer a more casual conversation with Spirit. Still others do it through dance, singing, chanting, or running. If you're interested in prayer but don't know how to begin, consider this basic format for meditative prayer, and feel free to change it however you like.

   1. Remove yourself from distractions if possible.
   2. Say hello. Open the connection.
   3. Welcome the intelligence, love, and guidance that are available to you.
   4. Express what you're ready to let go of—blocks, limiting beliefs, damaging behaviors, emotional pollution— and ask that it be taken away.
   5. In the *space* that has been made, ask a question or make a request for something you wish to invite into your life. See it in your mind's eye, feel it, intend that it shows up in a way that is healthy and supports the common good.
   6. Be open. Listen.
   7. Say thank you.

6. **Repeat mantras, names of the Divine, blessings, or prayers.** This is something of a combination of meditation and prayer, and a bit different than either. In Catholicism it's called praying the rosary, in Buddhism and Hinduism it's called *japa*, and similar traditions exist in other religions. A string of beads (rosary, or *mala* in Sanskrit) is customarily used to count the repetitions, though it's not required. The value of repetition of mantras or prayers isn't just in the meaning and energetic influence

of the sounds, but perhaps even more in the effect on your con-sciousness. It can put you in a deeply peaceful and connected meditative or trancelike state. It gives the busy mind something to focus on, and in the process you're liberated from its mono-logue. Some common mantras from various traditions include: Om (Aum), Maranatha, Om Namah Shivaya, Om Mani Padme Hum, God, Nam Myoho Renge Kyo, Elohim, So Ham, Om Shanti Shanti Shanti, Sat Nam. You can find more ideas and interpretations at www.thewelllifebook.com/resources.

7. **Connect to what encompasses and guides you.** Although it seems that between you and the nearest objects is just empty space, imagine that Spirit is meeting you at every point on your body, that you're fully held and embraced from all sides. Feel the flow, the trajectory by which your life moves along. See if you can become aware of its contours, its gentle nudges.

8. **Expect magic.** Ask Spirit to reveal itself to you in the form of coincidences, gifts, and serendipities. Your Higher Self wants to be seen. Tune in and open your awareness to the ways you're taken care of, the lessons you're shown, the answers you're given, and the delight and humor that's sprinkled throughout your days. If you believe in this magic, you start to see it eve-rywhere, and ultimately it doesn't matter if you're making it up or not because it has a positive subjective impact either way.

9. **Go to holy places and sites dedicated to spiritual practice.** Even if it makes you a little uncomfortable, check out beauti-ful, spacious old churches. Visit a Jewish synagogue, a mosque, an ashram, Hindu and Buddhist temples, a zendo. If you like travel, see some sacred shrines and natural places of power, such as Mount Kailash, Giza, Chichén Itzá, the Ganges River, Glastonbury Tor, Lake Titicaca, or Machu Picchu.

10. **Do something charitable, help someone, serve your world.** These kinds of actions have the potential to align you with Spirit because you're doing "God's work" by making your-self an emissary of love and kindness. Plus, you're serving the common good, which can only benefit you. Finally, there's

little opportunity for connection when you're immersed in your small self's worries and interests all the time. Broadening your awareness to include others is a valuable first step to opening to Spirit.

11. **Make an offering.** Offer up a dance, offer your sweat, offer your exhale, offer your time, offer your labors, offer your tears, offer your love. It's a symbolic thing we do out of reverence for Spirit, for our Highest Self. Your intention can be to offer yourself for Divine infusion. You can offer your pain, your karmic residue, or your sadness to be liberated from it. Connection through exercise can be powerful because you're naturally breathing deeply, you're focused, you're sweating, and your body is open and in the flow. It's easy to get out of your mind and to give yourself over to the activity. Connection through your work is also potent, as it inspires you to work hard, to do it with care, and to feel grateful in the process. Give everything to this moment in recognition of the tremendous gift that it is.

12. **Let yourself fall in love.** Rather than confining your devotion to a particular image or idea of God, realize that God is in everything. Therefore, you can pick the sweetest thing, the easiest to love, and love it purely, deeply, and unconditionally. Then use this as a portal to loving and connecting with the greater Whole. As you effortlessly experience love in relation to this expression of Spirit, allow this love connection to open up into a broader connection with the Totality. Love the flowers. Love the children. Love the animals. Love your family members. Practice perfect love. Love the ugly parts as well as the pretty ones. Then recognize that this small part of the Divine is connected to all the other parts.

13. **Practice mind-body arts that cross over into the spiritual, such as *Qi Gong*, tai chi, *yi quan*, and yoga.** These disciplines promote the perception of energy, expand your awareness, and help you integrate the nonphysical into everyday life. The East Asian arts specifically train in the cultivation and focus of power, while yoga is also especially good at promoting flexibility and

openness and undoing resistance (the single greatest impedi-
ment to your power). Try both yoga and *Qi Gong* or a martial art, since they develop you in different ways. You can find
some basic *pranayama* (yogic breathing) and *Qi Gong* exercises at www.thewelllifebook.com/resources.

As you start to trust more in the broader awareness in which you're
held, you'll begin to recognize that you don't have to figure everything
out yourself. You don't need to control all the variables in order to
succeed. Guidance is available, and it's all around and within you.

After you have explored different approaches to connection, revisit
the "*space* approach" to finding your Life Purpose in Chapter 8.

What Do We Do with This Connection?

We hope you have a sense of the great value that spiritual connection can bring to your life. In terms of *what to do* with this connection, we advise you foremost to *allow it to wake you up*. Allow it to
guide you to notice the incredible beauty that surrounds you, the
magic that connects everything, and the utter gift of life. The more
you're able to receive this, the more you'll recognize that there's
nothing, really, to ask for.

We recognize, however, that most people are in a place of wanting certain changes to their circumstances, so let's address that first.
Please, don't restrain yourself from asking for your life to contain
the elements you desire, such as love, food, money, meaningful work,
and family. These things are expressions of Spirit like everything else.
There's nothing inferior about wanting to experience life in a pleasant
way. Just remember that your connection can be more than just the
means to help you achieve your desires.

Magnetize

With the power, alignment, and clarity imparted through your
connection, you can set your intentions into motion and imbue them

with a gravity or "magnetism" that effectively guides you to their fulfillment. Magnetization is our term for a ritual to potentiate an intention in order to more effectively bring a desired state into being. We believe these practices work best at helping you achieve a certain *experience* – e.g., happiness, peace, abundance, inspiration, love, etc. And this, when you think about it, is the real reason why you might want to, say, hit the bull's-eye or get the new house.

The Magnetization Process

In this process, you'll be empowering an intention. We say *magnetizing* because the idea is that you'll add so much energy or magnetism to the idea of *you, in the attainment of your goal* that you will be drawn toward it like metal shavings to a strong magnet. Following are step-by-step instructions for this process. Read through them before beginning the process so that you'll be able to stay in a meditative state

> Magnetization is our term for a ritual to potentiate an intention in order to more effectively bring a desired state into being.

and will only need to glance at them from time to time. For the best experience, download the audio version from www.thewelllifebook .com/resources, which will guide you through the process. However, you should still read the following text to familiarize yourself with the concepts involved.

Before you begin, choose an intention to magnetize. As we discussed in Chapter 9, this should be phrased in positive language and directed at how *you* will become the person who receives and integrates the goal or circumstances you desire. It should not focus on manipulating anyone else. Also, it should issue naturally from the values, gifts, and purpose you defined in Chapter 8. Remember that the alignment of your intention with the core truth of who and what you are is essential for it to be empowered.

This process is based, in part, on *Qi Gong* techniques. As we explained in Chapter 5, there are three energy centers, called the three *dan tians*, that are an important focus of many *Qi Gong* practices. The *dan tians* (which literally mean "alchemy field," "elixir field," or "cinnabar field,") are like cauldrons where energy is stored and transformed.

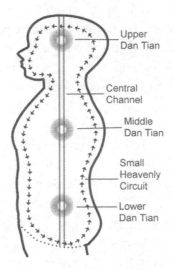

The lower *dan tian* is located about two inches below the navel, deep at the center of the body. The middle *dan tian*, which can be thought of as the heart center, is located also at the midline of the body, roughly at the level of the nipples. The upper *dan tian*, which can be thought of as the third eye, is located between the two eyebrows.

All three *dan tians* are about halfway between the front and back of the body along the Central Channel. The Central Channel (*zhong mai*) is the central vertical axis of the torso. It runs from a point at the very top of the head (called *bai hui*—"hundred convergences") to the bottom of the torso at the perineum, halfway between the genitals and the anus (called *hui yin*—"sea bottom"). Think of it as a column of light and energy. When your energy is strong and consolidated in the Central Channel, you're more centered, resilient, and stable. Some teachers feel that the Central Channel carries inherited patterns and memories of trauma.

The loop of arrows shown in the diagram represents the Small Heavenly Circuit (also known as the Microcosmic Orbit), an energy pathway formed by two major acupuncture channels. Opening this circuit and moving energy along it is one of the foundational Daoist

Qi Gong practices, which is said to build power and broaden your spiritual awareness. The two acupuncture channels involved are called the Governing Vessel and the Conception Vessel and they're located on the midline of the torso. The Governing Vessel runs from the tip of the tailbone, up the spine, over the top of the head, down the forehead and nose, to end at the upper gum. The Conception Vessel portion starts just below the lower lip and runs down the throat, chest, abdomen, and sex organs to the perineum. In order to connect these two energy pathways, the tip of the tongue must be resting on the upper palate, just behind the front teeth.

In the following process, you'll be utilizing each of the *dan tians,* the Central Channel, and the Small Heavenly Circuit to imprint or program yourself with your intention. Essentially, you're refining your energetic *structure* in a way that makes you better able to receive and embody this goal.

Make sure that you have already done the counter-intention process in Chapter 9 so that when you bring your intention to mind, you feel peaceful yet enthusiastic about it. Write your intention down on a nice piece of paper. Find a setting that feels good to you, where you won't be disturbed. Bring something into your *space* to set it apart from your everyday experience, such as a candle, a special piece of clothing, a flower, a pretty bowl of water or stones, or another unique natural object. If you feel dizzy or lightheaded at any point, take a break. Make sure the tip of your tongue is touching your upper palate and breathe deep into your belly, letting the exhale portion of the breath extend as long as possible.

Now, let's begin.

STEP 1

Sit comfortably in a chair with your feet flat on the floor, or cross-legged on the floor with a straight spine. Open the ritual. In whatever way feels significant and natural to you, state that you hereby begin this ritual to initiate and empower this intention for a positive change in your life. Invite Spirit (God, Highest Self, etc.) to join you in this *space* and process.

STEP 2

Place the tip of your tongue on your upper palate, just behind your front teeth. Relax your body from your head to your feet. You can spend several minutes focusing on each part of your body and releasing it, or if you're adept at relaxing quickly, you can simply imagine a warm wave of light or a golden fluid pouring over you from the top down and clearing any tension.

STEP 3

Activate your intention. Bring your intention to mind and imagine that you've already attained it. Whatever feelings this brings up in you, allow yourself to be absolutely immersed in them—excitement, satisfaction, ease, delight, relief, gratitude, peace. Let yourself drop into the bodily sensations that go along with having reached your goal, and let these feelings spread over every cell of your body. Feel it, hear it, see it, smell it, and taste it. Spend a few minutes here. In each of the following programming processes, remember to program yourself with not just the intention statement, but the full body experience of its attainment.

STEP 4

Activate your lower *dan tian*. Now bring your focus to your lower *dan tian*. Allow energy to flow into this area. As you inhale, imagine that you're drawing energy in the form of light from every direction into the lower *dan tian*. Let your breath go deep into your pelvis, expanding your belly. As you exhale, imagine that the energy in your belly is being condensed into a point the size of a pearl. With each breath, imagine that the lower *dan tian* becomes stronger and glows more brightly.

STEP 5

Program your lower *dan tian*. As you continue to breathe into your lower *dan tian*, you'll now begin to speak your intention into this region and to pour in the good feelings you associate with its attainment. With each breath, mentally state your intention and imagine the words entering the lower *dan tian*. Smile. As you inhale and your belly fills up with light, imagine that it also fills with this intention. As you exhale and the light becomes consolidated into a pearl, imagine that your intention is also becoming consolidated into the pearl. For instance, if your intention was, "I allow myself to be peaceful and happy," you would imagine that you're speaking this into your lower *dan tian* and allowing it to be incorporated into the lower *dan tian* with each breath into this region. Do this for about a minute.

STEP 6
Program your Central Channel. Now, become aware of your Central Channel. As you sit upright, you can visualize it as a vertical column of light that connects your perineum at the very bottom of your torso with the point at the very top of your head. It's the central axis of your torso. Imagine that the memories of all your wounds are stored here. Visualize a healing light running up and down this channel, repairing these wounds and erasing their scars from your records. Intend that this light also clears any negative patterns or beliefs from this column. Next, as you continue to breathe fully and deeply, imagine that you're speaking your intention into your Central Channel. Smile. Imagine the energy of the words and the feeling of attainment, like pure light, running up and down your Central Channel. With each breath, send your intention up and down your Central Channel, as if you're programming it, and in the process, the love and light within your intention opens and heals your Central Channel.

STEP 7
Program your DNA. Now imagine that you're able to look deeply into your Central Channel, and that within this column you see a long spiral of DNA. It curls around and around from your perineum to your head like a long spiral staircase. Imagine that this is the template of the DNA that's in every cell of your body. Make sure your tongue is still touching your upper palate, and as you inhale, speak your intention into this spiral staircase of your own DNA and

instill it with the feeling of its attainment, beginning at your perineum and spiraling up to the top of your head. On your exhale, speak your intention into your DNA again as you ride the spiral back down to your perineum. Smile. Inhale and spiral the intention up. Exhale and spiral the intention down. Imagine that your intention is made of pure love and light, and that as it runs through your DNA, it repairs any weaknesses, it heals any damage, and it changes you into someone who fully allows light and love into every part of your being. Continue for a minute or so.

STEP 8

Activate your Small Heavenly Circuit. Next, you're going to run your intention through the Small Heavenly Circuit that loops around the midline of your torso and head. Focus again on your lower *dan tian* and allow your energy to gather there again. Be sure that the tip of your tongue is still pressing gently against the roof of your mouth, just behind your front teeth, and allow the root of your tongue to relax. Now imagine that you're sending the energy from your lower *dan tian* down to your perineum, and then back to the tip of your tailbone. Slowly, intend that you're moving the energy, like a white or golden light, up the sacrum (the plate of bone at the base of your spine), and then bringing it up your spine, one bone at a time, like sucking some liquid up a straw. Move the energy up your lower back, up your mid back, up your upper back, up your neck, and then up the midline of your skull, coming over the top of your skull. Then allow the energy to pour down the midline of your forehead and nose, through your tongue, down your chin, your throat, chest, abdomen, and pelvis, to where it began at the perineum. Then continue the loop.

At first, it's common to not feel the whole pathway clearly. The more you practice, the smaller the unfeeling regions will be, until eventually you'll be able to perceive energy along the entire loop. Classically, there are three points or "gates" along the circuit that are integral in opening the circuit as a whole. These are the tailbone, the midpoint of the spine—halfway between the skull and the tailbone— and the base of the skull.

As your awareness of the pathway begins to feel more natural, you can increase the speed at which you're moving through it, so that with every inhale, you bring your energy from your perineum all the way to the top of the head, and as you exhale, you move your energy all the way back down. If you encounter numb or stuck places, you can spend a little longer there, inviting them to open up.

STEP 9

Program your Small Heavenly Circuit. After spending a couple of minutes opening and enlivening this circuit, you can begin to speak your intention into it. Smile as you feel the attainment of your intention. With each breath, mentally speak your intention into the circuit and imprint it with the feeling of the attainment of your intention. You can do this once on the inhale and once on the exhale, or if it takes you longer than half a breath to state your intention, you can just do it over the course of each full breath. Imagine the words and the feeling they invoke circulating through this loop. Do this for about a minute.

STEP 10

Program your bone marrow. Now visualize your skeleton. See all your bones in your mind's eye. Smile as you allow the feeling of the attainment of your intention to spread over you. Now speak your intention deep into your bones, as if programming the crystalline matrix of the bones. Imagine that the calcium crystals that make up your bones are now carrying this message. Then imagine the intention going deeper, into the center of the bones, to the marrow, and it fills the hollow centers of your bones with light and the feeling of attainment. Stay here for a few breaths.

STEP 11

Program your three *dan tians*. Now bring your focus to your upper *dan tian* behind the third eye. Make sure your tongue is still touching your upper palate. Smile as you recall the feeling of the attainment of your intention. Speak your intention into your upper *dan tian* and instill it with the feeling and image of its attainment. Stay here for a few breaths.

Next, bring your focus to your middle *dan tian* at your heart center. Let your heart open as you smile into it, speaking your intention into it and filling it with the feeling of attainment. Let yourself experience the *knowing* in your heart that this intention is aligned with self-love and your highest good. Stay here for a few breaths.

Finally, bring your attention back to your lower *dan tian*. Imagine that all the charged energy from within and around you is being funneled into your lower *dan tian* and anchored there. Speak your intention again into this point and instill it with the feeling of attainment. Stay with this for a few breaths. Then place your palms on your belly, directly over this area, one hand on top of the other, and intend for your energy to become stored and condensed in the lower *dan tian* until it's the size of a pearl, like a tiny blazing star.

STEP 12

Close the ritual. Let yourself be peaceful for a minute in the feeling of your new attunement to your intention, the deep knowing that your highest good is ensured, and the experience of groundedness in your lower *dan tian*. Express thanks to Spirit (God, Highest Self, etc.) for being the Divine container in which this work could occur and infusing it with love and truth. And make a closing statement, such as, "I hereby seal this work and ask that it be protected from interference by anything that is not of Love and Truth, including my own negative thoughts. And I allow myself to fully and gratefully receive the positive changes and blessings that are coming."

You just did something powerful. This process works. You may repeat the process as often as you like. Once is enough to send your message to the universe and the depths of your being, but doing the process repeatedly may help make you stronger and more *receptive* with regard to your intention. And receptivity is no small thing.

Receive

Receiving is half of the equation of creating something new or initiating a change. The receiving is an opening, a welcoming, a willingness, and an invitation for the goal to enter your life. It's the act of making spiritual *space* for your intentions. When changes don't come, or when they come but don't last, it's more likely that you're not receiving than it is that you're not asking properly.

Some of the best lessons in initiating and managing change can be found in one of the oldest books on the planet, the *I Ching* (*Yi Jing*) or *Book of Changes*. This ancient Daoist text is a study of nature and how the qualities and dynamics of the natural world exist also in the human world. The book defines sixty-four fundamental states—such as Conflict, Peace, Waiting, Danger, Gathering, Abundance, and Limitation—and it explains how best to navigate each of these states in areas such as business, politics, relationships, and personal growth. The sixty-four states are presented in a special order, with the two most important first, since these two can be understood as giving birth to the other sixty-two. The first is called The Creative, and the second is called The Receptive.

1. **The Creative** is considered to be an expression of pure *yang*—an emanation of expansive, active, powerful creative energy. In his interpretation of this state, Confucius said, "Great indeed is the generating power of The Creative; all beings owe their beginning to it."
2. In contrast, **The Receptive** is an expression of pure *yin*. It's like an open vessel. Its qualities are soft, yielding, and accepting.

These two states are considered to perfectly complement each other. If The Creative is the activating force of change, The Receptive is the ability to accept and respond to this force. Each needs the other. Conception works the same way, and it's an apt metaphor for initiating change. Sexual reproduction is the interaction of The Creative and The Receptive. It involves an external and an internal component; a giving and a receiving; a penetrating and a yielding. A seed by itself is useless without the earth to receive it, hold it, and nurture it. If you want something, you need not only to be able to make a request but to fully accept its fulfillment.

The Creative and The Receptive are our basic design. Each of us is somewhere on The Creative spectrum, from being profoundly obstructed to unrestrainedly expressive, and on The Receptive spectrum, from fighting, closing, and rejecting, to absolute openness and trust. In this section, we'll explore ways to improve receptivity.

Being Receptive Isn't Lazy

It's natural after setting an idea into motion to focus on figuring out what actions you must take, who you need to win over, and, in various other ways, how you can control the situation to ensure it turns out the way you want. However, there is much to be gained by simply allowing yourself to receive—to receive guidance, support, wisdom, and the fulfillment of your request. This is not to discredit the value of taking action, but even your actions have the potential to be informed by insight, which is only available through receptivity. What you're looking for may be right at the door, just waiting to be invited in. There are tremendous gifts in store for you. The more receptive you become, the more you receive.

Make sure you can see yourself as *someone who has attained the intention you've chosen*. If you don't feel entirely at peace with the idea of being this person, ask yourself, "What do I believe it will *mean* about me if I attain this?" Whatever you come up with, ask yourself if it's really true. You may be applying a stereotype or outdated belief to yourself in your imagined future. You may have a persistent image of yourself in a state of lack. Or, you may simply need more practice at receiving an updated version of You. On the other hand, the receiving process can sometimes reveal that your chosen intention is itself outdated or inconsistent with your Values, Gifts, and Purpose. What was the *state* you believed this intention would facilitate? Return to the questions and counter-intention process of Chapter 9, and consider a revision of your intention.

The Creative   *The Receptive*

Receptivity is *space*. The *I Ching* depicts its sixty-four states through a primitive "language" of whole and broken lines. The symbol for The Creative is six solid (*yang*) lines, indicating the utmost of directive, purposeful energy, whereas the symbol for The Receptive is six broken (*yin*) lines, forming a *space*—a channel or vessel—in the center. When you think about your intention, make sure this *space* exists in you, an opening for the intention to enter. One of the best ways to cultivate receptivity is meditation—when we stop talking, stop doing, and stop focusing on our thoughts.

Meditation for Receptivity

Try this meditation, derived from Kundalini yoga:

1. Sit cross-legged, in lotus position (feet on thighs as in the picture), on your knees, or in a chair.
2. Cup your two hands together to form a bowl.
3. Lift your hands to the level of your heart.
4. Close your eyes.
5. Smile gently.
6. Imagine that you're making yourself an open vessel.
7. Allow whatever comes to come.

Let Go

Pretend your intention is a paper airplane. You wrote your intention on the paper, you folded the paper as well as you could. Now, don't be so afraid that your airplane isn't going to fly that instead of letting it go, you just run around the room with it pinched between your fingers. As you get ready to throw the plane, you're saying, "Here you go, Universe! I did my best! It's up to you now," and then it's, "Wait, no. It's still up to me. I won't give up control." It's needlessly effortful for you. You never actually get to see what the airplane could do on its own. And you miss out on an opportunity to build your trust in Spirit (which is really just trust in yourself), which lends a great sense of ease to your life.

Certain aspects of the creative process are within our control and others aren't. There's an ancient parable by the philosopher Mencius about a farmer who can't let go. After planting his seeds, the farmer digs them up each day to check whether they have sprouted yet, and then buries them again. When they finally do sprout, he walks up and down the rows, tugging on each tiny seedling to help them grow. Eventually, his plants wither and die from too much meddling. Mencius advises that we should neither abandon our seeds completely nor try to pull on the seedlings to make them grow. The happy medium he offers is to weed around them—in this way, you don't forget what you're working toward, yet you let go of trying to do the growing for the plant.

You've probably heard the parable about the student who seeks instruction from an esteemed teacher, but is so full of his own ideas that there's no *space* to receive the teacher's wisdom. The teacher demonstrates this by pouring tea into a cup until it overflows. Look back at the symbols for The Creative and The Receptive. This student is imbalanced to the side of The Creative—always wanting to run the show, even when under the guidance of another. Only The Receptive is *open*, a vessel with *space* to accept more "tea."

We're saying the same thing in so many ways with the hope that one of these examples will jog something loose in you. So many people are "full cups." We're brought up with an emphasis on always knowing the right answer, like we're perpetually on a TV quiz show, and this can make us closed to new ideas and unwilling to be wrong. We're always babbling in our minds, which impairs our ability to receive what's coming in. We're often wanting to control life so that it goes our way. And as much as we may criticize ourselves, we're also quite attached to the personality and beliefs we've cultivated. These characteristics impair receiving and make us reluctant to let go.

If you feel tight, doubtful, anxious, and untrusting with regard to your intention, you have closed the *space* for receiving. The more intense your desire for something, the greater is the likelihood that you're strongly opposed to the idea of not getting it, and opposition, too, isn't conducive to receiving. Therefore, if you're trying to figure out what to let go of, this is a good start: *Let go of your resistance to not getting what you want.* Feel what comes up in your body when you bring your intention to mind. Close your eyes and see if you can perceive an area that is clenched or closed. As you take a deep breath, does it feel free, open, and unrestricted? Or is there a tightness or congestion somewhere? Wherever you feel something other than openness, imagine that you're smiling into this place. If you can't spontaneously muster a smile, recall a happy or funny memory, or bring to mind someone who puts a smile on your face.

Whatever you feel, invite the feeling to be felt. Let it open up. Welcome it with your entire being. Let it spread over you without any resistance. And let it go. Next, bring to mind the idea of not attaining your intention, and repeat this releasing process. Then bring to mind an undesired circumstance that you imagine might occur if you were to not achieve this goal, and release. Consider all the things you don't like about the idea of failing to get what you want, and consciously let go of whatever arises in your body when you hold them in your mind.

The more you let go, the easier it is to receive, and the lighter you feel. Much of our resistance to letting go stems from our attachment to the things we become familiar and comfortable with. But if these familiar things include, say, negative emotions, or an image of yourself being overweight, poor, sick, or unhappy, letting go is a necessary step toward positive change.

Live It

Rehearsing for the quality of life you desire (and expect) is one of the best ways to facilitate receiving and to make it a reality. Besides enabling you to immediately experience an expanded perspective and the opportunities it brings, it highlights any resistance or judgments you may hold about who you would become if your life were to change in this way, or about others who have the kind of life you want. Discovering and amending or releasing these beliefs is essential to allowing yourself to have this life without sabotaging it.

Don't Wait

Humans tend to think that they'll start acting and feeling elevated as soon as their circumstances become ideal. However, as we mentioned in the section on positive thinking, it more often works the other way around. When we think about the successful people we knew before they became successful, nearly all of them were already trying on success before it arrived.

If you wait to shift your perspective because you expect your circumstances to *do it to you*, you delay feeling better and you miss out on an opportunity to recognize and hone your ability to shift your perspective. Furthermore, there's no guarantee that a change in circumstances is going to make you feel differently. Ultimately, it's up to you to choose your point of view.

Living it is the art of bringing the *sweetness* into the present that you believe is conditional upon *someday's* circumstances. If your intention is to have more money, living it isn't accomplished by spending more money "because that's what a rich person would do." You *can* spend more money if that helps you embody this state of attainment. But it's deeper than that. Living it requires *becoming* that person. The *you* that has already achieved this. You're not pretending to be someone else. You're not adopting the mannerisms of some caricature of a rich person. You're becoming who *you* would be with more money. And to get even more particular, rather than being who you "would" be with more money, you're going to be who you *are* with more money.

Get Inspired

Sometimes you may not have a clear sense of how you would feel or what you would do upon attaining a goal. If this is the case, you may benefit from some research. Find people who already seem to embody the qualities and lifestyle you desire, and let yourself be inspired by them. They could be people you're able to meet and converse with in person, or ones you read about in interviews and biographies. Seeing other humans model altruistic or heroic behavior can awaken something in you—a sense of what you're capable of. There are so many people living life in beautiful ways.

Don't let yourself get down by comparing yourself in a way that disparages either you or them; just notice what's possible. You may not be able to attain the same body or specific state of affairs that they have, but it's the inner experience that matters, and you can absolutely live with the same courage, grace, and enthusiasm. Just remember that it will be the same you inside. You don't have to sacrifice what is authentically you, and you don't have to become pretentious or shallow. You get to do it your way.

Perspective-Tuning

If you need help with the *living it* part, try this *Perspective-Tuning* exercise. In the positive thinking section, we advised that if you're feeling like a two on a happiness scale of one to ten, you're more likely to be successful at shooting for feeling like a three than you are at shooting for a ten. Perspective-tuning is a similar concept. While it can be challenging to make a dramatic perspective change, a subtle shift is usually pretty easy. Multiple small steps ultimately amount to a big step, and the process can eventually be compressed in order to accomplish these steps in a short period of time. Also, with practice, you'll be able to shift perspective with greater ease.

1. Get a piece of paper and pen. On a scale of one to ten, where one represents the most hopeless negative perspective you could imagine and ten represents the most ecstatic positive perspective you could imagine, rate your current perspective with regard to your intention. In the middle of the page (leaving room above and below), write, *Perspective 5:* or whatever number you came up with. Then write a few sentences about how you currently feel with regard to your intention. Specifically, describe your point of view, and name the emotions that come up around it.

2. Below this, write, *Perspective 4:* or whatever number is *one less* than the rating you just gave to your current state. Here you'll write a few sentences from the state that's just below your current state. You probably occupy this level on a bad day. Imagine you got up on the wrong side of the bed—describe your point of view and name the emotions you're feeling.

3. Next, above your first perspective, write, *Perspective 6:* or whatever number is *one more* than the rating you gave to your current state. Here you'll write a few sentences from the state that's just above your current state. Imagine you're having a good day and feeling more positive than usual. Describe your point of view and name the emotions you're feeling.

4. Now, imagine, like twisting the tuning knob of a radio, that you're tuning your perspective down from your current state and occupying the thoughts and feelings this lower state brings. Then tune back up to your current state and occupy the thoughts and feelings this state brings. Then tune to the next state up and occupy the thoughts and feelings this state brings. At the beginning, the knob is rather tight. It's something of a challenge to tune yourself up and down, and you can only shift about one value in either direction. As you continue

to practice this, you'll find that your knob loosens up, and you're able to more easily glide down and up.

5. After you've played with adjusting your tuning, imagine that you're tuning yourself to the state that's just above your current state (i.e., Perspective 6 in the example), and locking the knob in place. Practice occupying this state for an entire day, then several days. It's not magic—you have to consciously *choose* this state. It's an ongoing choice you'll make over and over by opting for perspectives, feelings, and behaviors that are in line with the frequency you're working on. It may take a few days or even a week of consistently shifting your perspective before it begins to stick.

6. When you have been relatively successful at this, return to your paper, and above your previous text, write, *Perspective 7:* or whatever number is *two more* than the rating you originally gave to your current state. This would have previously represented a *really* good day, but should now seem well within reach. Write a few sentences while embodying this elevated state, describing your point of view and emotions.

7. Practice loosening the tuning knob again, feeling the state you first described, then the state you've been practicing, and the state you've just written about. Go up and down a couple of times. See how pliable your perspective can be?

8. Now, imagine you're tuning yourself to the elevated state you described today and locking the knob in place. Practice occupying this state for an entire day, then several days, until it feels comfortable. Then, return to your page and write about the next stage up. Practice tuning up and down, and then occupying increasingly elevated states.

Use whatever tools work for you to remind yourself of the process you're engaged in. You're changing habits of thinking. It requires discipline and consistency, but it's not actually that hard. Set an alarm to go off every fifteen minutes or half hour to tell you to bring yourself back to your new perspective. Or hang up stickers in your living space, workplace, and car, and every time you see one, it means, "check in and shift your awareness." Soon you'll be *living it* with ease.

On our site you'll find a worksheet for this process, which you can download and print at: www.thewelllifebook.com/resources.

Part of why perspective-tuning is a useful exercise is that it gives you a break from thinking about what you *don't* want. If your intention is to feel vibrantly healthy, chances are some of the time you're dwelling in thoughts like, "I don't want to be sick. I don't like feeling tired. I don't like feeling incapable." You know these kinds of thoughts never help your body or mind. Besides the other techniques we have presented (the inner critic processes, positive thinking approaches, letting go, etc.), living an elevated perspective, even for just a minute, pulls you out of the mental muck, and this is relieving to your whole system. Remember, it should be enjoyable. You're playing—with purpose!

Treat Your Intention As Non-Negotiable

As you live your intention, practice having a non-negotiable mindset around it. We make all sorts of things non-negotiable, like always being there for our family or having a clean living space. But we don't always hold our dreams in the same uncompromising way. Frankly, you may not get *that particular guy* or *that particular house* or *that particular job*, but the experiences that these objects represent for you—love, happiness, abundance, purpose, self-worth—are most definitely available to you.

There are two key elements in relating to your goal in a non-negotiable way: planning and loosening up. First, the planning. If you invited a friend over for dinner, you'd buy groceries, prepare a meal, and set the table. You wouldn't think, "I'll wait until they show up, because maybe they just won't come." If you planned to get a car, perhaps you'd clean out a space for it in the garage. If you intended to get a dog, maybe you'd want to put a fence around your yard. So, what could you do in anticipation of the attainment of your goal to make it feel like it's a definite *yes* rather than a maybe? Get a larger bed in anticipation of the person who will soon be sharing it with you?

Second, the loosening up. If you *truly* believed your goal was non-negotiable, if you knew you'd bring it into reality regardless of the means or time frame, you'd relax about it. You'd be patient. When you fully anticipate that things will work out, there isn't worry, concern, or a tight grip on the outcome. Relaxing into the results allows them to just show up, unobstructed. Pushing, pushing, pushing with seriousness and stress leaves little *space* for magic to enter the equation. Be open and ready to receive with grace. Without becoming rigid about it, stop entertaining thoughts about the possibility of failure or the option of aborting your plan, and instead practice a feeling of expectant gratitude.

What about Taking Physical Action?

Now that you've done so much work in the nonphysical realm, perhaps you're wondering whether to continue working toward your goal in the physical world. Some teachers insist that there's no need to do any physical work once you've set your intention, as long as you control your thoughts. There's even a popular notion that if you continue to do physical work toward the goal, you're undermining the nonphysical efforts you've made; you're telling yourself and Spirit that you don't trust it; and you're interfering with the universe's ability to deliver it to you.

But it all depends on where you're coming from. The key is to notice the attitude with which you're approaching these actions. If you trust, if you're able to let go, if you're living it and you feel willing and positive about receiving—even if you're not there 100 percent of the time—you're not going to impede the process. But if you're taking action because you don't trust the process, you feel you need to do more, and you want to control it, then you might be getting in your own way. The important thing is that such an attitude highlights a need to let go of the fear of not achieving your goal. Trust. Relax. Accept. Be patient. Get out of the way and receive.

As long as you continue to bring yourself back to receiving and trusting, there are plenty of good reasons to take action in the physical realm toward your goal:

- You increased the magnetism of the next evolution of *you*. As you put yourself out into the world, it's like waving a magnet around. You're giving a tug to the fabric of space-time and bending it in your direction. In more mundane terms, doing your physical work brings you in contact with people and resources that may be integral to your purpose and goals.
- Putting yourself in the world gives Spirit avenues through which to bring you what you've asked for, *structures* through which to deliver blessings to you.
- The physical and nonphysical worlds, like your body and your mind, are completely intertwined. You wouldn't operate in one world to the exclusion of the other anymore than you would try to live entirely through your body to the exclusion of your mind, or vice versa. If there are necessary steps to be taken in the physical world, take those steps. If you want to become a banana farmer, it's reasonable to look for land in a tropical place and buy a few cans of monkey repellant.
- Sometimes Spirit parts the waters for you, but you still have to walk through. Just because you put it out there for Spirit to take care of doesn't mean its manifestation can't take place through you and your physical efforts. If you put an intention out to the universe that you wanted to receive a million dollars, and then you started a business, worked hard, and made a million dollars, you could conclude, "That intention setting really worked well!" or you could conclude, "That intention setting was worthless. I just ended up doing it all myself!"
- Few people truly believe they can bring something into their life through intention alone. Staying busy (in a balanced way) can be beneficial if you use it to settle down that doubtful

part of your mind. Taking measurable action quells the urge to manipulate, and in the process it gives you something to focus on instead of scrutinizing the process. Sometimes, if you throw your mind a bone it stops choking the process. Finally, your work is connected to your purpose—to serve. We believe there's value in doing work in the physical world. Work that connects you to the creatures you share the planet with. Work that is purposeful and efficient. Work that's balanced with the rest of your life. Kahlil Gibran wrote: "You work that you may keep pace with the earth and the soul of the earth. For to be idle is to become a stranger unto the seasons, and to step out of life's procession, that marches in majesty and proud submission towards the infinite." Doing the work that's an expression of your values, gifts, and purpose is a profoundly empowering form of action. It's the work you're here to do. It aligns you with Spirit in a way that you can feel, and this makes you more effective at attaining whatever you intend.

⬥

Talking about spirituality is tricky. Everyone experiences it in their own way; feathers are easily ruffled; and ultimately, it's impossible to truly express Spirit through words. But there would have been a gaping hole in this book without this chapter. Despite its ability to elude the mind, this divine *space* represents a constancy that has a way of holding us, even when the bottom drops out of life. So we urge you once more to make a place for it in your life—you get to choose the terms.

CHAPTER 12:
INTELLIGENT LIFE ARCHITECTURE

PLANNING FOR SUCCESS

Planning Pays Off

Now that you've chosen the *sweet* details of the life you'll bring into being, and you've activated an intention by consciously accessing *space,* we'll help you build healthy and intelligent *structure* to promote the realization of your Well Life and your specific intentions. We'll begin where any construction project would start—the planning.

Why Should You Plan?

The most critical factor in planning effectively is *doing it.* If you're not a planner by nature—Peter isn't—there's no getting around this.

If you don't write down your plans, you're putting yourself through needless difficulty. You probably experience some confusion, because it's hard to see the plan when it's entirely in your mind. You may feel anxious or overwhelmed, because you're constantly engaged in mental tracking, and perhaps fear that you're missing something. And you've probably had your share of disappointment, because mental plans don't often work out the way you want them to. Writing out your plans will enable you to escape these unpleasant situations.

Here are some of the things planning can do for you:

- **Writing down a plan makes it real.** It's one thing to have a thought; it's another thing to write out a plan. Like drawing up blueprints before building a house, making a plan forces you to see the entire *structure* before you even begin. It hugely improves your chances of ending up with a house, rather than, say, a sculpture made of bricks, pipes, and wire. Planning is an investment of time and energy into your future, whether that future is tomorrow or ten years from now, and it nearly always pays off.

- **Planning asserts your position as the creator of your life.** You aren't just a spectator. The drafting pencil is in your hands. You're a maker. A visionary. Planning is an act of affirming this role. Taking the time to plan is also an act of honoring your soul, your purpose, your potential, and your loved ones. Especially if there are others who depend on you, making plans is one of the most caring and respectful things you can do for them.

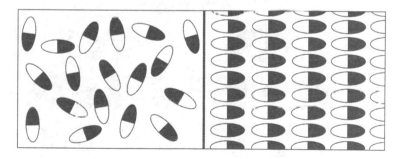

- **Planning generates momentum.** To use another magnetism analogy, the diagram above shows the difference between the molecules in an ordinary piece of iron (on the left) versus those within a piece of iron that has been magnetized. At first, the molecules are arranged in a haphazard way, but as the metal is magnetized, this coaxes all its molecules to become oriented in the same direction. Creating and abiding by a plan has a similar effect, by orienting our thoughts, actions, agreements, and environment in the same direction. The "magnetism" that results tends to attract circumstances and resources that facilitate the process.

• Planning not only allows you to do *big* things effectively, it's hugely important in managing a life with many moving parts in a balanced way. When you embrace planning and you do it with clarity and consciousness, it makes life simpler. The *structure* leads the way. If you have any resistance to planning, we have a mantra for you: "My plan is the clear path to the life of my dreams."

It's the *structure* that enables the integration of *sweetness* and *space* in your life, so it's a precious thing. And it gets easier the more you do it.

The Planning Process

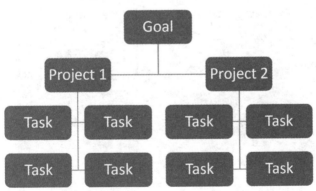

The Hierarchy of a Plan

A plan starts with a goal. Ideally, your goals should be aligned with your vision for the future, which you expressed in Chapter 9. A goal consists of one or more projects, each of which involves multiple tasks. When you plan, the key is to break down the goal into the simplest possible elements, which we call tasks. Tasks should be *immediately actionable* with little to no additional planning.

Plan When You're at Your Best

Research in cognitive function has shown that the slow, analytical thinking that's required to solve problems and make big decisions occurs in the prefrontal cortex of the brain. It's the "high maintenance" part of the brain, and it's what sets us apart from other animals, yet it demands the most resources in order to operate. If you're tired, sick, poorly fed, upset, or stressed in some other way, your tendency is to let the more primitive parts of the brain—the "animal brain"—run the show. But the animal brain is terrible at understanding perspective, consequences, and complex decisions. When the animal brain is in charge, we make impulsive, emotional choices, and we aim for survival, pleasure, and avoidance of pain.

It's smart to prepare for a dumb brain. It's like having a roll of toilet paper in your glove compartment—you hope you'll never need it, but boy will you be glad it's there if you ever do. If you do your planning when you're at your best, you can schedule tasks for yourself that involve minimal thinking.

How to Figure Out Which Projects Will Help You Achieve Your Goal

Find a time when you're well rested, well fed, sharp, and in a good mood. Set the stage for a productive planning session by making your space special in some way. Spend a few moments relaxing and tuning in. Begin by choosing a goal. You could form the goal from the intention you worked with in Chapter 10, or return to the material you came up with in Chapter 9 for other ideas. Write it down.

Next, list the projects that you believe are necessary to achieve the goal. You can think of these projects as mini wins to achieve along the way. Some goals, like remodeling your kitchen, will be fairly easy to break into projects: find a contractor; choose colors, appliances, and materials; figure out how you'll manage without a functional kitchen during the remodeling process; etc. Other goals, like finding a spouse, may be more difficult because there's no straightforward or "right" way of doing it. Let's look at a few different approaches for challenging goals.

1. The first approach is to **work backward from the attainment of the goal to the present**. Imagine that you just achieved your goal. What would have to happen right before that? Write it down as a project. What would have to happen right before that? And right before that? Keep working back to step one. This method is effective for most material goals.

2. When you're unsure of the means to achieving your goal, but you know some ways that it's been done by others, you can try the "spray approach": **tackle the goal from many angles.** With this method, your projects may not build on each other in the sequential manner that usually occurs with other goals. Instead, you'll be betting on several horses (luckily, they're all running in the same direction). If your goal is to meet your soul mate, you might create projects based on many of the ways people find a partner. For example: ask your friends to set you up, attend more events (especially where single people are likely to be), take classes, check out social clubs (such as fitness groups, gaming groups, dog groups, community betterment groups, etc.), try online dating, try speed dating, hang out at more roadside taco stands. You might also consider ways to make yourself more receptive and appealing to your future partner, such as improving your hygiene, building confidence, and making *space* in your life for a relationship. If you're truly committed to getting your goal, you won't scoff at any opportunities. You can't know exactly how things will go, so you have to let go of the idea of getting it perfect. The plan gets you moving toward your goal, gives you lots of options, and provides opportunities to change or refine your course along the way.

3. If you don't know how someone might achieve what you're after, **do research**. Study the ways others have attained it (or something similar) and choose your projects based on the factors that made it possible for them. Read biographies and memoirs, interview your heroes, and ask a mentor, "What do *you* think I need to do?" There are so many inspiring, triumphant stories out there. Don't get lost in the sea of information; just learn what you can from others' successes and make your own plan.

4. As you become more adept at planning, you may occasionally want to break goals into projects in the **"choose your own adventure"** style. It's ideal when the outcome of one project will dictate the projects that follow. When you map this out, you can draw two (or more) stems from each pivotal project to represent the different outcomes. From each outcome, a certain set of projects will follow. This diagram shows the simplest version—a single pivotal project with just two possible outcomes.

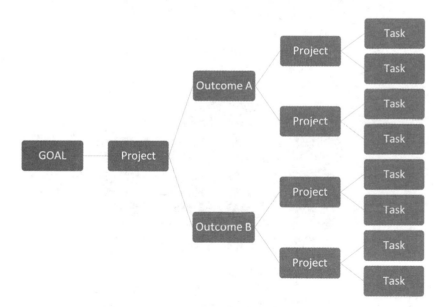

5. **Use a visual scheme that helps you feel you can grasp the whole picture.** The mind map style shown here allows for a

more creative visual representation of the plan. If you wish, next to each project, you can write the date when you plan to have it completed.

Mind map

Linear goal/project/task breakdown

A combination of research and spray is also appropriate when your goal is to *feel* a certain way. For instance, if your goal is to feel light, happy, or peaceful, there's no single method for achieving this, but there are many proven contributing factors. A little investigation will reveal how others have done it: exercise, dietary changes, psychotherapy, acupuncture, herbs, nutritional supplements, meditation and prayer, community engagement, exposure to sun and nature, serving others, behavior modification, mindfulness practices, and uplifting surroundings. Formulating projects based on these approaches is a logical start.

Planning Builds Momentum

Planning in this way brings structure to your goals:

1. The projects get you focused on what to do next.
2. You complete your tasks as scheduled.
3. Then momentum kicks in.

You're not depending on any single act to produce the goal. Instead, it's the *convergence of many influences.*

It begins with the contract you make with yourself as you embark on this plan: to participate fully, in both body and mind. Countless times, we've seen people achieve amazing things through excellent plans and solid follow-through.

Breaking Projects Into Tasks

After determining all the projects involved in your plan, the next step is to break these projects down into the tasks they comprise. Remember that tasks must be *actionable*. They will be scheduled into your calendar, and when you see one, you'll know exactly what to do without further analysis. If it's not actionable, dissect it into smaller parts.

If you encounter a task in your schedule that's actually a *project*, two inefficient things are likely to happen:

1. **You'll have to switch modes.** If you've been cruising through your day, knocking out tasks like nobody's business, the shift from *action mode* to *analysis mode* disrupts your momentum.
2. **You'll need your "high maintenance thinking" to translate this project into tasks.** If you don't have the mental resources available at the time, you'll get stalled. For instance, most people would be stalled by a calendar event called "Make Halloween Costume." The tasks involved could include choosing the costume, figuring out what supplies are needed, buying these supplies, and assembling it. If these tasks were scheduled individually, you'd be able to take immediate action on each one.

Don't go overboard on breaking down tasks into tiny subtasks unless it's helpful to have these smaller tasks scheduled individually. Assuming you have stationery, an envelope, a stamp, and her address on hand, a task such as, "Write a Letter to Aunt Mabel," doesn't need to be reduced to smaller steps unless you're extremely distractible.

Don't Forget to Add in *Sweetness*!

Now is the time to incorporate *sweetness* into your *structure*. Here is a list of suggestions—we call them Rituals for Thriving—taken from our *Rituals for Living Dreambook*. You might recognize some of them from Chapter 2.

- Exercise
- Meditate/breathe
- Journal
- Dance
- Go on a date
- Connect with nature
- Visualize
- Family time
- Cook/eat a healthy meal
- Organize my space/life
- Get rid of things I don't love
- Be with friends
- Play
- Let go/forgive
- Sing/make music
- Create art
- Read for enjoyment
- Connect/pray
- Call someone/write a letter
- Stretch/do yoga
- Massage/exchange touch
- Serve my community

Be sure these types of tasks are incorporated into your projects.

Scheduling Tasks

Once you've broken your projects down into tasks, it's time to schedule them. It's important to put these tasks in your calendar rather than working directly from a to-do list. Scheduling them further reduces the need for analysis during the flow of your workday. Also, because you're always adding new tasks to your to-do list, if you work directly from a list, there's not much sense of progress because you never complete the whole thing. When your tasks are scheduled into your calendar, you'll have a feeling of accomplishment and of being *done* at the end of each day. Scheduling your day in a detailed way also enables you to be more present. At any given moment, you'll know exactly what you should be doing—and this goes for both work and play.

Maintain a running list of tasks that you'll review when deciding which tasks you'll take on for the week. You can use a digital task list, such as Google Calendar's Task List; or a note app, such as Evernote; or a small paper notebook. During the week, whenever a new task comes up, you can quickly add it to your running task list, let it go, and get back to what you were doing.

> **GUIDELINES FOR SUCCESSFUL SCHEDULING**
> - Set up a time once a week when you'll schedule the forthcoming week.
> - Make a list of all the tasks from your goal breakdown that you'll be doing this week.
> - Add to your list items from your running task list that you'll tackle, plus all other necessary work and life tasks for the week.
> - Add in *sweetness* practices.
> - One of your tasks will always be "schedule next week."

Add Tasks to Your Calendar

Now, for the calendar part. You must have either a paper calendar or a digital calendar. Go through your list of tasks for this week and put a star next to the items you want to prioritize—specifically, the tasks that are most important to achieving your goals and facilitating your Well Life. The starred tasks will go into your calendar first—before it fills up. This is how *sweetness* moves to the forefront of your life and goals get accomplished.

As you schedule the tasks on your list for this week, be sure to set both a start time *and an end time.* One of the most common impediments to healthy *structure* is undefined end times. If you don't contain them, your tasks tend to sprawl and consume as much time as you have available.

Analyze Your Task List Thoughtfully

Putting all these tasks into an already full calendar can feel overwhelming, but we're not asking you to work harder; we're simply suggesting that planning can bring you peace of mind. We're asking you to adopt a new way of structuring your life, where you'll gain time by reducing inefficiency, and you'll gain energy and inspiration by prioritizing *sweetness*. If you're finding that you literally have too many tasks and not enough time, it's okay to move some tasks out to the next week. But please ask yourself if there's anything you're devoting time to that doesn't nourish you on some level, get you closer to your goals, or make your life run smoothly. (If you need to go to work to earn money, this is something that makes your life run smoothly. The same goes for picking up your children from school or walking the dog.) We suggest removing any tasks that don't qualify. Next, go through your list and ask yourself if there's a way to get your tasks accomplished with less investment of time and/or energy. Could you get groceries delivered to your house instead of shopping? Are there any tasks you could delegate to someone else? If so, try it out.

Your Tasks Are Agreements

Once you have your tasks in your calendar, think of them as agreements with yourself. Not only will these agreements keep your life working and advance your goals, they will also help you build self-trust and personal power. Treat these agreements with respect, as we explained in Chapter 4: Stay conscious of what you've agreed to. If you anticipate that you won't be able to keep an agreement, communicate ahead of time and look for ways to make it work and avoid a loss of trust. Clean up broken agreements. And don't make more agreements than you can handle.

We strongly recommend that you create a ritual around planning (we'll explain how to do this later in the chapter), which will help it become a more integrated, positive part of your life *structure*.

In order to accomplish big things while maintaining a clean mental space, planning must become an integral part of your life. There's no reason to dread it—it can be enjoyable and will actually help you feel lighter. As soon as events change and the plan you've been working from needs modification, you'll likely feel a certain sense of unease until you check in and update the plan. It might be a very subtle feeling that's easy to ignore, but when you have major plans, the unease can feel quite strong. If you feel "off," check in with your plan: Is something out of sync? Have you broken an agreement? Do you have a need that isn't being met? Revise the plan and/or your attitude. Clarity always feels good. It takes practice, but you'll get better with time, and as you experience its value this will boost your enthusiasm to stick with it.

Be One with the Tree

Now, let's give your analytical left brain a little break and invite your right brain to the conversation. In Chinese Five Element philosophy, each of the elements—water, wood, fire, earth, and metal—presides over a certain arena of our lives, and *wood* is the element most closely associated with planning and *structure*. Wood is represented by all plant life, and is profoundly sophisticated in its cellular and life *structure*—especially in comparison to the other four elements.

Plants are rooted in the earth and grow upward toward the sun; their lives abide by this *plan* and never waver. Human lives aren't much different—we're grounded in our bodies, our tangible surroundings, and our material needs—yet we grow and aspire toward something less tangible, toward our own source of light and accomplishment. That's our version of following the plan. When we speak of your relationship to your plan, we mean *all* the plans—the plan to get yourself from bed to work and the capital-P Plan of your whole life.

A healthy relationship to your plan is characterized by several of the qualities that distinguish healthy plant growth—tenacity, perspective, and flexibility. Explore and cultivate these qualities as you pursue your plan.

- **Tenacity:** When a plant is healthy and strong, it can break through frozen soil. It can get trampled, nibbled, even chopped to the ground, and still rise up with new shoots. It knows where it wants to go and it's determined to get there. When it encounters an obstacle, a healthy plant will find a way to *grow around it*. We urge you to do the same. Don't see obstacles as injustices; see them as a reason to grow. Perspective and flexibility make this easier.

- **Perspective:** The wood element is considered to preside over our sense of vision, and this gives us the perspective to see clearly where we are, our destination, and what's in the way. It's like the perspective from the top of the tallest, oldest tree in the forest. This noble view lets us see our hurdles as part of the *big picture* of our life path—and helps us avoid needless suffering and confusion. *Space* is the key to backing up enough to get such perspective.

- **Flexibility:** The wind may blow it and snow may weigh on its branches, but a healthy plant bends without snapping, and in this way it preserves its ability to pursue its plan. If you're rigid around every detail, you become brittle and more apt to snap under life's demands. Likewise, fixed attitudes and resistance are a clear indication that you're fighting the organic nature of life rather than dancing with it. Flexibility around your plan allows you to stay light and loose, open to new possibilities and novel solutions.

STRUCTURE, SWEETNESS, AND SPACE

Remember, there should always be *space* in your *structure*. Over-planning can impinge on this *space*. It's important to allow for an openness where life gets to do its thing. You don't need to control everything. Think of your plan as a graceful piece of architecture. At most, you need four legs to hold up a chair. Six legs are excessive. Fifty legs are absurd.

Many architects look to biological structures to inform their designs because the biomechanics of living organisms make them resilient and self-stabilizing. We introduced the wood metaphors to give you ideas of how to respond *organically* when your *structure* is threatened by disruptive forces. A plant wouldn't abandon its plan entirely just because of a bad day—or month—and you shouldn't either. If you get off track and overwhelmed, *rearrange, get help, and adapt.* You might have to reschedule some tasks for later—that's okay. Just stay in the spirit of participation, to the best of your ability.

How to *Live Your Plan* with Greater Efficiency

Feeling chronically overwhelmed, beset by obstacles, and short on time can really get in the way of living a Well Life. Obstacles are unavoidable, but these issues can often be effectively managed by simply improving your efficiency. Here are some of the best approaches we've found for becoming more efficient and reclaiming your time.

Better Decision-Making

Tenacity, perspective, and flexibility help foster one of the greatest assets to a smooth plan: the ability to make conscious and efficient decisions with a minimum of deliberation. We're not saying you shouldn't take your time on big decisions, but most decisions aren't big. And we have to make them all day. In fact, we're bombarded with more choices than humans have ever known. The vast number of options is meant to feel like freedom, to help us customize the exact experience we desire, but in practice it's like a continuous series of speed bumps, often leading to what's been dubbed "decision fatigue."

Overcoming Decision Fatigue

Studies show that after making numerous decisions, the quality of our decisions begins to decline. An analysis of 1,100 cases at a parole court found that prisoners who were seen in the morning received parole about 70 percent of the time, but those whose cases were reviewed later in the day received parole less than 10 percent of the time. Researchers attributed the disparity in verdicts to the judges' decision fatigue. The same phenomenon explains why we're susceptible to impulse purchases at the end of a shopping trip—after having made dozens of decisions on products. Not only do our decision-making faculties suffer as decisions mount, sometimes we avoid making any decision at all—we just stick with the default because it takes less effort. But when it comes to decisions affecting your life direction, taking the default is like driving with closed eyes.

The simplest solution to decision fatigue is to reduce the number of decisions you need to make each day. One way to do this is by "automating" recurrent decisions so you can conserve mental freshness rather than using it on insignificant decisions:

- Preplan meals, outfits, carpools, bedtime, wake-up time, and any other routine events.
- Take the same route to work and school, eat mostly the same foods that you enjoy and feel energized from.
- Make rules to reinforce healthful habits—such as not working on the weekends, or exercising every day at a certain time.

Automating decisions doesn't make life boring; it simply frees your consciousness to be more present in the experiences—and decisions— that matter most.

It's valuable to be able to quickly identify when the decision at hand is unimportant. Which is a better deal—thirteen ounces of soup for $2.99 or seventeen ounces of soup for $3.99? Unless you're on an *extremely* tight budget, just grab the amount of soup you need and move on! Don't just *physically* move on to the next item on your grocery list, *mentally* move on, because—besides needlessly adding to your decision fatigue—being that nitpicky about money is a hindrance to having an experience of ease and abundance. When you give undue attention to an unimportant decision you constrain your own flow. Giving it your time, energy, and focus is a rip-off because the investment greatly exceeds the return.

Create a Morning Ritual

We recommend creating a morning ritual to set the tone and help align your intentions and actions for the day. This can facilitate easier decisions and a smoother overall flow. Rather than waking up and immediately presenting your mind with a pile of decisions, fill these precious first moments of wakefulness with something centering and meaningful. A ritual as simple as a few deep breaths and a good morning message to yourself can affect the quality of your whole day. If you want to go further with it, another idea is to "rehearse" the day with a visualization of yourself moving efficiently through all of your tasks.

Do your big decision-making when you're at your best—well rested, hydrated, fed, calm, sharp, and clear. For most people, this means making your most important decisions early in each day—before you've exhausted your decision center. Fresh air also helps—recent studies show that high levels of carbon dioxide indoors can impair decision-making. Create your schedule for the week in this state (or as close to it as you can get). If you schedule well, you'll eliminate the need to make many decisions throughout the week.

Bend Time

Time is more malleable than you might think. In Ayurvedic medicine, the movement of time is seen as being proportional to our speed and depth of living. If you're living fast and furious, and engaging with the world at a shallow level, time passes more quickly and you even age faster. But if you slow down and go deep—*dropping in* to the present experience and really feeling and breathing into it—then time slows down and expands. Try it while engaged in your tasks. Multitasking is a myth, so forget about anything other than the task at hand. Instead, try to keep your attention on *what you're actually doing and feeling* and broaden your perception. At first, this practice may seem forced, but over time, you'll notice that there's a greater degree of satisfaction and peace to your activities, and time stops feeling like your dominatrix. This is the infusion of *space* into *structure.*

We tend to underestimate how long things will actually take, especially when gear-switching is factored in. So, schedule *more* time than you think you'll need. If you believe you can paint the bathroom in two hours, give yourself three hours. This way you'll create more spacious containers for your activities, and if you finish early, you can always use the extra time to rest, take some deep breaths, stretch, or walk. Meanwhile, pay attention to the accuracy of your time estimates and let this inform your scheduling practice.

Know Your Rhythm

All of your faculties wax and wane. If you pay attention, you can learn when you're at your best with regard to focus, creativity, sociability, and other key skills for life management. Once you have a sense of your rhythm, plan your tasks to align with the peaks of relevant aptitudes. For instance, if you're most gregarious in the evening, try to schedule networking events around happy hour. If you're most creative around dawn, do your visionary work then.

Learning your rhythm will also show you your optimal *work interval*—how long you can sustain uninterrupted focus before you start losing efficiency. When your math skills decline or you've spent five minutes trying to find the right word, notice how long it's been since your last break. If you have a brain-intensive activity scheduled for a couple of hours, plan breaks based on your work interval. Test your interval and adjust it if necessary. Most of us have a work interval of only twenty to forty minutes! As you become better able to preschedule your breaks, you can begin to maximize their usefulness by planning short self-care activities during these times.

Chunkify

Some people find it useful to group or "chunk" their tasks based on where or how they will be performed. For instance, all the tasks that involve calling someone could be grouped under Phone, all the tasks that involve errands out of the house could be grouped under

Errands, and all the tasks that need to be done on a computer could be grouped under Computer. Choose categories that make sense to you based on convenience. If many of your tasks involve e-mailing, you might want an E-mail category. You can mark the tasks in your list with a letter or symbol to designate each category, or if you use a digital task list, you can create a list for each category.

There are three main benefits of this practice.

1. It facilitates scheduling. For example, if you've marked the tasks in your running list with the categories they belong to, you can readily find all the phone calls you need to make and set up one session to take care of them.
2. Even more valuable is that when you perform several similar tasks as a chunk, you get into a flow that makes you more efficient because you don't have to switch gears.
3. Chunking can help you knock out a few extra tasks here and there. If you have to run an unexpected errand, you might want to take a look at your Errands category to see if there's anything you can easily take care of while you're out. If you find yourself with a few spare minutes, you can check your Phone or E-mail lists if you feel like being productive.

Redefine "Emergency"

Some of the worst hijackers of attention are "urgent" matters and "emergencies." Most alleged fires that need putting out are more like sparks, or just dry logs handed to us by someone who's feeling emotional. Don't let emotion dictate priority. Your attention is exceedingly valuable. Just because someone writes you an e-mail in capital letters doesn't mean they get to derail your schedule—the *agreements* you made to support your Well Life.

Don't let emotion dictate priority.

There are very few genuine emergencies in life, but when one happens, you'll know that it's worth dropping everything. As for all the pseudo-emergencies, give them some breathing room before assessing whether a rearrangement of your schedule is warranted. And, regardless of whether or not it's a true emergency, when it has blown over, go back to any agreements that were broken and clean them up.

Honor Your Boundaries

Good boundaries aren't hostile, they're just clear and consistent. Believe in what you've established. This may mean saying no to requests on your time—sometimes by people you care about, sometimes by people who really need help, and sometimes for opportunities that seem promising. It also means saying no to your own temptation to blow off your plan, to let yourself be distracted, or to turn a quick search into a Wikipedia research marathon. We're not saying you should only do things that are self-serving. By all means, help friends and serve the world! Just don't undermine your own agreements for it.

STRUCTURE, SWEETNESS, AND SPACE

Healthy *structure* not only serves to contain and organize the *space, sweetness*, and purposeful work you invite into your life, it should also protect the contents of these containers. It's kind of like a wilderness refuge—the fence is there so the goodness inside can thrive without getting tampered with—but, it's up to you to honor the boundaries you've established.

Delegate

Most of us grew up in cultures that highly value independence and individual achievement, so it's not uncommon to feel that we only get credit for what we accomplish if we do it without help. The "every man for himself" mentality may also cause you to feel that you're burdening others if you ask for help. But for optimal efficiency and ease—and especially if you want to make big things happen, learning to delegate is essential.

Any work that doesn't require *you*—your particular knowledge or skills—can be delegated to someone else. You have to be willing to let go of doing it yourself, which can be challenging, but this frees your energy to be focused on the things you enjoy more and the tasks you're uniquely qualified to do.

Be Disciplined

Discipline is one of the most valuable human attributes. Whether it's the discipline to meditate, to exercise, to eat well, to overcome negative thoughts, to learn a language, to always speak kindly, to hone a skill, to lose weight, to train your dog, or to love yourself relentlessly, this quality is often the determining factor in many forms of success. Behind every accomplished person—from Salvador Dalí to Mother Teresa—is a story of discipline. Discipline is, in essence, a commitment to adhere to some *structure*, and the heart of every *structure* is an agreement. When you commit to a *structure*, you build yourself into it.

Discipline goes hand in hand with the ability to delay gratification. In Walter Mischel's famous experiments, preschoolers were given a marshmallow and instructed that if they could sit in a room with it for fifteen minutes without eating it, they'd get a second one. When Mischel followed up decades later, he found that, in general, the kids who delayed gratification turned into adults who were less likely to abuse drugs, had higher self-esteem, had happier relationships, had a healthier body mass index, were better at handling stress, obtained higher degrees, and earned more money.

Discipline is great stuff, but it's not always there when we need it. Like the decision-making mechanisms discussed earlier, discipline originates in the prefrontal cortex of the brain, which is a resource hog. You need to be in good shape in order for it to perform well, and it gets worn out from continuous use. Similar to decision fatigue, you can also experience discipline fatigue. The longer and more tightly you *control* yourself—like sitting in a long, tense meeting, or acting like you fit in at a party—the higher the demand on your discipline battery. Researchers have theorized that the massive number of stimuli and choices modern humans are exposed to is a likely explanation for why we seem to be less disciplined than our grandparents were.

When you're in demanding circumstances—stressed, tired, hungry, eating poorly, drunk, or in pain—it's more of a challenge to remain disciplined. In these times, people tend to default to the impulsive animal brain, fall off the wagon, and make poor choices. Thus, being disciplined is not only the determination to stick with the plan, but also the ability to resist impulses that would sabotage it.

Just to be clear, the positive self-discipline and impulse control we're speaking of are quite different from a *need to control life.* We want you to be able to make conscious choices and to follow the course you set out for yourself without being undermined by emotions and distraction. But we also want you to be able to go with the flow and make the most of what life brings.

SEVEN TIPS FOR IMPROVING YOUR SELF-DISCIPLINE

1. **Attach your discipline to things you really care about.** You can be disciplined by attraction or repulsion, by negative thoughts and feelings or by positive ones. Would you rather quit smoking out of a fear of cancer, or because of a love for life? The former involves an ongoing relationship with fear, and the latter an ongoing relationship with love. Therefore, know *why* you want what you want. If it's motivated by negativity, see if you can begin to frame it in positive terms. Connect your dream to your Values, Gifts, and Purpose. Make it something that goes beyond your own personal satisfaction. Every task and project isn't likely to be delightful, but if you keep your eye on your *why* then at least the grunt work will feel purposeful.

2. **Support your health.** Eat well, breathe deeply, get enough sleep, do tai chi, de-stress, stay hydrated, avoid low blood sugar, and above all, meditate. These practices will improve physical and mental functions conducive to sustained discipline.

3. **Know yourself.** Become more self-aware. Understand your impulses. Pay attention to the triggers that tempt you to break your agreements. In the moment when you're considering abandoning your agreement, slow down. Shift your awareness to your body and see what sensations are there. Let yourself experience them fully, without any resistance. Perhaps there's some restriction, heaviness, or another unpleasant feeling. Breathe into it, then let it go. Don't let it sabotage you from below the radar. Maybe you'll still choose to give in to temptation, but at least it's a conscious choice now—and, this awareness may be the start of a new freedom—to do something different

4. **Strengthen your discipline muscle.** Building discipline is like improving your physical fitness. It takes time and you have to increase the challenge level gradually. You wouldn't give a full-time job, a baby, and a demanding fitness regimen to someone whose *structure* currently consists of playing video games all day. Add these items one at a time. Luckily, improving discipline in one area of life tends to spill over into others. When you're on the verge of giving in, what would a trainer say? Stick with it for five more minutes! If you want to cut your workout short, give it five more minutes. If you planned to write a chapter of your book and you're considering blowing it off, just do it for five minutes. If you're trying to shop less but you really want that dress, just leave the store for five minutes.

5. **Approach it as a matter of integrity.** Be clear about the agreements that underlie your discipline. Honoring them is a demonstration of love and respect for yourself and builds your self-trust.

6. **Craft your self-talk wisely.** As we explained before, when faced with the temptation to be distracted or break an agreement, people are more likely to stay the course when the language they use with themselves is framed as *"I don't—break my agreements, get on Facebook during my workday, eat gummy bears, skip my workouts, etc."* rather than *"I can't—"* Choose empowering language.

7. **Create conditions that will reduce the need for discipline in the first place.** This may take some discipline at the outset, but will protect your resources for when you really need them. Here are some examples:

- Avoid situations that tax your willpower—like going to a candy store. If you can't avoid it, spend a few moments beforehand mentally rehearsing yourself navigating it in a positive way.
- Set up an undesirable consequence. We don't like to have to use this approach, but sometimes it works, especially for short-term plans. For instance, you could promise a friend that if you break your agreement, you'll clean up all the dog poop in their yard. (At least it's a positive for your friend.) Sticking with the plan then becomes an easy choice.
- Earmark time in your schedule and/or arrange the necessary resources for what you've agreed to do. Don't give yourself the (bullshit) excuse of being unable to stick with the plan because of circumstances beyond your control.
- Make it as easy as possible. The more convenient it is for you to do what you really want for yourself, the more likely it is that you'll do it. We're ruled by convenience much more than we'd like to admit.
- Create ritual and routine. If you can turn your plan into a series of *habits,* they become "toll free" and the need for discipline disappears. The next section will explain how to forge rituals to add *sweetness,* depth, and purpose to everyday tasks.

We know it's not easy, but you can do it. It might even be terribly uncomfortable to learn to live by a plan and practice discipline, especially if you aren't used to it. But it's not unlike the discomfort you'd feel in your lungs if you were learning to run, or the discomfort in your fingertips if you were learning to play the violin. Don't convince yourself that discomfort means it's wrong. It's simply part of the growth process. The world needs your greatness. Let it be your guiding light.

Ritualize

For modern humans who are driven toward speed, convenience, and self-sufficiency, rituals can seem a clunky and unnecessary add-on. They demand time and energy without seeming to offer a value you can easily identify. This is especially true for those who have lost touch with their cultures of origin.

STRUCTURE, SWEETNESS, AND SPACE

Rituals can be one of the most valuable ingredients in your life *structure*. They're the ultimate balancer, because, besides clarifying and stabilizing our *structure,* they involve accessing *space* and invoking *sweetness.*

We propose a resurrection of ritual—on the terms that each user gets to define for themselves. Within your life *structure*, ritual has the properties of a most extraordinary building material—like pillars made of diamond. Imagine living in a home supported by a geometric arrangement of such pillars. They would lend a certain *consistency* to your habitat, as well as *stability* and *beauty*. And it's likely that as you passed one of these brilliant columns, you'd stop and pause. These are the roles ritual plays:

- It elevates the mundane.
- It serves as a checkpoint throughout our life.
- It provides an opportunity to orient ourselves.

When things get crazy, your rituals can keep you sane.

Rituals

When you forge a ritual, you're prompted to acknowledge *why* you're doing what you're doing. And amidst a sea of influences that might darken your consciousness, connecting with the *why* is like turning on a light. Sociologists say the loss of our bearings that has come with the decline of ritual makes us more prone to stress and drug addiction. In contrast, having rituals promotes psychological health and resilience.

Peter once had a patient with lung cancer who adopted two rituals after her diagnosis. First, she started making and drinking a quart of green juice every morning. If she came into The Dragontree before noon, she'd always be carrying a half-finished mason jar of murky green liquid. Second, she brought healthy treats to every chemo session to share with the other patients, and she became the unofficial cheerleader of the group.

It's hard to measure the health impact of these rituals, but they became her "thing." She was absolutely committed to them, and they kept her going through a challenging time. She had no fantasy that these practices would tether her to life, but she never lost her hair, she remained in great spirits, and after a year, she was declared cancer-free. Even if they didn't cure her cancer, these rituals had an undeniably positive effect on her quality of life.

If you want to establish a new habit, ritual can help. By *ritualizing* a chosen practice, you make it more than an everyday task—instead, it becomes an integral pattern in the tapestry of your life. Rituals even make a measurable difference in how you feel: Recent studies show that they are surprisingly effective at alleviating negative emotions such as anxiety and grief, improving confidence and focus, and enhancing performance.

The word *ritual* comes from the Latin *ritus* (rite), meaning a custom or performance. This seems to be derived from the earlier Sanskrit word *rta* (or *rita*). *Rta* is a term that appeared frequently in the *Rig Veda,* one of the oldest texts on the planet. It's variously translated as "natural order," "cosmic order," "truth," "universal law," and "harmony between all things." Quite in alignment with this idea, some scholars suggest that *rta* is the origin of the English word *rhythm*. Thus, you can think of your rituals as practices that establish and tune us in to the natural rhythm and order of life.

Finally, here's what we see as the quintessential reason and method for ritual—conscious ritual is, at its most fundamental, an act of creating specialness in your life. We know this logic is almost too simple to take seriously, but please just let it sink in: The more special moments you create, the more special your life will be. People tend to think they need to be lucky or skilled at working life the right way in order for special things to happen. Don't make it more complicated than it is.

How to Build a Ritual

There are all sorts of ways to perform a ritual, from solemn to light, and from simple to complex. You can make up a new ritual entirely. You can adopt or maintain rituals that work for you (from your childhood, your family, your heritage, or a culture you resonate with), and personalize them as you see fit. If you're trying to produce a psychological shift in yourself, research indicates that you may be more successful at enrolling your mind if your ritual involves several steps.

GUIDELINES FOR CONSTRUCTING RITUALS

1. A ritual can be an activity in itself or it can be based around some task or event. For instance, you could create a daily ritual for the specific purpose of setting a positive tone for each day. You could also create a ritual around eating or washing to make it a more deliberate and special event.
2. Seriousness isn't necessary—after all, some rituals are about rejoicing—but respect for the value and significance of what you aim to do makes a real difference in its impact.
3. In crafting a ritual, know why you're doing it. Consider how it fits with your emerging purpose and goals. Make it enjoyable

and meaningful. Experience it through your body, your breath, your mind, and your spirit. Savor the moment and the intention.

4. At the least, we recommend that your ritual has an opening and a closing. The opening could be as simple as acknowledging what the intention of the ritual is. You could state, "I'm grateful for this meal and I intend to be deeply nourished by it." Even better would be to also "tune in" somehow, such as taking a breath, closing your eyes, or relaxing your body. The closing of the ritual could be as simple as restating the purpose or expressing gratitude for what was done. You might just say, "That was really good, and I am thankful." Of course, you could get a lot more elaborate, too.

5. The main thing that makes a ritual stand out in our *structure* is that it's *different* from the surrounding material. The ritual may involve different scents, sounds, and materials than those of your usual life, and moreover, your *presence* is different. Consider incorporating one or more of the following elements (adapted from *The Rituals for Living Dreambook*) to make your ritual unique:

- **Fire:** A candle, a fireplace, an oil lamp, or the sun. Fire is a symbol of illumination, warmth, and connection.
- **Special words:** Set an intention, say a blessing or mantra, invoke a helper. Writing can make words even more real.
- **Food or drink:** Consuming a significant food or drink is special as it involves bringing something from the outside world into your body. Plus, it incorporates the senses of taste and smell, and may produce a biological response.
- **Beauty:** Adorning and beautifying your *space*, your things, your body, and your life is a way of uplifting them and of demonstrating gratitude and reverence.
- **Sound:** Trickling water, bells, chimes, chants, binaural beats, and favorite songs can all help tune our attention and elicit a shift of consciousness.

- **Garments:** Putting on a special piece of jewelry, hat, or superhero outfit may help you get into the right *space*.
- **Water:** Water symbolizes purity, cleansing, and flow. Bathe, dip your hands or feet in it, or splash some on your face. Natural water sources may help you connect more deeply.
- **Scents:** Flowers, incense, and essential oils have long been used to uplift our spirit and shift the *space* around us to designate a special purpose.
- **Gathering:** There is strength in numbers. Whether coworking or coritualizing, tuning in together can be stronger.
- **Location:** The right space can lend sanctity to your ritual. Go where you feel good—the woods, the beach, a church or temple, your bedroom altar. A consistent location can help anchor your ritual.
- **Objects of significance:** You may wish to bring something to your ritual that reminds you of the *why*, helps you connect, or charges you up. A flower, a photograph, a crystal, etc.
- **Timing:** Synchronizing a ritual with a particular season, the birthday of someone important, a historic event, a moon phase, time of day, the solstice, equinox, etc., may contribute to a sense of extra power and alignment.

If this is entirely new to you, start with one simple ritual around something you'd like to make more special. Choose the elements and format beforehand, follow the guidelines above, and let it flow naturally. Afterward, make note of what could have been better or smoother, and revise it over time.

Develop a ritual around planning, as well as any other practice that you want to make a stable fixture in your life. For example: exercise or cooking; any everyday act that you want to enhance the specialness of, such as mealtimes or bathing; and any act that you want to transform into a grounding or tuning-in point in your life.

❖

We presented many instructions in this chapter. If this work seems daunting, remember that you don't have to implement everything at once. You're not only building new *structure*, you're simultaneously dismantling old *structures*. It's a process that takes time. Like transitioning from a typewriter to a computer, there may be some clinging to what you know, but you'll be so much better off when you let go and evolve. You'll begin enjoying your improved efficiency and making progress on your plan, and as you work through updating your whole infrastructure, it will just get better.

CHAPTER 13.
EXPAND

Commit to Your Well Life

With all the pieces in place (or most of them), momentum, magic, and expansion start to happen. This chapter is about taking what you've set into motion and reinforcing your commitment and participation. It's about making refinements for enhanced results and being persistent. It's about opening your eyes to the abundance of opportunities available to you. It's about letting your Wellness extend to all parts of your body and mind, all facets of your life, and then taking it to the world at large.

STRUCTURE, SWEETNESS, AND SPACE

So, you've chosen a *sweeter* life, with a *structure* that supports you to take care of yourself and achieve your goals, and the *space* to connect and grow in this human experience. It's a good time to revisit the meaning of commitment. Now that the ball is rolling, what exactly does commitment entail and what will it do for you?

You've probably never had a job for which you committed to just clock in, contribute in the most minimal way, clock out, and collect your paycheck. No, when you were hired, there was an implicit understanding that you'd use all your skills and experience, you'd enhance the workplace, and you'd do your best. Likewise, anyone who is conscious during their wedding vows understands that "Till death do us part" is just a fraction of the commitment. You actually committed to cocreate a mutually positive experience. Without continuing to feed it and tend to it, *merely sticking around* isn't in the spirit of commitment. Commitment doesn't mean a relationship can never end, but as we see it, as long as you're committed, it makes sense to *act* like you're committed.

Commit: Do It for Yourself

When you sincerely commit, the heart of the commitment is the quality of participation you'll bring. Real commitment has more to do with the spirit of your presence than anything else. We often focus on the *structure* of the commitment while neglecting the *sweetness* and *space*.

For any number of reasons—it's hard, you're tired, you're bored, you're scared, you're underpaid, your partner doesn't participate at the same level you do—you may ignore your commitment and withdraw your participation. It's important to recognize how significantly this hurts your own happiness, self-trust, and sense of self-worth. It's like saying, "Because I dislike the terms, I'm going to stop participating in the enhancement of my own life."

> Real commitment has more to do with the spirit of your presence than anything else.

When you're functioning at this level, you often carry around a feeling of guilt or drudgery. Not only do you have a sense that your follow-through is half-assed, you know that you're really breaking a commitment with yourself. When you're struggling with pain, loneliness, or burden, you can forget that life is a gift. But if you become quiet, in the *space*, you eventually start to remember. With this recognition comes a feeling of gratitude and inspiration that makes you want to show up as fully as you can. Though it may be hard at times to see the incentive to show up fully for your boss or partner, you can always choose to do it for yourself.

Remember

If you notice that you're not following through on your commitment to your plan (your work, your partner, your kids, yourself), see if you can uncover what you've been committing to instead. Comfort? Control? Security? Facebook? Stay awake and *choose*. Every time you notice you've unconsciously eclipsed a true commitment with something else, make a mental or verbal statement of choice, such as, "I choose to be completely present with my kids right now," or "I choose to take care of myself," or "I choose to be happy."

The Quest for Happiness

Sometimes we get confused about commitment and feel trapped or restricted by it, which makes us restless and indecisive. It makes us want to push back and sabotage the *structures* we've chosen to build our Well Life. The paradoxical thing is that when we believe we're really, truly stuck with something, we're less likely to suffer than if we believe we *might* be stuck with something if we continue down the road we're headed on.

Dan Gilbert, Harvard psychologist and author of *Stumbling on Happiness,* has discovered some unlikely facts about happiness. First, humans greatly overestimate the impact that the outcome of a future event will have on us. Whether we win or lose, within a few months we're usually back to the same level of happiness we were at before the event. "A year after losing the use of their legs and a year after winning the lotto," Gilbert said in a TED talk, "lottery winners and paraplegics are equally happy with their lives."

This is due, in part, to our ability to "synthesize" happiness. It's a facet of what Gilbert calls the psychological immune system—the capacity to make a bad situation not so bad for ourselves. The tricky part is that this system works best when we think we can't get out of our situation. While we all want the freedom to change our mind (perhaps over and over), this actually impairs our ability to synthesize happiness. When we believe we have lots of options—including the option to return or exchange something, to divorce our partner and find a new one, or to move to a new town—we're more prone to feel unhappy. We may constantly go back and forth, wondering if we've made the best choice or if we should change something.

Committing Promotes Happiness

Take advantage of this psychological mechanism by *committing*. Think of commitment as *the continuous application of sincere participation*. When it comes to any big choice—your partner, your job, your town—buckle in and stick with it. Bring your *sweetness* to the table—your passion, your skills, your beauty, your love, and your mojo. You have the ability to make yourself happy regardless of the outcome. If you make a choice and don't give yourself an easy "out," you're more likely to be happy than you'd be if you kept your options open.

A commitment doesn't have to be forever; you might decide to give a situation a commitment of three months. Whatever the duration of the commitment, participate fully and aim to make it work. When it doesn't feel good, instead of entertaining the idea of *exiting*, first consider, if exiting weren't an option, what would you do to enhance the situation? Of course, it makes sense to end a commitment when someone's well-being is endangered by it—such as an abusive relationship. For nearly all other cases, we stand to gain more from staying and upholding our commitment than we do from leaving.

> Whatever the duration of the commitment, participate fully and aim to make it work.

When you stand behind your commitments, new possibilities arise. Figuring out a problematic relationship may seem impossible if you've already withdrawn your commitment. But when you renew your participation with humility, a willingness to be wrong, and an expectation that harmony and fruition are possible, the "figuring out" part usually just happens, perhaps in ways you couldn't have foreseen.

Difficulty Is Not a Sign That You're on the Wrong Path

As we explained in the section on the wood element in Chapter 12, healthy plants embody a combination of tenacity, perspective, and flexibility, which enables them to grow around obstacles rather than becoming stuck. Humans benefit from these virtues, too. There *will* be obstacles, and if you're rigid, shortsighted, or anger-prone, you'll see these obstacles as injustices. Whether the obstacle is getting pulled over for speeding, a broken leg, having mean parents, dirty dishes, or people not buying your product, there's a single (usually subconscious) belief that can prevent you from moving on: *I am right.* Even though it happened, you believe it *shouldn't* have happened; your plan was *right* and *life was wrong.*

Let Go of Having to Be Right

An attachment to your rightness is a hindrance to flexibility and growth. The popular business book *Who Moved My Cheese?* expresses this concept brilliantly through the analogy of mice running through a maze searching for cheese. When the scientist moves the cheese and the mice don't find it where they expect it, they don't waste a minute dwelling on it—they simply continue searching for the cheese until they find it. Only a human would stay glued to the spot where the cheese is "supposed" to be, shocked and outraged that someone moved it, hoping that our insistence that it should be here will make it appear.

An interesting thing happens when you loosen up about needing to be right. Whereas you may have thought it was your rightness that was making your plan work and giving merit to your position, without it, you suddenly find you're able to move forward with great ease and flexibility. You are able to be decisive because you don't get stuck on the obstacles. You develop like a healthy plant, for which obstacles are simply impetuses for increased growth.

Obstacles Make You Stronger

If we take another lesson from the plant world, we see that plants that have no obstacles are often weak or unprepared for challenges that arise. Without cold nights and strong breezes, your tomato plants will probably have stems that are too weak to support the weight of their own fruit. Some growers actually whack their plants with a broom—a manmade "obstacle"—because it's thought to stress them into building stronger stems and putting more energy into fruiting.

Humans also need obstacles to be our best. If we don't encounter any in everyday life, we start searching for them. We climb mountains and run marathons on the weekends. We get into relationships with people we know will be difficult to live with. Thus, it's possible for obstacles to be both the bane of our existence (when we resist them) and the means by which we grow and mature.

Most new relationships—whether with a career, a human, or a health practice—begin with some obstacles. But they're obstacles we're expecting, and we're up for doing the work to grow into them. We're excited about this person or endeavor, and we're clear about the payoff the relationship will yield for us. After a while, though, when the shine wears off a bit, we may expect the relationship to become easy, and this makes us reluctant to keep up the work—much less to double our efforts when the big growth periods come—as they inevitably do.

While we want you to experience *ease*, it's not the same as *easy*, and it's important not to confuse ease with a lack of work.

Work and Relaxation Can Go Hand in Hand

One of the greatest gifts we received from studying tai chi is the concept of simultaneous work and relaxation. Traditional instruction in tai chi relies on ideas that seem paradoxical, and the paradox of work and relaxation is most important. The key is to discover that these two qualities aren't really mutually exclusive. In tai chi, the entire body should be engaged. Every part of us should be working simultaneously, even our mental focus. Yet, we must also maintain slow, deep breathing and a state of inner peace. It can be difficult to accomplish because people so frequently equate working hard with being tense and stressed.

Our tai chi practice started out as four hours a week in the Chinese Benevolent Association building in downtown Portland, but over the years we noticed that it was less and less confined to just that time and space. When you're devoted to the practice of a body-mind art, such as tai chi, yoga, *Qi Gong*, or even ballet, it expands into your everyday life. It starts to affect the way you move, think, breathe, work, and communicate. And this is when it becomes truly transformative.

What would happen if you were to adopt this tai chi attitude of simultaneous work and relaxation—of total participation—in the way you relate to your plan, your job, your housework, your partner, kids, friends, parents, and yourself? Jump in and try.

Edit Your Life

Editing is essentially *structural maintenance*. In order to keep your *structure* from becoming rickety or inefficient, you must regularly edit your life. This entails *reflecting* on how you've been operating, *evaluating* what has and hasn't worked, and then *adjusting* for better results. Because you're undertaking some new approaches to life, we recommend doing this process on a monthly basis to begin. Later, when you're the embodiment of a Well Life, you may wish to do it just quarterly or semi-annually.

You can develop your own *life editing* process, or use these questions to guide you.

1. What was your biggest time and/or energy waster in the past month?

2. Which activities and rituals yielded the biggest "return" for you (either tangible or intangible) in the past month?
3. Is there anything you've been procrastinating over during the past month?
4. What possessions took time or energy to maintain, or cluttered your space or routine, but offered little value?
5. If anything happened in the last month that you'd like to reframe (i.e., change the story you tell yourself and others to hold it in a more positive light), please write how you intend to reframe it.
6. What has been infringing on your happiness, health, or productivity in the past month that you intend to let go of in the coming month?

Use your answers to shape your focus and refine your thoughts and behaviors in the coming month.

Reconnect to Your Growth Mindset

Let's look again at Carol Dweck's "growth mindset" research, which we touched on in Chapter 6. Dweck found that students either believed their intelligence was a fixed value ("fixed mindset") or that it was something that could be increased ("growth mindset"). Those with a growth mindset outperformed those with a fixed mindset.

Now that we've shown you so many ways to grow, we want to help you adopt a growth mindset. As we've seen in the years since Dweck published her findings, the fixed mindset is simply an untrue perspective. *Everyone* can grow. Dweck emphasizes that a growth mindset isn't just about working harder; it should also involve trying different approaches and getting input from others when you're stuck. Further, she holds that it's counterproductive to praise children for expending effort without learning—just to make them feel good in the moment—and the same applies to how we treat ourselves. If the learning isn't happening, something needs to be *changed.*

Rather than telling yourself that you're great just for trying, Dweck would advise that you start by telling the truth about your current achievement, and then change course as necessary. Part of the growth mindset is a healthy attitude around making mistakes: If you want to grow, you can't see mistakes as problematic or harmful.

In this task, watch for your "fixed-mindset triggers." Notice if you feel anxious when facing challenges—what do you believe a mistake will mean? Pay attention to your thinking after a setback—do you take it as an indication that you're incompetent? Do you look for excuses instead of trying to learn from the feedback? Remember that you can grow. If you're tempted to say, "I'm not good at marketing," add the word "yet" to the end of the sentence.

Spot Opportunities

Now that you've done so much work toward creating and receiving your Well Life, it's essential to notice when good things show up. Sometimes the biggest difference between a cursed life and a charmed life is that a person with the latter knows how to spot opportunities.

As we see it, opportunity is a state of mind, not a lucky set of circumstances. When you believe this, you'll see opportunities everywhere, in every moment:

- Opportunities to connect
- Opportunities to grow and learn
- Opportunities to contribute
- Opportunities to engage more deeply in the moment
- Opportunities to play
- Opportunities to let go
- Opportunities to enhance your circumstances
- Opportunities to experience love and beauty

If this sounds like someone else's life, it's only because you've forgotten. You've been seeing obstacles instead of opportunities, probably for most of your life. It's a habit of restricting your perspective.

It can be a difficult habit to break, but your perspective is *really, truly* a choice that's yours to make. You just have to open enough *space* to see the *sweetness*.

Here are three steps that will help you develop an opportunity-spotting perspective:

1. Know your purpose. Know it so well that you could recite it at any moment. Remind yourself of it every morning.
2. Stay "on purpose." Consciously choose to align your life with your purpose.
3. Remain open to the idea that opportunities are everywhere, and be willing to expand into a new way of being.

Have you ever ridden on a carousel and tried to snatch the golden ring as you whirled past it? Opportunities are like that—like golden rings hanging from hooks that are just about everywhere. They're up for grabs and are continually replenished. In fact, there's one hanging on every human.

Keep Your Eyes Open

Narrow, fixed thinking causes you to tune these rings out of your vision, like wearing blinders. It takes a massive toll. If you buy into restrictive interpretations of life, you can get caught in the compulsion to prove to yourself that you're right, because it would be sad and embarrassing if you had missed out on something great. The longer it goes on, the more that's at stake. You may even surround yourself with others in the same plight, so you never have to face the truth (which, of course, you know deep inside). So many people live lives of poverty—a poverty of love, joy, and connection—when they're surrounded by wealth. There are others right next to you, *stretching*, reaching out for those rings, and filling their lives with gold while you clutch your wooden pony's reins and insist that they got better horses.

Maintaining a campaign of blindness requires ferocious manipulation of your perspective. It's not just sad; it's exhausting. Why not concede your folly and join the party? Better late than never. Although it may initially feel like work to open your eyes wider than you've been accustomed to, it will come to feel like a relief. With the slightest shift in orientation, life can feel like a treasure hunt. It's a perspective that is actually *so close* that it's easy to miss. It doesn't require a pilgrimage and years of psychotherapy to get there; it's barely hidden by the veil you've created.

Finding Opportunities When Life Sucks

Of course, everyone has moments when their opportunity-spotting faculties seem to fail them. Even if you're fully onboard with us, chances are you'll someday ask, "How could I possibly see *this* as an opportunity? This just *sucks*. Where's the golden ring here?" But even at a funeral, the golden rings haven't disappeared. Chances are, the tears are clouding your vision, and that's okay.

The best answer we can offer is a question. When you're experiencing some struggle, ask yourself one (or more) of the following questions. Imagine that you're opening your heart and allowing the question to penetrate your soul. (If you're so inclined, bring your higher power, your superconsciousness, your angels, your inner wise one, your deceased loved ones, or any other helpers in on the question.) Then *listen* for the answer and *feel* what comes up in your body. Please resist the temptation to browse these questions and assume that you know what the effect of asking them would be. Experience it instead.

- How can I see this as an opportunity?
- What could I let go of in this moment in order to have a healthier point of view?
- How can I use this situation as a way of feeling more connected—to God, to my partner, to my community, to my family, to myself, etc.?
- How can I serve others in this situation?
- How can I use this situation as an opportunity to love myself more completely?

If one question doesn't elicit an answer or produce a positive shift, try a different one, or repeat the question throughout the day.

In your whole life, you'll never find yourself in a situation where there isn't an opportunity to connect, to grow and learn, to contribute, to engage more deeply, to help, to play, to let go, to enhance your circumstances, or to experience love and beauty. These are just a few of the golden rings available to you. The more rings you grab, the more immersed in the game you'll become. Not only will the quality of your existence change profoundly, you'll be an ever-brighter light in the world.

Expand

As you've been trying out the concepts and techniques in this book, chances are, the most accessible parts of yourself benefited the most readily. You probably implemented these ideas in the ways and places of your life that required the least adaptation, which was smart. The less disruption that's involved in making a change, the more likely it is to "take," and the easier it is for you to assess its value. It's like upgrading from version 14.0 to version 15.0.

STRUCTURE, SWEETNESS, AND SPACE

The expansion process is a unified expression of *space, structure,* and *sweetness.* It's what happens when you allow *space* to open every dimension of your life, *sweetness* to emerge from every atom, and *structure* to embody its own perfect design. All three occur simultaneously. When a person welcomes expansion, some people call it "coming into your power." We think of it as growing into who you really are—your unrestricted potential.

Little by little, however, you'll be prompted (by the part of you that wants to expand) to apply this upgrade to the less accessible parts of yourself—your deeper beliefs, your longstanding habits, the restricted parts of your body. Depending on how long it's been since you last upgraded these regions, this task may be more like upgrading from, say, version 7.0 to version 15.0. It's going to take longer to download, longer to install, and longer to get used to the new system. That is, it's going to take longer to understand what should change and how, longer to implement these changes in a comprehensive and lasting way, and longer to fully embody the evolving You. Sometimes it happens more quickly, but what's the rush?

There might even be parts of you that are still operating under, say, version 2.1—areas of your consciousness or behavior that never grew up. And, it's possible that there will be some discomfort involved in the expansion process, but the majority of it comes from the part of you that wants to cling to what's familiar. The more patient and open you can be, the more fascinating and gratifying the process will be.

We like Rabbi Dr. Abraham Twerski's lobster metaphor for the growth process: A lobster is a soft creature living in a rigid shell that can't grow. As the creature inside gets bigger, it experiences pressure as the shell becomes confining and uncomfortable. This is how the lobster knows it's time to shed its shell and grow a new, more spacious one. As Twerski summarizes, "The stimulus for the lobster to be able to grow is that it feels uncomfortable." If the lobster tried to avoid the discomfort (with a painkiller, for instance), it would never grow. We're not saying it's a bad thing to take an aspirin for a headache—especially if it can be easily explained by the coconut that just fell on your head. But if you're experiencing discomfort, it's always worthwhile to take a look inside and see if there's a growth opportunity there.

The Metta Tradition: Start with You

The *metta* tradition of Buddhism is a good framework for the expansion process. The monk Acharya Buddharakkhita defined *metta* as "loving-kindness," "an altruistic attitude of love and friendliness," and a "strong wish for the welfare and happiness of others." The *metta* practice involves directing loving-kindness to every aspect of your life and being totally committed to the expression of universal love in everything you do.

If you aspire to treat people well—with kindness, love, support, and patience—doesn't it make sense to start with the person closest to you? (We're talking about *You*.) You're always available for practicing, and, if you're like the rest of us, you've probably spent much of your life depriving yourself of love and approval. But your effectiveness as a conduit for the outward expression of love can be limited by your inability to love yourself. Therefore, the *metta* path always begins with directing benevolence toward yourself.

Once you are able to love yourself—to expand into yourself— entirely and without exclusion, the practice broadens to include the outward expression of loving-kindness toward your circle of friends and family. Then there are those you see regularly in your workplace. Eventually, you can expand your focus to include more distant acquaintances, then strangers, then enemies, and eventually the entire world.

You Are the World

Let's now look at this expansion process through the metaphor of the body. Extending from your heart in every direction is your *vascular tree*—the intricate network of vessels that distributes blood. The heart's job is to be absolutely *inclusive*—sharing its love with every single cell of your body. Imagine that, in a similar fashion, your job is to extend your consciousness, your love, and your awakening to all parts of yourself. Would you ever dream of deliberately restricting blood flow to a certain part of your body? Of course not. So, don't exclude your evolution from any part of your being.

Expansion Meditation

As an expansion meditation, take a few minutes to close your eyes and hold all of yourself within your awareness. Imagine that even the nonphysical aspects—your mind, personality, and spirit—are part of your body. You may see yourself as extending beyond the borders of your physical body.

Next, instead of blood, visualize your heart as a pump of *light* to all of your many parts, and know that this light is synonymous with *love*. Ask yourself, as you consider each facet of yourself—even the parts you might dislike—"Is this part being circulated with light? Have I accepted and expanded into this part of myself? Am I loving this part completely?" Your evolution depends on not depriving any part of yourself of acceptance, awareness, and love. Restricting a part of yourself is like depriving one of your toes of blood.

The next frontier is your local sphere—your household, your workplace, your friendships, and your close community. As you operate in these realms, consciously include them in your growing perspective, healthy habits, rituals, and emerging purpose. Try applying the expansion meditation practice to this portion of the world: Notice who and what you resist including. Visualize an expanded image of yourself that integrates you with these difficult people and situations. Imagine that they are an inextricable part of You. Again, just as you wouldn't restrict blood from your own toe, don't restrict them from your inclusion. Also, you may find it easier to encompass them in your love if you see them not as a distant part of you, but host them instead within your heart.

Gradually, you can allow your practice to contain a larger and larger sphere. See the entire planet as an extension of you. Challenge yourself to accept and include even the people and practices you have an aversion to. Denying or despising them won't make them go away any more than hating cancer makes it leave a body. But ending your internal conflict with these rejected aspects of the world will free up your energy, allowing you to make a bigger difference and to experience more complete peace and happiness.

Contraction

After an experience of expansion, it's extremely common to *contract*. You feel you're making great progress, you're in balance, you're in love with the world, your hair looks amazing, and then . . . it seems to fall apart. Suddenly you're strikingly unenlightened. You're hollowing out sacred texts so you can hide candy in there. You can't connect to the Mother Ship. You're critical of yourself and others. The money stops coming in. Perhaps you even spiral into despair.

It's useful to understand why this is happening. One mechanism, which we could call "small mind contraction," occurs because your expansion feels uncomfortable or unsafe to your subconscious mind. Maybe having extra money worries you or makes you think you're going to become shallow. Maybe being light and happy is unfamiliar. Maybe it's scary to come into your power with others watching you.

Another mechanism we might call "existential contraction" happens because your ego feels its very existence is threatened as you begin to grow out of it. In an effort to assert its realness and pull you back in, it generates conflict and pain.

It's natural to resent contraction. Things were going well and now they seem not to be. But, as in all things, hating and resisting it won't resolve it. Here's the approach we recommend for moving through contraction:

1. **Name it.** It's easier to avoid wallowing in it if you see it for what it is—a mere hiccup. This contraction is a reaction by your small, scared mind to your having made real progress.
2. **Stay the course.** Contraction is not unlike what follows an intense workout. After stretching and working your muscles to their limit, they may stiffen up to the point of hobbling you. Even though the micro-tears you've made will stimulate increased growth, in the short term you may feel like you were hit by a truck. Most people know to expect this effect with exercise, so they don't interpret it as a sign that they should stop working out. Treat your psycho-spiritual contraction the same way. Rest a little, keep stretching your mind, nourish yourself with good food and water, stick with the plan, and reassure yourself that this is natural.
3. **Keep powerfully choosing.** You always have a choice of following your heart—i.e., Spirit, Truth, God—or your ego. Your

ego is extremely limited and unable to *wake up* to the vastness of what you really are, but you can choose to transcend it. As often as you remember, state your choice by saying (inwardly or aloud), *I choose Spirit!* or *I choose Love!* or *I choose Freedom!* or *I choose Truth!* or whatever wording feels strongest to you.

4. **Turn toward the conflict.** Asserting the choice of Spirit and ignoring your ego can take a lot of willpower, but there is a *softer* way: turn *toward*, rather than away from, the contraction that's occurring. Be curious without resisting. See how your ego screams for attention? See how it generates conflict in order to reinforce a reality in which it is needed? See the silliness and confusion of what you're mired in? See how you fall back into old habits because of fear and limiting beliefs? What else does your curiosity reveal? What happens when you say YES—*Yes, I am ready for whatever comes along because I trust that I'm being guided to greater peace and fulfillment*—instead of NO?

An experience of contraction does not mean your hard work was in vain. In fact, the process of navigating a period of contraction can lead to tremendous healing and increased freedom. Li Hongzhi, creator of a popular form of *Qi Gong* called *Falun Gong*, describes a similar process as one progresses in one's practice. He explains that whenever we *level up*, meaning we make a significant leap in our development, we have to *relearn* certain things that we learned previously, because we're operating from a somewhat different perspective. The apparent loss of these functions can feel like a major setback until we relearn them, but in actuality, it's a good sign.

Raise the Stakes

Throughout this book, we've encouraged you in various ways to *raise the stakes*—to dream bigger, to include more of the world in your dreams, and to embody the most powerful and evolved form of yourself. The wonderful thing about raising the stakes in these ways is that, while your potential "winnings" increase greatly, your potential losses don't. While playing bigger than ever, you become more supported and more resilient. And if you fall, you'll fall more softly.

When we started The Dragontree, we had many conversations about what the whole purpose of the business was. For years, we had been doing the work that's laid out in these pages, and we realized that it wasn't work we could just do in our spare time. It was a full-time job, and therefore, we needed to begin to treat our careers (and every other facet of our lives) as an extension of the personal urge to heal and evolve.

The broader our perspective became, the more convinced we were that our overarching purpose was to promote peace. All the problems of the world would either disappear or be overcome by a global community of peaceful, united individuals. Our motto became, "A peaceful world begins with a peaceful you."

From that point onward, our efforts took on new meaning. When we stayed up all night to paint the walls of our spa, it wasn't just so that we'd be able to pay our rent—we were doing it out of commitment to our purpose. The business acquired a life of its own. We raised the stakes, and the prizes got bigger. The spa attracted staff members who were as passionate about cultivating peace as we were. Every decision was informed by the mission. Opportunities arose, resources became available—sometimes as if by magic—for us to help more people. We've overcome obstacles that appeared insurmountable, and the only explanation that makes sense is that our purpose pulls big strings in the world.

While we attempt to stay clear and grounded, of course we have times when we're destabilized by our circumstances and our own runaway minds, and sometimes we act like cranky babies. But when we remember our commitment to peace, this usually brings us back into alignment rather quickly.

We have noticed that our personal fluctuations are reflected in our relationship with the world. When we get off track internally, we see it reflected externally. Whether this comes from a shift in the way we treat the world or a subtler push-and-pull between us and our environment, it reminds us that we are inseparable from our container. Which is precisely why a peaceful world must begin with a peaceful us—and a peaceful you.

Our Shared Well Life

You probably have a desire to affect the world in a positive way. It may be a desire that's hidden or long ago deemed unrealistic. You may be unsure about how to make it happen, you may doubt that it's possible, and you may feel a little sheepish about dreaming so big. But why do you think you were attracted to a book like this? Now that you've begun tending to the health of your mind and body, releasing the snares of your past, living with integrity, fortifying your resources, honoring your values, gifts, and purpose, clarifying your true desires, connecting to your highest self, practicing rituals to anchor meaning and magic into every day, magnifying your intentions, honing your efficiency skills, and opening yourself to opportunity, there's no good reason to deprive the world of your greatness.

You might want to argue that you still have a long way to go on these aspirations. It's true. We all have a lifetime's worth of growth ahead of us, which is why it makes no sense to wait until you're finished before you'll start including the world in your Well Life. We come back to these principles over and over, growing in new ways, remembering things about ourselves that we hoped never to forget, and we invite you to join us. Treat this material not as something to learn and master once and for all, but as a resource that will always steer you toward the truth.

> Treat this material not as something to learn and master once and for all, but as a resource that will always steer you toward the truth.

⊰✦⊱

Your Well Life is interconnected with the wellness of the world. Supporting the peace, balance, and happiness of the world around you is integral to having these qualities in a genuine way in your own life. Likewise, cultivating these qualities within yourself—by being an enthusiastic participant in this lifetime of work—helps engender them in the world. Ultimately, you see, your *personal* Well Life is inseparable from *our* collective Well Life. Let's make it exceptional together.

ACKNOWLEDGMENTS

We would like to thank:

The Divine Source/Our Highest Selves.

Our parents—Kit, Kate, Rick, John, and Ann—for loving us, teaching us, encouraging us, and guiding us. You have served as an example of what kind, freethinking, and inspired people can do with their lives. Bill and Judy for believing in us and pushing us to grow. Abe and Desiree for supporting our work and dreams in so many ways.

Our dear friends in our Boulder community who have become our family here in the mountains, and all our loved ones in Portland, whom we miss always.

Peter Eschwey, the quintessence of *friend*, who has been instrumental in our evolution.

Nathan and Heather, for loving us endlessly and always being there when we need you.

Many teachers have shaped the course of our lives and played a pivotal role in our development. Matt Garrigan comes to mind first, a man whose passion for life and human potential changed us forever. Sifu Fong awakened our fierceness and taught us the dichotomies of power and softness, and of humor and pain.

Our Dragontree team: Robert, you are a dream, and not a day goes by that we aren't aware of our immense gratitude for you. Phil, we appreciate the many ways you beautify, execute, and expand our vision. Cheri, you're like family, and you manage all the nuts and bolts with such grace. Our management team, your dedication to our mission and your huge hearts are such a gift to us. All the practitioners who've been with us for years, you do powerful healing, and we're honored to work with you. Our receptionists, spa attendants, customer service team, and product crafters, you serve with selflessness and love, and do important healing in your own ways.

The Dragontree clients. We're honored to have the opportunity to be part of your path toward balance, and are moved by your strength, kindness, and enthusiasm.

Our book agent, Steven Harris, for believing in us and our message, and for being such a wonderful person to work with.

Our editor, Laura Daly, for helping to refine our message, and our publisher for seeing something in our work that needed to get out in the world in a big way.

Peter would also like to thank:

Nature, you are the greatest instructor, and I am your perennial student. Divine Light, I am eternally grateful for your love, guidance, and creative flow. SiriNam Singh Khalsa and Gurunam Kaur Khalsa, you showed me how to live with intention. Huixian Chen, you embody the power of the human spirit in a way that changed what I think is possible. To my many other teachers, including Guohui Liu, Hong Jin, Joe Coletto, Khosrow Khalighi, Joe Soprani, Allen Barker, Laurie Hodin, Mitch Stargrove, Paul Greenbaum, J.R. Worsley, Yogi Bhajan, Sri Karunamayi, Adyashanti, Dan Axelrod, Tomo Schramm, Mary Clare, and Brandy Keller, you've all played a role in my awakening, my development as a healer, and my understanding of myself and the human condition. I have the deepest appreciation for what you have offered.

To Briana, I feel tremendously lucky to have you as my partner and friend, to support each other and revel in this crazy, beautiful life.

Briana would also like to thank:

My siblings for protecting me, loving me, and laughing with me: Maurika, your enthusiasm and grit are truly awesome and inspirational. Abe, thank you for taking risks on me and metaphorically holding my hand through some incredibly difficult times. Hannah, you are purely "good," as Abe would say, and I value your insight like gold.

My close Mastermind sisters for your support, your brainstorming, your love, and your encouragement. Emily Rosen, for your honesty, your brilliance, and for being such a true friend. Anna Doogan, for showing me how to live with incredible grace as a mama while chasing my dreams. Nisha Moodley, for being a true soul sister and for caretaking my heart. Sarah Jenks, for your endless creativity and for navigating this world with me in such a deep and centered way.

My mentors and teachers: TJ Ford, for introducing me to the idea of combining the physical work and energetic work of healing; Marie Forleo, for your inspiration and really seeing me and my potential; David Howitt, for believing in us and being a beacon of light in our lives; and Hiro Boga, for reawakening some of the sweetest parts of my soul and for clearing out old shit so I can shine.

And Peter Borten, writing this with you has just shown me even more that you are the greatest choice I ever made, my best friend, and my forever love.

Finally, our deepest gratitude goes to you, the reader, for picking up this book, being open to what we have to teach, and believing in your ability to achieve your Well Life.

SOURCE MATERIALS

Chapter 2

Chaddock, L., Erickson, K.I., Prakash, R.S., Kim, J.S., Voss, M.W., Vanpatter, M., . . . Kramer, A.F. (2010). A neuroimaging investigation of the association between aerobic fitness, hippocampal volume, and memory performance in preadolescent children. *Brain Research, 1358*, 172–183.

Chevalier, G. (2015). The Effect of Grounding the Human Body on Mood 1. *Psychological Reports, 116*(2), 534–543.

Chevalier, G., Sinatra, S.T., Oschman, J.L., & Delany, R.M. (2013). Earthing (Grounding) the Human Body Reduces Blood Viscosity—a Major Factor in Cardiovascular Disease. *The Journal of Alternative and Complementary Medicine, 19*(2), 102–110.

Chevalier, G., Melvin, G., & Barsotti, T. (2015). One-Hour Contact with the Earth's Surface (Grounding) Improves Inflammation and Blood Flow—A Randomized, Double-Blind, Pilot Study. *Health, 07*(08), 1022–1059.

Chevalier, G., Sinatra, S.T., Oschman, J.L., Sokal, K., & Sokal, P. (2012). Earthing: Health Implications of Reconnecting the Human Body to the Earth's Surface Electrons. *Journal of Environmental and Public Health, 2012*, 1–8.

Dishman, R., & Sothmann, M. (n.d.). Exercise fuels the brain's stress buffers. *American Psychological Association*. Retrieved from www.apa.org/helpcenter/exercise-stress.aspx.

Dwyer, A.A., Caronia, L.M., Lee, H., Nathan, D.M., & Hayes, F.J. (2012, June 25). Lifestyle modification can reverse hypogonadism in men with impaired glucose tolerance in the diabetes prevention program. *The Endocrine Society's 94th Annual Meeting & Expo; Houston*.

Eriksson, K., & Lindgarde, F. (1991). Prevention of Type 2 (non-insulin-dependent) diabetes mellitus by diet and physical exercise The 6-year Malmo feasibility study. *Diabetologia, 34*(12), 891–898.

Gottfried, S. (2013, April 06). The Horrors of Hair Loss. Retrieved from www.huffingtonpost.com/sara-gottfried-md/women-hair-loss_b_2597382.html.

Hannan, J.L., Maio, M.T., Komolova, M., & Adams, M.A. (2009). Beneficial Impact of Exercise and Obesity Interventions on Erectile Function and Its Risk Factors. *The Journal of Sexual Medicine, 6*, 254–261.

Lytle, M.E., Bilt, J.V., Pandav, R.S., Dodge, H.H., & Ganguli, M. (2004). Exercise Level and Cognitive Decline. *Alzheimer Disease & Associated Disorders, 18*(2), 57–64.

Mayo Clinic. (2014, October 10). Depression and anxiety: Exercise eases symptoms. Retrieved from www.mayoclinic.org/diseases-conditions/depression/in-depth/depression-and-exercise/art-20046495.

Mayo Clinic. (2015, August 06). Exercise: A drug-free approach to lowering high blood pressure. Retrieved from www.mayoclinic.org/diseases-conditions/high-blood-pressure/in-depth/high-blood-pressure/art-20045206.

Moore, S.C., Patel, A.V., Matthews, C.E., Gonzalez, A.B., Park, Y., Katki, H.A., . . . Lee, I. (2012). Leisure Time Physical Activity of Moderate to Vigorous Intensity and Mortality: A Large Pooled Cohort Analysis. *PLoS Med PLoS Medicine, 9*(11).

Myers, J. (2003). Exercise and Cardiovascular Health. *Circulation*. Retrieved from http://circ.ahajournals.org/content/107/1/e2.full.

Otto, M.W., & Smits, J.A. (2011). *Exercise for mood and anxiety: Proven strategies for overcoming depression and enhancing well-being.* (New York, NY: Oxford University Press).

Petty, K.H., Davis, C.L., Tkacz, J., Young-Hyman, D., & Waller, J.L. (2009). Exercise Effects on Depressive Symptoms and Self-Worth in Overweight Children: A Randomized Controlled Trial. *Journal of Pediatric Psychology, 34*(9), 929–939.

Physical Activity and Cancer. (n.d.). Retrieved from www.cancer.gov/cancertopics/factsheet/prevention/physicalactivity.

Reid, K.J., Baron, K.G., Lu, B., Naylor, E., Wolfe, L., & Zee, P.C. (2010). Aerobic exercise improves self-reported sleep and quality of life in older adults with insomnia. *Sleep Medicine, 11*(9), 934–940.

Reynolds, G. (2014, April 16). Younger Skin Through Exercise. Retrieved from http://well.blogs.nytimes.com/2014/04/16/ younger-skin-through-exercise/?_r=0.

Roberts, V., Maddison, R., Simpson, C., Bullen, C., & Prapavessis, H. (2012). The acute effects of exercise on cigarette cravings, withdrawal symptoms, affect, and smoking behaviour: Systematic review update and meta-analysis. *Psychopharmacology, 222*(1), 1–15.

Steinberg, H., Sykes, E.A., Moss, T., Lowery, S., Leboutillier, N., & Dewey, A. (1997). Exercise enhances creativity independently of mood. *British Journal of Sports Medicine, 31*(3), 240–245.

Taylor, A.H., Oh, H., & Cullen, S. (2013). Acute effect of exercise on alcohol urges and attentional bias towards alcohol related images in high alcohol consumers. *Mental Health and Physical Activity, 6*(3), 220–226.

University of Georgia. (2006, November 8). Regular Exercise Plays a Consistent and Significant Role in Reducing Fatigue. *ScienceDaily*.

Chapter 4

Khalsa, G.K. (1991). *Energy Maps I*. (La Crescenta, CA: Cyber Scribe).

Chapter 6

Baumeister, R.F., Campbell, J.D., Krueger, J.I., & Vohs, K.D. (2003). Does High Self-Esteem Cause Better Performance, Interpersonal Success, Happiness, or Healthier Lifestyles? *Psychological Science in the Public Interest, 4*(1), 1–44. Retrieved from http://files.clps.brown.edu/jkrueger/journal_articles/ baumeister-2003-doeshigh.pdf.

Bronson, P. (2007, August 3). How Not to Talk to Your Kids: The Inverse Power of Praise. *New York Magazine*. Retrieved from http://nymag.com/news/ features/27840/.

Formica, J.J. (2008, May 17). Self-esteem doesn't make better people of us. *Psychology Today*. Retrieved from www.psychologytoday.com/blog/ enlightened-living/200805/self-esteem-doesnt-make-better-people-us.

Newsom, C.R., Archer, R.P., Trumbetta, S., & Gottesman, I.I. (2003). Changes in Adolescent Response Patterns on the MMPI/MMPI-A Across Four Decades. *Journal of Personality Assessment, 81*(1), 74–84.

Patrick, V.M., & Hagtvedt, H. (2012). "I Don't" versus "I Can't": When Empowered Refusal Motivates Goal-Directed Behavior. *J Consum Res Journal of Consumer Research, 39*(2), 371–381.

Storr, W. (2014, February 25). The Man Who Destroyed America's Ego. *Medium.* Retrieved from https://medium.com/matter/the-man-who-destroyed-americas-ego-94d214257b5#.lt046yt0q.

Twenge, J.M., Konrath, S., Foster, J.D., Campbell, W.K., & Bushman, B.J. (2008). Egos Inflating Over Time: A Cross-Temporal Meta-Analysis of the Narcissistic Personality Inventory. *Journal of Personality, 76*(4), 875–902.

Twenge, J.M., Miller, J.D., & Campbell, W.K. (2014). The narcissism epidemic: Commentary on Modernity and narcissistic personality disorder. *Personality Disorders: Theory, Research, and Treatment, 5*(2), 227–229.

Twenge, J. M. *Generation me: Why today's young Americans are more confident, assertive, entitled—and more miserable than ever before.* (New York: Free Press, 2006).

Chapter 7

McKnight, John. *The Abundant Community.* (Oakland, CA: Berrett-Koehler Publishers, 2010).

Putnam, Robert. *Bowling Alone.* (New York: Simon & Schuster, 2000).

Chapter 8

Joseph Campbell and the Power of Myth with Bill Moyers, edited by Betty Sue Flowers. (New York: Doubleday and Co., 1988).

Clifton, Donald and Marcus Buckingham. *Now, Discover Your Strengths.* (New York: The Free Press, 2001).

Pavlina, Steve. www.stevepavlina.com.

What the Research Says About Character Strengths: Overview. (n.d.). Retrieved from www.viacharacter.org/www/Research/Character-Strengths-Research-Findings-Summary.

Chapter 9

Garrigan, Matt. www.radiantlightministries.com.

Gurdjieff, G.I. www.gurdjieff.org.

Uspenskï, P.D. *In Search of the Miraculous; Fragments of an Unknown Teaching.* (New York: Harcourt, Brace, 1949).

Chapter 10

Our perspective-tuning technique was based, in part, on the writings of Vern Black and the teachings of Matt Garrigan. If you're looking for more detailed instruction, we encourage you to check out the writings of Frederick Dodson and Greg Kuhn, both of whom have developed similar techniques, to which they have dedicated entire books.

Allison, P.J. (2003). Disposmonal Optimism Predicts Survival Status 1 Year After Diagnosis in Head and Neck Cancer Patients. *Journal of Clinical Oncology, 21*(3), 543–548.

Geers, A.L., Wellman, J.A., Fowler, S.L., Helfer, S.G., & France, C.R. (2010). Dispositional Optimism Predicts Placebo Analgesia. *The Journal of Pain, 11*(11), 1165–1171.

Geers, A.L., Wellman, J.A., Helfer, S.G., Fowler, S.L., & France, C.R. (2008). Dispositional Optimism and Thoughts of Well-Being Determine Sensitivity to an Experimental Pain Task. *Annals of Behavioral Medicine Ann. Behav. Med, 36*(3), 304–313.

Gibran, K. *The Prophet.* (New York: Knopf, 1952).

Ironson, G., Balbin, E., Stuetzle, R., Fletcher, M.A., O'Cleirigh, C., Laurenceau, J.P., . . . Solomon, G. (2005). Dispositional optimism and the mechanisms by which it predicts slower disease progression in I IIV: Proactive behavior, avoidant coping, and depression. *Int. J. Behav. Med. International Journal of Behavioral Medicine, 12*(2), 86–97.

Kim, E.S., Smith, J., & Kubzansky, L.D. (2014). Prospective Study of the Association Between Dispositional Optimism and Incident Heart Failure. *Circulation: Heart Failure, 7*(3), 394–400.

M., & Van Norden, B.W. (2008). *Mengzi: With selections from traditional commentaries.* (Indianapolis: Hackett Pub).

Matthews, K.A., Räikkönen, K., Sutton-Tyrrell, K., & Kuller, L.H. (2004). Optimistic Attitudes Protect Against Progression of Carotid Atherosclerosis in Healthy Middle-Aged Women. *Psychosomatic Medicine, 66*(5), 640–644.

Räikkönen, K., Matthews, K.A., Flory, J.D., Owens, J.F., & Gump, B.B. (1999). Effects of optimism, pessimism, and trait anxiety on ambulatory blood pressure and mood during everyday life. *Journal of Personality and Social Psychology, 76*(1), 104–113.

Ranganathan, V.K., Siemionow, V., Liu, J.Z., Sahgal, V., & Yue, G.H. (2004). From mental power to muscle power—gaining strength by using the mind. *Neuropsychologia, 42*(7), 944–956.

Scheier, M.F., Matthews, K.A., Owens, J.F., Magovern, G.J., & Al, E. (1989). Dispositional optimism and recovery from coronary artery bypass surgery: The beneficial effects on physical and psychological well-being. *Journal of Personality and Social Psychology, 57*(6), 1024–1040.

Sidaway, B., & Trzaska, A.R. (2005). Can mental practice increase ankle dorsiflexor torque? *Physical Therapy, 85*(10), 1053–1060.

Yao, W.X., Ranganathan, V.K., Allexandre, D., Siemionow, V., & Yue, G.H. (2013). Kinesthetic imagery training of forceful muscle contractions increases brain signal and muscle strength. *Frontiers in Human Neuroscience Front. Hum. Neurosci., 7.*

Zijdewind, I., Toering, S.T., Bessem, B., Laan, O.V., & Diercks, R.L. (2003). Effects of imagery motor training on torque production of ankle plantar flexor muscles. *Muscle & Nerve Muscle Nerve, 28*(2), 168–173.

Chapter 12

Baumeister, R.F., & Weir, K. (2012). The Power of Self-Control. *American Psychological Association, 43*(1), 36. Retrieved April 13, 2016, from www.apa .org/monitor/2012/01/self-control.aspx.

Chao, J. (2012, October 17). Elevated Indoor Carbon Dioxide Impairs Decision-Making Performance. *Berkeley Lab News Center.* Retrieved April 08, 2016, from http://newscenter.lbl.gov/2012/10/17/ elevated-indoor-carbon-dioxide-impairs-decision-making-performance/.

Damisch, L., Stoberock, B., & Mussweiler, T. (2010). Keep Your Fingers Crossed! How Superstition Improves Performance. *Psychological Science, 21*(7), 1014–1020. doi:10.1177/0956797610372631.

Esfahani Smith, E. (2014, March 14). In Grief, Try Personal Rituals. *The Atlantic*. Retrieved from www.theatlantic.com/health/archive/2014/03/in-grief-try-personal-rituals/284397/.

Gino, F., & Norton, M.I. (2013, May 14). Why Rituals Work. *Scientific American*. Retrieved April 13, 2016, from www.scientificamerican.com/article/why-rituals-work/.

Tierney, J. (2011, August 17). Do You Suffer from Decision Fatigue? *The New York Times Magazine*, MM33.

Vohs, K.D., Baumeister, R.F., Schmeichel, B.J., Twenge, J.M., Nelson, N.M., & Tice, D.M. (2008). Making choices impairs subsequent self-control: A limited-resource account of decision-making, self-regulation, and active initiative. *Journal of Personality and Social Psychology*, 94(5), 883–898.

Chapter 13

Buddharakkhita, A. (1989). *Mettā: The philosophy and practice of universal love*. Kandy, Sri Lanka: Buddhist Publication Society.

Dweck, C. (2015, September 22). Carol Dweck Revisits the 'Growth Mindset' Retrieved from www.edweek.org/ew/articles/2015/09/23/carol-dweck-revisits-the-growth-mindset.html.

Gilbert, D. (2004, February). The Surprising Science of Happiness. Retrieved April 18, 2016, from www.ted.com/talks/dan_gilbert_asks_why_are_we_happy?language=en.

Twerski, A. Lobsters and Salmon. Retrieved April 28, 2016, from www.abrahamtwerski.com/index.php/writings/essays/57-self-esteem/126-lobsters-and-salmon.

INDEX

Agreements
  broken agreements, 45, 55,
    64–65
  changes in, 62–63
  defining, 61–62
  honest agreements, 58–60
  importance of, 58–61
  integrity and, 55, 58–66
  self-trust and, 58–66
  trustworthiness and, 55, 58–66
Ayurveda, 8, 13, 15, 21, 70

Balance
  achieving, 8–10, 14–17, 146–47,
    268–69
  dynamic balance, 15–17
  enjoyment and, 15–20
  maintaining, 14–17
  optimal balance, 16–17
  theories of, 15–16
  true balance, 15–17
Blame
  emotional baggage and, 49–56
  forgiveness and, 49–56
  self-blame, 53–54, 188
Bliss, 147–50. *See also* Happiness
Boundaries, 142–44, 148, 239
Breathing techniques, 31–33

Challenges, 14, 86–88, 123,
  254–55
Commitment
  expansion and, 250–69
  explanation of, 250–51

happiness and, 251–54
  reinforcing, 250–52
  to Well Life, 250–69
Communal energy, 79–80, 83, 88
Community
  current communities, 119–20
  ideal community, 120–22
  intentional communities,
    117–19
  local community, 116–17
  need for, 116–17
  as resource, 67, 116–22
  social connections, 41–44, 120,
    160
  supportive connections,
    116–22
Competence, 104–7
Concepts, applying, 21–22
Confidence
  assessing, 114–15
  building, 89–115
  competence and, 104–7
  courage and, 107–14
  defining, 89–90
  ingredients for, 89–115
  as resource, 67, 89–115
  self-esteem, 90–94, 99, 106
  self-trust and, 90–91, 100–108,
    113–15
  self-worth and, 90–99, 105–6
Connection. *See also* Community
  with others, 41–44, 120, 160
  social connections, 41–44, 120,
    160
  spiritual connection, 10, 15, 20,
    191–219

supportive connections,
116–22
Contraction, 264–66. *See also*
Expansion
Core values, identifying, 129–31
Counter-intentions, 167–72, 201,
209. *See also* Intentions
Courage, 107–14
Creativity, 161, 207–10

Decision-making, 234–35, 240
Desires, 151–67, 184–85. *See also*
Goals; Prizes
Discipline, 240–44
Dreambook, 9, 134, 153, 156, 228,
247
Dream life, 151–53, 164. *See also*
Well Life

Elements, 232–34
"Emergencies," 238–39
Emotional baggage
blame, 49–56
consequences, 54
daily baggage, 56–57
identifying, 47–49
negative emotions, 47–54
reducing, 56–57
releasing, 45–57
unresolved issues, 45–49,
54–56
Energy
communal energy, 79–80, 83, 88
deficit of, 73–76
fatigue and, 69–79
life energy, 80–81
optimal energy, 76–86
quest for, 69–70
as resource, 67, 69–88
savoring, 82–83

space for, 84–88
structure for, 76–79
sweetness for, 79–82
understanding, 70–73
Enjoyment
balance and, 15–20
happiness and, 15–20, 24–26,
39–41
laughter and, 26, 39–41
life purpose and, 135–36
nutrition and, 30–31
play and, 15, 26, 39–41, 153
Environment, 13–14, 37–39
Equilibrium, 15–17. *See also*
Balance
Essence, concept of, 70–71,
155–57, 162–63
Exercise benefits, 33–35
Existential contraction, 165–66
Expansion
benefits of, 15, 250, 261–69
commitment and, 250–69
contraction and, 264–66
explanation of, 15, 250
happiness and, 250–69
meditation and, 263–64
of perspective, 266–67
space and, 20–21

Failure, fear of, 171–72, 217
Fatigue, 69–79, 234–35, 240
Fearful thinking, 187–90. *See also*
Negative thinking
Feedback, 131–32
Financial concerns, 15, 77, 108,
153, 158. *See also* Money
concerns
Five-element philosophy, 15,
232–34
Flexibility, 197–98, 232–34,
254–55

Forgiveness
    importance of, 53–55
    power of, 49–56
    practice of, 55–56
    withholding, 45, 49–52

Gifts, identifying, 131–34
Goals. *See also* Prizes
    achieving, 8–10, 14–18, 163–65,
        218–31, 250–51
    advancing, 179–84, 231, 246–47
    breaking down, 222–25
    for dream life, 151–53
    establishing, 15
    importance of, 125–26
    intention statements for,
        165–73
    letting go of, 157–58
    life architecture and, 226–28
    life purpose and, 18–20, 174–
        76, 218–23, 230–31, 246–47
    mind map for, 226
    outdated goals, 157–58
    revisiting, 164
    structure for, 18–20
Gratitude, expressing, 83, 145,
    162, 189, 247, 252
Growth mindset, 106–7, 257–58

Habits, changing, 21–22, 123,
    212–13
Happiness
    attaining, 17–20, 250–69
    bliss and, 147–50
    commitment and, 251–54
    enjoyment and, 15–20, 24–26,
        39–41
    expansion and, 250–69
    forgiveness and, 52
    meditation and, 227, 263–64

options and, 253
peacefulness and, 162–64, 203,
    227
quest for, 252–54
spiritual connection and,
    191–217
synthesizing, 252–53
unhappiness and, 23, 212,
    253
Health
    environment and, 13–14,
        37–39
    exercise, 33–35
    imbalances, 13–14
    mind–body health, 23–44
    nutrition, 28–31, 77–78, 82
    physical health, 23–44, 127,
        155, 160–61
    play and, 39–41
    psychological health, 23–44,
        127, 162, 245
    self-care, 24–26
    sleep, 24–28, 70–74, 78, 82
    spiritual health, 155, 162
    whole health, 14
Healthy plants, 232–34,
    254–55

Illusions, 188–89, 193
Imbalance, 13–14
Inspiration, 20–23, 189, 199, 213,
    231, 252
Integrity, 14, 55, 58–66
Intentions
    counter-intentions, 167–72,
        201, 209
    desires and, 184–85
    letting go and, 210–12
    living, 212–19
    magnetizing, 198–206
    space for, 207–10

spiritual connection and,
191–206
statement of, 165–73, 191–206

Laughter, 26, 39–41
Law of Attraction, 18, 24, 177–80,
183–85, 187
Life, quality of, 187, 212–13, 245.
See also Well Life
Life architecture. *See also*
Structure
art of, 10
discipline for, 240–44
explanation of, 19–20
goals and, 226–28
mind map for, 226
momentum, 227
planning process, 220–30
projects, 226–29
rituals, 236, 244–48
tasks, 226–29, 237–40
visualization, 225–28
Life-editing process, 256–57
Life energy, 80–81. *See also*
Energy
Life Purpose
bliss and, 147–50
enjoyment and, 135–36
finding, 136–45
goals and, 18–20, 174–76,
218–23, 230–31, 246–47
integration of, 146–47
knowing, 15, 136–42
love and, 139–45
space for, 135–36, 139–45
statement for, 136–39, 142,
145–46
structure for, 18–20, 136–39
understanding, 135–48
Light, spreading, 125–28,
149–50

Love
choosing, 265–66
life purpose and, 139–45
for others, 159, 197
spreading, 125–28
truth and, 125, 189–90, 206
virtue and, 125–26, 149–50

Magnetization, 198–206
Manifestation, 163, 177–82
Mantras, 56, 195–96, 222, 247
Meditation
expansion and, 263–64
happiness and, 227, 263–64
peacefulness and, 169, 195–96
position for, 209
for receptivity, 209
for releasing resistance,
167–72
space for, 175
Mind–body health. *See also*
Health
breathing techniques, 31–33
connecting with others,
41–44
laughter, 39–41
movement/exercise, 33–35
nature, 37–39
nutrition, 28–31
play, 39–41
practices for, 23–44
self-care, 24–26
sleep, 24–28
stillness, 35–37
Mind map, 226
Momentum, 227
Money concerns, 167, 171–72,
176–77, 212–13. *See also*
Financial concerns
Morning rituals, 236
Movement/exercise, 33–35

Nature, enjoying, 37–39
Negative emotions, 47–54. *See
    also* Emotional baggage
Negative thinking, 77, 79, 85, 97,
    118, 180, 187–90
Negativity, 180, 187–88, 206,
    240–41
New Thought movement, 177–78
Non-negotiable intention,
    216–17
Nonphysical realm, 176–78, 184–
    86, 190, 197, 217–18
Non-truths, 188–89
Nutrition, 28–31, 77–78, 82

Obstacles, 86–88, 123, 254–55
Openness, 10, 14, 21, 175, 233
Opportunities, experiencing, 15,
    25–26, 39–42
Opportunities, finding, 54–56,
    111–12, 258–61

Pain
    avoiding, 147–48, 223
    positive thoughts and, 182
    reducing, 31, 74, 127, 165, 197
    sleep deprivation and, 26–27
    stress and, 187
Passion, following, 147–48, 253
Past, releasing, 45–57
Peacefulness
    breathing techniques for,
        31–33
    happiness and, 162–64, 203,
        227
    meditation for, 169, 195–96
Perspective
    benefits of, 232–34, 254–60,
        266–67
    expansion of, 266–67

forgiveness and, 52
growth mindset and, 257–58
maintaining, 87
perspective-tuning exercise,
    213–16
positive thoughts and, 118–19
shifting, 212–15
spiritual connection and, 191
Physical action, 217–19
Physical health, 23–44, 127, 155,
    160–61
Physical realm, 176–78, 182–86,
    218–19
Pitfalls, avoiding, 186–90
Planning process, 15, 220–30,
    234–35
Plants, 232–34, 254–55
Play
    balance and, 15–20
    creativity and, 161
    enjoyment and, 15, 26, 39–41,
        153
    exploration and, 161
    laughter and, 26, 39–41
    opportunities for, 258, 261
    work and, 229–30
Positive thinking, 118–19, 179–
    84, 187–89, 212–14
Positivity, 179–84, 241
Prayer, 195, 227
Prizes. *See also* Goals
    choosing, 151–73
    clarity and, 153–54
    desires and, 151–67
    intention statements for,
        165–73
    prize-winning life, 163–65
    resistance to, 167–72
    taking action on, 153–54
    visualizing, 154–58
Psychological health, 23–44, 127,
    162, 245

Receptivity, 206–12, 217–18
Rehearsal, 109, 183, 212–13, 236, 243
Relationships, fulfilling, 15, 159
Relaxation, 14, 183, 255–56. See also Peacefulness
Religion, 191, 195–96. See also Spiritual connection
Resistance, releasing, 167–72
Resources
    community, 67, 116–22
    confidence, 67, 89–115
    cultivating, 67
    energy, 67, 69–88
    importance of, 86–88
    as structure, 67
    for thriving, 67
Rituals, 236, 244–48
Rituals for Living Dreambook, 9, 134, 156, 228, 247

Self-alignment, 123
Self-assessment, 92, 105, 114–15, 132–33
Self-blame, 53–54, 188
Self-care, 24–26
Self-discipline, 240–44
Self-esteem, 90–94, 99, 106
Self-trust, 58–66, 90–91, 100–108, 113–15
Self-worth, 90–99, 105–6
Sleep, 24–28, 70–74, 78, 82
Social connections, 41–44, 120, 160
Space
    accessing, 88
    benefits of, 10, 20–21
    description of, 10, 20–21
    elements of, 13–22
    for energy, 84–88
    expansion and, 20–21

explanation of, 10
for intentions, 207–10
for Life Purpose, 135–36, 139–45
for meditation, 175
need for, 174–75
opening, 22, 174–75
receptivity and, 207–10
spiritual connection and, 10, 20
terms for, 20–21
for Well Life, 174
Spiritual connection
    benefits of, 191–92, 198–219
    experiencing, 15
    fulfilling intentions, 191–206
    happiness and, 191–217
    intentions and, 191–206
    letting go and, 210–12
    magnetization process, 198–206
    non-negotiable intention, 216–17
    physical action, 217–19
    receptivity, 206–12, 217–18
    religion and, 191, 195
    space and, 10, 20
    strategies for, 194–98
Spiritual health, 155, 162
Stillness, 35–37
Stress
    breathing techniques for, 32–33
    negative thinking and, 187–90
    pain and, 187
    relieving, 34–38, 74–75, 241
    response to, 32
Structure
    benefits of, 10, 18–20
    description of, 10, 18–20
    elements of, 13–22
    for energy, 76–79
    explanation of, 10
    good structure, 19–20

Structure—*continued*
  for Life Purpose, 18–20, 136–39
  resources as, 67
  for Well Life, 174–75
Success, planning for, 220–30, 240
Success, understanding, 176–77
Superpowers, 125–28
Sweetness
  benefits of, 10, 17–18
  description of, 10, 17–18
  elements of, 13–22
  for energy, 79–82
  explanation of, 10
  for Well Life, 174

Tai chi, 109, 197, 241, 255–56
Tasks
  breaking down, 226–29
  chunking, 237–38
  delegating, 239–40
  scheduling, 229–32, 236–37
Tenacity, 232–34, 254
Time, scheduling, 236–37
To-do list, 229–30
Touch, benefits of, 42–44
Traditional Chinese Medicine
  (TCM), 13, 15, 33, 70, 79
Trustworthiness, 55–66, 90–91,
  100–108, 113–15
Truth
  choosing, 265–66
  following, 149, 265–66
  illusions and, 188–89, 193
  love and, 125, 189–90, 206
  positive thoughts and, 188–89
  spreading, 125–28, 149–50

Unhappiness, 23, 212, 253. *See
  also* Happiness
"Urgent" matters, 238–39

Values, identifying, 129–31
Virtue
  following, 149–50
  love and, 125–26, 149–50
  spreading, 125–28, 149–50
Visualization, 154–58, 225–28

Weaknesses, 134
Well Life
  achieving, 8–10, 17–20, 163–65,
    250–69
  commitment to, 250–69
  concepts of, 21–22
  defining, 151–73
  dream life and, 151–53, 164
  elements of, 10, 13–22, 28,
    174–75
  expansion and, 250–69
  foundation for, 23–26
  integrating, 250–69
  living, 212–19, 234–49, 268–69
  nonphysical realm, 176–78,
    184–86, 190
  physical realm, 176–78, 182–86
  practicing, 21–22
  principles of, 10, 13–22, 28
  prizes for, 151–53
  success with, 176–77, 220–30,
    240
Wood element, 232–34, 254–55
Work. *See also* Life Purpose
  play and, 229–30
  purposeful work, 218–19, 239
  relaxation and, 255–56

Yin and yang, 15, 207–9
Yoga, 175, 197–98, 209, 256

ABOUT THE AUTHORS

DR. PETER BORTEN became interested in healing at a young age, writing his first report on acupuncture at age twelve and acting as counselor to his peer group in high school. Growing up in the Boston area, he frequented the witchcraft stores of Salem as a young adult, which kindled his interest in herbal medicine. He received his B.S. in botany from the University of Massachusetts at Amherst. He earned his master's and doctorate in acupuncture and Oriental medicine at Oregon College of Oriental Medicine (OCOM), where he also became a certified *Qi Gong* instructor under Professor Huixian Chen.

He has been in private practice since 2000, and taught Chinese medicine and Daoist philosophy at Lewis and Clark College, National University of Natural Medicine, and OCOM. He has authored hundreds of articles on all facets of health, and has produced a wide array of educational resources for natural healthcare practitioners.

In his focused *sweetness* time he builds things out of wood, makes music and art, and studies health, nature, and spirituality with endless fascination. Throughout every day he endeavors to make his wife and daughters laugh.

BRIANA learned early on that she is capable of creating her own destiny. When she was eighteen, she broke her neck in a debilitating car accident. It derailed her college career, but she unexpectedly discovered the power of positivity and the profound rehabilitative benefits of massage. She attended massage school and established a busy private practice in Portland. But she yearned to create an environment where clients could have a more comprehensive and transcendent healing experience. This came to fruition when, at age twenty-three, she opened The Dragontree Spa.

She went on to attend California College of Ayurveda, where she earned the degree of Clinical Ayurvedic Specialist. Her health-care practice and the ongoing expansion of The Dragontree stoked her deepening passion for assisting others to reach their full potential. Redefining her career as a wellness entrepreneur and peace engineer, she has now opened four spas; writes extensively on personal development; started a wellness product line; and created several magazines, books, and online programs to help people achieve their dreams and live extraordinary, healthy lives.

During her focused *sweetness* time, Briana loves to swim in natural bodies of water, hike in the mountains, dance, create art, and cuddle with her daughters. She loves natural medicine, holidays, salted caramels, innovative design, and fresh flowers.

Peter and Briana live in Boulder, Colorado, with their two daughters, Sabina and Sailor.